RENEWALS 458-4574.

DATE DUE

DEC 1 7 2008			
DEC 0 8 2008			
GAYLORD			PRINTED IN U.S.A.

Music in Imperial Rio de Janeiro

European Culture in a Tropical Milieu

Cristina Magaldi

The Scarecrow Press, Inc.
Lanham, Maryland • Toronto • Oxford
2004

SCARECROW PRESS, INC.

Published in the United States of America
by Scarecrow Press, Inc.
A wholly owned subsidiary of
The Rowman & Littlefield Publishing Group, Inc.
4501 Forbes Boulevard, Suite 200, Lanham, Maryland 20706
www.scarecrowpress.com

PO Box 317
Oxford
OX2 9RU, UK

British Library Cataloguing in Publication Information Available

Library of Congress Cataloging-in-Publication Data

Magaldi, Cristina.
  Music in imperial Rio de Janeiro : European culture in a tropical milieu /
Cristina Magaldi.
     p. cm.
  Includes bibliographical references and index.
  ISBN 0-8108-5025-7 (hardcover : alk. paper)
  1. Music—Brazil—Rio de Janeiro—19th century—History and criticism. 2.
Music—Brazil—Rio de Janeiro—European influences. 3. Rio de Janeiro
(Brazil)—Social life and customs. I. Title.
ML232.8.R5M34 2004
780'.981'5309034—dc22

2004004745

♾ ™ The paper used in this publication meets the minimum requirements
of American National Standard for Information Sciences—Permanence of
Paper for Printed Library Materials, ANSI/NISO Z39.48–1992.
Manufactured in the United States of America.

Contents

Illustrations

Acknowledgments

This book was made possible by the financial support of various institutions in Brazil and in the United States. I express my gratitude to the Brazilian institution CAPES (Coordenação de Aperfeiçoamento de Pessoal de Nível Superior) and the Center for Latin American Studies at UCLA, which, in 1994, awarded me fellowships that made possible my work in various libraries and archives in Rio de Janeiro. I am equally thankful to the Guggenheim Foundation, which granted me a postdoctoral fellowship in 1996, allowing me to continue my work in Rio de Janeiro on music in the comic theater. I am also grateful for the financial help from the Towson University Faculty Development Program (1998–1999), which allowed me to work on early drafts of this book. Finally, I am indebted to the Manfred Bukofzer Publication Endowment Fund of the American Musicological Society for their financial assistance.

The help from the staff of the UCLA music library, research library, and special collections was invaluable. I am also immensely grateful to the staff of the Biblioteca Nacional in Rio de Janeiro, and in particular to the library's music division (Divisão de Música e Archivo Sonoro).

My colleagues at Towson University have been especially helpful; my thanks go to James Anthony and Jonathan Leshoff for offering their comments on early drafts. I am also grateful to Walter Clark for reading and commenting on the final draft. My deepest gratitude goes to my advisor and friend Dr. Robert Stevenson, whose valuable intellectual help and constant incentives and support were a vital part of this laborious work.

This book would not be possible without the support of friends and family. Carmem Nava has been there for me since the inception of this work and has ever since followed all the steps that led to the book publication. I thank my husband, Keith, and our son, Alexander, with all my heart. This book would not have reached print without their constant support, patience, understanding, comfort, and selfless love.

Introduction

CULTURE OF IMITATION

In 1935, the French anthropologist Claude Lévi-Strauss went to Brazil eager to experience the exotic "perfumes of the tropics."[1] However, having disembarked in the Brazilian capital, Rio de Janeiro, one of Latin America's largest cities and an important international port, he reported with disappointment: "The tropics are less exotic than out of date."[2] The anthropologist was looking for a radically different civilization, but found instead a cosmopolitan city replete with "impoverished imitations of his own [European culture]."[3] Like Lévi-Strauss, Europeans who visited Rio de Janeiro in the nineteenth century were invariably struck by the city's odd familiarity. The façades of public buildings, the neoclassical architecture and decoration of theaters and elite houses, the dress fashion, and the music performed at theaters and concert halls unmistakably recalled Paris and London. But the tropical climate and vegetation, alongside an overwhelming number of Africans and Afro-Brazilians, gave Rio de Janeiro a particular characteristic that set it apart from contemporary European capitals. To the outsider, the city was "almost the same, but not quite."[4]

Daunted by the place's familiarity, most European visitors looked with contempt upon the European element in the context of Rio de Janeiro. The German painter Johann Moritz Rugendas (1802–1858), who visited the capital in the first part of the nineteenth century, for example, described Rio de Janeiro with a mix of awe and disappointment: "The foreigner cannot help but feel appalled to encounter, in the midst of such a grand and original nation, the same shabbiness of the European society. Thus, for example, it is not a pleasant view to the [European] artist to see the people walking around, as it is very common here [in Rio de Janeiro] . . . dressed in the latest fashion from Paris or London."[5]

It was with similar reluctance that Brazilian nationalist intellectuals in the 1920s and 1930s saw the appropriation of European cultural imports in nineteenth-century Brazil. The dominance of European culture was then interpreted as a manifestation of colonial shame that needed to be excised from the process of building a Brazilian national cultural identity. In their search for an "authentic" local culture that could represent a new, unified nation, Brazilian nationalists saw "no future in the [local] past,"[6] a past that included a unique New World experience with monarchy (1822–1889) and a conspicuous cultural link to the Old (European) World. Looking at nineteenth-century Brazil's cultural milieu through the framework of their agenda, Brazilian nationalists largely underestimated the social, political, and cultural role that European cultural imports played in shaping the local society. Their views, echoed in Brazilian scholarly writings throughout the twentieth century, helped perpetuate the idea that the culture of nineteenth-century Brazil was nothing but a "culture of imitation."[7]

This is particularly true with respect to music. Most contemporary interpretations of music making in nineteenth-century Brazil are still, directly or indirectly, dependent on the ideas put forward by Mário de Andrade (1893–1945), one of the leaders of the modernist and nationalist movements. His ideas about music, outlined in seminal works such as *Ensaio sobre a música brasileira* and *Aspectos da música brasileira,* were written when defining Brazilianess was a central issue for intellectuals and artists.[8] Andrade's writings are prescriptive texts that define what Brazilian music should be (and what it should not be) and set guidelines for art music production and criticism. However, his interpretation of the musical past is vague and problematic. As Christopher Dunn points out in *Ensaio* Andrade suggests that there were no Brazilians in the nineteenth century, only Indians, blacks, and Europeans without a cultural (and racial) unity. Given that Brazilian music, as he defined it, had to reflect the nation's racial and cultural identity, Andrade asserts that before the advent of modernism in the 1920s, Brazilian culture—and, by association, Brazilian music—did not exist as such.[9] How to justify a past in which national music, as Andrade understood it, was admittedly nonexis-tent? How to assign worth to a past where local artists and musicians attempted to occupy "a space that was already occupied by European masters?"[10]

This approach misconstrued the complex impetus that motivated the spread and the appropriation of European culture, and specifically European music, in postcolonial Latin American cities, and has hindered fresh scholarly scrutiny. There are but a few studies that address specifically the cultural interchanges that took place in urban areas like Rio de Janeiro, and that confront the role of European cultural artifacts, architecture, and music as more than impoverished imitations, or as more than cultural texts that tell tales of power enforcement and/or instigate local resistance.[11]

Although a tangible result of European expansion, the dissemination and appropriation of European culture in Latin American cities was a process that found complicity on both sides. From a Latin American perspective, the dominance of European culture came as a kind of welcome fate. Kirsten Schultz has referred to the process as "the post-independence Latin American paradox" in which "to no longer be colonial meant embracing a colonial project: to 'civilize' [according to European precepts]."[12] Thus, European architecture and other cultural artifacts, European fashions, and music so prevalent in nineteenth-century Rio de Janeiro were more than cheap counterfeits; they were sound paradigms that brought about a whole set of new local practices and thus served as keys to how "local choices and alternative practices . . . were constructed historically and politically."[13]

The force with which European imports, both manufactured goods and cultural artifacts, influenced the construction of nineteenth-century Rio de Janeiro has nonetheless captured the attention of several cultural historians in recent years.[14] The more they delve into Rio de Janeiro's cultural history, the more it becomes evident that an understanding of the city's local culture cannot be achieved without considering its drive toward Europe. Because Rio de Janeiro was the capital of the country and the seat of a nineteenth-century New World monarchical government, the presence of European culture in the city was not simply an exterior element, out of context in a radically different society; nor was it merely an eccentricity of the local elite, as many have claimed, but rather it was a vital part of local cultural life. Throughout the nineteenth century, a small elite and an emergent middle class perceived European culture as symbols of "civilization," fashion, "modernity," and power. They fantasized about European culture for the opposite reasons that Europeans exoticized their Other; their embodiment of European culture reflected a candid urge "to be included," to be aligned with what they perceived as a more "civilized" world. And while most *Cariocas* (residents of Rio de Janeiro) longed for an idealized European culture, they also constructed a complex web of internal identifications and cultural associations with it, which in turn reflected their political, socioeconomic, and ethnic fabric.

Because of its uncanny ability to help people pretend they are somewhere else,[15] music played a pivotal role in this process. As a product of European culture, European music was used by many Cariocas to construct their own image as Europeans. By attending an opera or a concert in which European music prevailed, or by composing or performing homemade European-style music, Rio de Janeiro residents could share with those in European centers of power, namely Paris and London, the ownership of something that for them represented "civilization" and "modernity." At the same time, by immersing themselves in the music arriving from Europe, Cariocas avoided the general feeling of being left out on the periphery, and shunned the prospect of "not being" European. In sum, European music served some Cariocas well in their attempts to disguise the sharp, local distinctions between "here" and "there."

Given the subjective way in which music takes meaning at the time of its reception, Cariocas's identification with various European musical styles depended on a complex, internal idealization of "European music." For them, as for those living in Paris or London, opera was the ultimate symbol of power; but Cariocas would attach similar meanings of worth to other genres and styles imported from Europe, regardless of the connotations Europeans gave them. The different spheres in which the adoption and local perception of a variety of European musical genres and styles took place in nineteenth-century Rio de Janeiro existed in relation to a mythical representation of European music as "civilized" and modern.[16] Thus, identification with the imported music did not stem from the idea that musical works were devised for aesthetic contemplation. For a majority of Cariocas, the various European musical styles arriving in their city embodied a particular "cultural appeal" and "social cachet" that rested solely in their European status.[17]

Most important, European music imported to imperial Rio de Janeiro played a vital part in both the local "management of culture"[18] and in constructions of identity. Although only a small percentage of the city's population actually adopted European music as their own, it was exactly those sectors in charge of establishing policies and maintaining the status quo—namely, a white elite and a local bourgeoisie made up of intellectuals and politicians—who immersed themselves in the imported music and used it as a valuable tool for transmitting and enforcing specific values. Those immediately outside the restricted circle of power were subject to the elite's preferences, but were not alien to the process. Because people establish their identities in relationship to the identities of others, as Kay Shelemay eloquently points out,[19] Cariocas from different social classes and ethnic groups directly or indirectly used European culture to interpret their own differences, and ultimately to claim their own culture. Thus, the process by which European music was appropriated and imitated in nineteenth-century Rio de Janeiro offers a valuable insight into what has been described as "the negotiations [taking place] on a cultural level between dominant and subaltern groups."[20]

This book is primarily concerned with how European culture, and particularly European music, related to the social and cultural experiences of residents of nineteenth-century Rio de Janeiro. The focus is on how Cariocas received, perceived, selected, used, and imitated different musical styles imported from Europe, and especially from Paris. A large part of the book focuses on the musical preferences of the local elite, of those who held political and/or financial power and were involved, directly or indirectly, in the process of decision making; they were the local "cultural managers." One will realize that in many ways the Brazilian aristocracy conspicuously mirrored Parisian aristocracy of the Second Empire and that the aspirations of the Carioca elite paralleled those of the European urban elite. In Rio de Janeiro, however, the group that has been broadly defined as *elite,* about 2 percent to 5 percent of the total urban population,[21] was small enough to suggest a much more homogeneous group, linked by close ties of family, friendship, or animosity.

Given that it was this elite who first instigated the local penchant for and appropriation of European music, the first three chapters of this book focus on the musical preferences and practices of this small but influential group. The first chapter introduces the local musical milieu and shows how musical life in imperial Rio de Janeiro reflected Parisian models. It focuses on a few Parisian musical institutions that were emulated in the imperial capital, and on the most significant media where Cariocas experienced the imported music: the piano and the theater. Chapter 2 deals with the imported operatic repertory and how it shaped tastes inside and outside the opera house. Chapter 3 traces the social organization of leading private musical societies and shows how the Rio de Janeiro elite used these organizations—and a repertory that emphasized (German) classical music—as a means to separate themselves from the less affluent. This chapter also focuses on how the cultivated discussions about music on a local level reflected the ideas brought to Rio de Janeiro in imported music literature.

Although the musical preferences of the Carioca elite were somewhat consistent with those in Paris, and were therefore largely predictable, Cariocas did not consume European music as a homogeneous repertory; not all musical styles and genres imported to Rio de Janeiro fitted the description of "high art," and most could be enjoyed in contexts that were far from exclusive. This is to say that the imported music did not remain in the strict domain of the rich and powerful. In fact, European music imported into nineteenth-century Rio de Janeiro allowed for a spectrum of social perceptions. Thus, chapter 4 examines the role of European music in a more inclusive environment: the theater. It shows how the social symbols and satires in Offenbach's operettas were reinterpreted and used in Rio de Janeiro to articulate local social and ethnic issues. This chapter also focuses on how local musical practices, particularly those derived from the Afro-Brazilian tradition, were combined with European music on the stages of imperial Rio de Janeiro. It shows that the consistent use of black dances in local theaters not only reflected a trend from Europe, but also marked the growing interest in black culture by the Brazilian white bourgeoisie. The last chapter addresses the idea of "local," "national," "foreign," and "European" music as perceived by local residents. It examines both the musical characteristics and the historical moments that made different musical works come to represent "national" music.

The examination of past repertories and musical practices cultivated outside central areas of dominance but fashioned on similar grounds to European music is a field that has yet to be fully embraced by music scholarship.[22] The challenges are plentiful: for a start, there are practical difficulties in retrieving and accessing primary sources; probably because the music has been considered unworthy of study, it still awaits proper preservation and cataloguing.[23] But the greatest obstacle lies in the traditional view that European musical works are "masterworks" standing on pedestals indifferent to time and, in our case, to place. Leo Treitler eloquently points out that investigation outside the "masterpiece" framework not only endangers claims of ownership but also threatens to disrupt "the myth through which Western European civilization contemplates and presents itself."[24] This book is not intended as a comparative history based on a monolithic aesthetic picture of how European music should sound and what images are associated with it. On the contrary, the main goal is to keep sight of the multiplicity of meanings European music has engendered outside its social-cultural-historical context and, specifically, how, in nineteenth-century Rio de Janeiro, European music was reshaped by a local culture to mean something else.

From the perspective of studies dealing with nineteenth-century music in Rio de Janeiro, the focus on the European element has also been limited. The emphasis has always been on the local musical production and performance practices. Perhaps as a way to avoid dealing with "impoverished imitations,"[25] one has been bound to look at European musical traditions in Latin American cities insofar as they were altered by some kind of "cross-fertilization" with the local element.[26] This study will consider several non-European musical practices, particularly those of Afro-Brazilian derivation. Nonetheless, rather than attempting to address the uniqueness and the authenticity in these practices, the focus here is on how they were articulated in the context of a European-minded society and amid different styles of European music.

A NEW WORLD EMPIRE

The pungent spread of European culture in nineteenth-century Rio de Janeiro was the result of political events that started in Europe. Napoleon's invasion of Portugal in 1807 prompted the Portuguese royal family to set sail for Brazil, their largest colony, and to transfer the court from Lisbon to Rio de Janeiro. The move resulted in an unprecedented event in the history of European colonialism, for the

Braganzas were the only European monarchs to rule from one of their colonies.[27] This strategic political maneuver, as Schultz points out, also gave rise to an extraordinary "inversion of the political, economic, and cultural hierarchies that had guided three centuries of European expansion."[28] For not only had the relationship between mother country and colony been altered, but it was on Brazilian soil that João VI, the prince regent of Portugal, and the Portuguese aristocracy celebrated the salvation of the independent European monarchy, as well as the promise of imperial renovation, with the re-creation in Rio de Janeiro of a European court that represented a New World empire.[29]

Nowhere in the country did the relocation of the Portuguese royal family cause deeper social and cultural impact than in Rio de Janeiro. Although the city had been a strategic port and the vice-regal capital since 1763, when the royal family arrived in 1808, Rio de Janeiro was still a small city, subdued by cultural and intellectual isolation. Its colonial setting hosted a small aristocracy of wealthy landowners served by a majority of blacks, mulattos, slaves, and freedmen, and only a thin stratum of middle-class workers. With the arrival of the Braganzas, Rio de Janeiro was transformed from a "backward" city into the capital of the Portuguese worldwide empire. To do justice to the city's new status, upon his arrival, João VI opened Brazilian ports to foreign trade and ordered several improvements to the city's infrastructure, including illumination and paving. He then endowed the new capital of the empire with several cultural venues such as public libraries, schools, theaters, and philosophical and scientific academies. He also established a printing press, thereby starting the official publishing of newspapers and books in the country.[30] João VI also saw to it that Rio de Janeiro enjoyed the same artistic development as European capitals; thus, in 1816 he sponsored a group of French artists to start a royal academy of arts and architecture in the capital.

As the large hegira that accompanied the prince regent tried to make the new setting as much like their home country as possible, European cultural and stylistic models became increasingly available. From booksellers to hair stylists to private French teachers, a new stratum of local commerce led by immigrants fulfilled the local demand for "things European." Rio de Janeiro's local white elite soon came to view their city as not merely the capital of the country, but as the capital of a New World empire. Following the example of the newly arrived aristocrats, they began to look across the Atlantic for inspiration, to adopt European manners and modes of thinking, and to view themselves as Europeans.[31] Cariocas then began to refer to Rio de Janeiro as the *corte* (the court): after all, their city was now a "Tropical Versailles."[32]

Since the beginning, music was vital in the city's transformation into a European-style court. Three months after his arrival, João VI inaugurated the royal chapel, which boasted a choir of thirty-eight singers and an orchestra of forty-one instrumentalists.[33] Several musicians imported from Portugal and Rome joined the best singers and performers available in the Brazilian capital to provide members of the court and European visitors with music that paralleled that of the royal chapel in Lisbon. One of João VI's most daring initiatives was the building of the Theatro São João, a project aimed at endowing Rio de Janeiro with a lavish theater that could rival those in Lisbon. With the inauguration of the new theater on October 12, 1813, Rio de Janeiro's residents could brag about possessing the venue necessary to transplant across the Atlantic one of the most imposing symbols of European (elite) culture: opera. With a stage capable of hosting large opera companies hired in Europe,[34] the Theatro São João was vital in starting an operatic craze in Latin American cities that would continue well into the twentieth century.

In 1815, in an attempt to consolidate Brazil's position within the empire and to further strengthen links with Europe, João VI raised the country's status to "Kingdom of Brazil," equal to and united with that of Portugal. However, with the defeat of Napoleon in Europe, João VI's stay in Brazil was no longer required; politics in Portugal went sour as the Portuguese aristocracy fought to regain control of the empire. Under constant pressure from Portugal to return to Lisbon, João VI bid farewell to Rio de Janeiro in April 1821, after thirteen years of residency. He left behind his son Pedro I as prince regent of Brazil. Not willing to give up Rio de Janeiro's status as a metropolis, Carioca elite overwhelmingly supported Pedro I, who openly identified more with Brazilian causes than with Portuguese interests. In January 1822, he challenged a direct order from Portugal and refused to return to Lisbon; in September of that year, supported by the local elite, Pedro I declared Brazilian independence from Portugal and was proclaimed "constitutional emperor and perpetual defender of Brazil."[35]

That the Brazilian independence was declared by the heir of the House of Braganza with massive support from elite landowners and merchants started Brazil along a different path than that of its Latin American neighbors. At a time when most Spanish courtly models were being dismantled and independence movements were stirring political unrest in other parts of South America, the transition from colony to independence in Brazil was a fairly peaceful process, marked by remarkable degrees of political, economic, and social continuity.[36] Furthermore, the establishment of a monarchical government in Brazil served as a symbol of stability, guaranteed local and international legitimacy to Pedro I's rule, and continued to link the country with the Old (European) World.[37] More than anywhere in Latin America, nineteenth-century Brazil remained directly responsive to European economics and politics, and its society remained solidly grounded in European culture.[38]

As the seat of a New World empire, now independent from Portugal, Pedro I's Rio de Janeiro (1822–1831) developed a rich cultural life, with the royal government as "the center of cultural patronage."[39] The royal family regularly attended plays, operas, and concerts— thus formally and publicly demonstrating their support for such cultural undertakings. As a composer himself and a personal friend of Rossini, Pedro I was well known for his commitment to music.[40] His wife, Empress Leopoldina, was the daughter of Franz Joseph I of Austria and shared the musical taste of the Habsburgs in Vienna. She tirelessly promoted musical performances at the court, in particular the Viennese classics. Through her contacts, the Austrian composer Sigismund Neukomm (1778–1858), a disciple of Haydn, came to Rio de Janeiro where he lived from 1816 to 1821 and taught several members of the royal family. In 1819, under his guidance, the local aristocracy heard the performance of Mozart's *Requiem,* and, in 1821 they were privileged to hear the first New World Italian performance of Mozart's *Don Giovanni.*[41]

Pedro I's initial political accomplishments did not last long, however. In 1831, after regional disturbances and difficulties in reconciling political disputes, Pedro I abdicated and departed for Lisbon, leaving the throne in Rio de Janeiro to his five-year-old son, Pedro II. A native Brazilian, Pedro II was proclaimed emperor of Brazil in 1840 at the age of fourteen, and for almost half a century (1840–1889) he governed Brazil with a personal commitment that gained him wide-ranging respect and strong political deference. In a short period the young emperor consolidated the process of independence, overcame regional rebellions, and brought political stability and some economic prosperity to the country. His efforts to modernize and "civilize" Brazil were under way by midcentury with the construction of railroads, the establishment of regular steam service to France and England (1843 and 1851), the improvement of the banking system and creation of the Bank of Brazil (1851), and the commencement of telegraphic communication and a mail system (1852).[42] These and other accomplishments led Brazilians to believe that Pedro II was capable of building a nation on par with the most powerful European countries.

The fast Europeanization and consequent transformations of the Brazilian capital became more evident during Pedro II's government, both as a reflection of the emperor's individual efforts and as a result of a new wealth derived from coffee production in the surrounding province. European ideals of modernization proposed by Pedro II were easily seen around the capital, where improvements in transportation (mule-drawn streetcars), gas lighting, and an underground sewage system helped the urbanization of the city, although benefiting mostly elite residential areas. The young emperor devoted special attention to the development of the arts and music, patronizing the Academia de Belas Artes and, in 1848, subsidizing with two lotteries the foundation of the Imperial Conservatory of Music, an initiative of composer Francisco Manuel da Silva (1795–1865).[43] Pedro II showed his personal goodwill toward the arts by also offering his personal patronage in the form of travel grants to students who distinguished themselves in the academia and in the conservatorio and who wished to study in Europe.[44]

The emperor also made it a priority to promote and subsidize European immigration. In addition to the aristocratic crowd that vaunted their way through the streets of the capital, Rio de Janeiro of the Second Empire was greatly transformed by a large number of European immigrants, especially Portuguese and Italians, who quickly responded to the country's expanding economy and flooded the city. From 100,000 inhabitants at the time of independence in 1822, the population of Rio de Janeiro grew to 275,000 in 1872, of which some 84,000 were foreign-born. From 1872 to the proclamation of the republic in 1889, the population of the city almost doubled.[45] The immigrants were predominantly professionals: artisans, doctors, musicians, tailors, merchants, bankers, small businessmen, and bureaucrats. They formed a middle class that helped transform the capital into a cosmopolitan center. European urban culture easily made its way into the lives of these new Cariocas, and unequivocally also helped delineate the values, behaviors, and tastes of Rio de Janeiro's emerging middle class.

European culture did not come to Rio de Janeiro unfiltered, however. Not every European fashion appealed to Cariocas, but primarily those emanating from England and France, the centers of economic and cultural power that directly affected nineteenth-century Brazil. England, Portugal's longtime commercial partner, not only orchestrated the Braganzas' move and helped transport the royal family to their New World colony, but also greatly benefited from trading privileges with Brazil throughout the nineteenth century. After Napoleon's defeat in Europe, an intense commerce with France strengthened French commercial and cultural connections with imperial Brazil, while boosting the longtime Portuguese Francophile on the other side of the Atlantic. From England came heavy machinery and industrialized items, fine china, and masculine fashion. But it was the French courts of the restored Bourbons and of the Second Empire that set the fashion for most Brazilian imperial institutions, fueling the ideas and ideologies of local politicians, intellectuals, artists, and musicians.

Under Pedro II, Brazil was destined to become "the France of South America," and imperial Rio de Janeiro a "Tropical Paris."[46] Pedro II himself projected the image of "a solidly bourgeois king, in tails, top hat, and carrying an umbrella in the manner of France's Louis-Philippe."[47] He maintained regular correspondence with several French intellectuals such as Arthur de Gobineau and Victor Hugo,[48] although to satisfy his intellect, he needed go no further than his own surroundings, for French literature and French writings were widely available in local bookstores. In 1838, the American Rev. Parish Kidder noted that the "increase of readers in Brazil is . . . an extension of the Parisian [book] market."[49] The "Frenchification" of imperial Rio de Janeiro could be easily seen in the local neoclassical architecture, the dress and hair styles of elite women, the paintings of artists trained in French *ateliers*, and in the sanctioning of music and literary fashions streaming from Paris.[50] The construction of opera houses, the proliferation of theaters, ballrooms, and concert halls, offered Cariocas myriad musical options, all of which mirrored Parisian musical institutions and gave Cariocas a delightful taste of musical Paris. The parallel between imperial Rio de Janeiro and Paris was evident enough to elicit comparisons by French visitors, who noted that the two busiest streets of the imperial capital, Rua do Ouvidor and Rua Direita, recalled the rue Vivienne and rue Saint-Honoré in Paris.[51] The French immigrant Adèle Toussaint-Samson reported in midcentury that the Rua do Ouvidor was "essentially a French street," which "although narrow and ugly, is in some sort the Boulevard des Italiens of the capital of Brazil."[52]

Behind the Parisian *façade*, however, the glamour of the imperial capital could not parallel that of major European capitals. At midcentury, Rio de Janeiro was indeed the largest city in Latin America, but its population was still very small by European standards. In 1860, London had some 3 million inhabitants, the population of Paris totaled 1.6 million, but Rio de Janeiro had only 250,000. Given that the segment of the population that promoted and attended artistic events was a meager part of that already small number, the city's parochialism had no counterpart in contemporary Paris. Furthermore, the French architecture barely sheltered a city that lacked the most basic urban infrastructure. Visitors and locals alike could not help but eagerly complain about Rio de Janeiro's dirty streets, lack of sewage, and inadequate water system, which made the yellow fever epidemics appear impossible to eradicate.[53]

Figure I.1. "Provisory Acceptance of the Lisbon Constitution." Largo do Rocio in 1821 with the front terrace of the Theatro São João in the background. Jean-Baptiste Debret, *Voyage pittoresque et historique au Brésil* (Paris: Firmin Didot Frères, 1834–1839), vol. 3/45. Library of Congress.

But the city's urban milieu contrasted most conspicuously with that of contemporary Paris in that, at midcentury, nearly half of Rio de Janeiro's population was composed of blacks, slaves, and freedmen, the majority of which were Africans and first generation Afro-Brazilians.[54] As the capital of a country that imported more Africans than any other in the Americas, the city clearly displayed nineteenth-century Brazil's racial relations: a slave society ruled by a minority of whites who relied heavily on patronage to maintain social and political control. That harsh reality hardly escaped foreign visitors, for whom the "tropical Paris" was incongruently also an "African city in America."[55] Gaston d'Orléans, prospective husband of Pedro II's daughter Isabel, wrote to his father in Europe that "[Brazil] is magnificent and much more advanced in civilization than I expected," but that he was most struck by "the overwhelming presence of people of wholly or partly African descent."[56] It was not the encounter with blacks per se that most struck visitors, but the disturbing presence of slavery, which persisted in Brazil until 1888. Toussaint-Samson reported in 1850 that "the sight of slavery was, during the first years of my sojourn in Brazil, one of the torments of my life. . . . At every instant my heart revolted or bled when I passed before one of those buildings, where the poor Negroes, standing upon a table, were put up at auction, and examined by their teeth and their legs, like horses or mules.[57]

There was no escape from the scenario. Africans and Afro-Brazilians, slaves, and freedmen were present in just about every aspect of Carioca life: in the streets they were seen escorting white, middle- and upper-class families, selling food on sidewalks, and *capoeira* dancing[58] accompanied by their drums in the city's large squares. Out of the public eye, they worked as servants in the houses of well-to-do families, in the manufacture of shoes and clothing, and in a variety of other artisan crafts, and provided labor for the city's incipient industry. Although excluded from all aspect of the city's decision making, their way of life and culture permeated the city's milieu to a degree that European-minded Cariocas could only begin to understand. If, on the one hand, black culture sharply contrasted with European buildings and fashions, on the other it managed to maintain an uncanny coexistence with the French façades. Unlike Paris, Rio de Janeiro society was deeply marked by the institution of slavery, and was shaped by a constant observance of black culture,

Figure I.2. "Os refrescos da tarde no Largo do Palácio," (afternoon refreshments at the Largo do Palácio) where individuals from various social classes and ethnic groups met during leisure times. Jean-Baptiste Debret, *Voyage pittoresque et historique au Brésil* (Paris: Firmin Didot Frères, 1834–1839), vol. 2/9. Library of Congress.

which, from the perspective of the ruling classes, was the object of constant disparagement and disapproval.

The massive presence of European models in a non-European setting undoubtedly magnified Cariocas's sense of "here" (as the periphery) and "there" (as the center). It also created peculiarities that in themselves marked the local culture as distinct from its Parisian counterpart.[59] The European liberalism advocated by Brazilian intellectuals, for instance, was always limited and contradicted by the institution of slavery. Local artists and intellectuals, strongly dependent on state patronage, provided an ambiguous interpretation of the imported culture. Brazilian novelist Machado de Assis (1839–1908) often endowed his characters with two contradictory perspectives to emphasize the conflicts between the aristocratic and bourgeois classes who lived in Brazil but chose Europe as their point of reference.[60] In the theater, European music mingled with songs and dances of Afro-Brazilian derivation, a combination that marked less of a fusion than a clash between the Carioca elite European fantasy and the Brazilian social and ethnic reality.

The clash between these different realities became more acute during the 1870s and 1880s. Pedro II's Rio de Janeiro was then quite a different place from the city that had embraced his rule thirty years earlier. Politically exhausted by a war against Paraguay (1864–1870), the imperial government now faced serious financial problems that intensified partisan strife.[61] Furthermore, an ever-growing middle class made up of wage-earners was challenging the monarchical government with increasing activism. Another middle stratum of the population consisting of students, intellectuals, and artists, now perceived the emperor and the established ruling classes as their "natural" opposition: "with republican and abolitionist ideals, they saw the monarchy as a force holding Brazil back."[62] It was during these decades that the various European theatrical, literary, and musical fashions played a most significant role in demarcating tastes and preferences. Explored as more than entertainment or art, European music was used both as a powerful social symbol and as a tool for articulating political statements in a period of fast socioeconomic and political changes.

NOTES

1. Claude Lévi-Strauss, *Tristes tropiques,* trans. John and Doreen Weightman (New York: Penguin Books, 1992 [1955]), 37.

2. Lévi-Strauss, *Tristes tropiques,* 87.

3. Clifford Geertz, *The Interpretation of Cultures* (New York: Basic Books, 1973), 348–49.

4. Homi Bhabha, "Of Mimicry and Man: The Ambivalence of Colonial Discourse," in *Tensions of Empire: Colonial Cultures in a Bourgeois World*, ed. Frederick Cooper and Ann Laura Stoler (Berkeley: University of California Press, 1997), 153, 156.

5. J. M. Rugendas, *Viagem pitoresca através do Brasil,* trans. Sérgio Milliet (São Paulo: Editora da Universidade de São Paulo), 203; cited in Jean M. Carvalho França, *Literatura e sociedade no Rio de Janeiro oitocentista* (Rio de Janeiro: Imprensa Nacional, 1999), 34.

6. Néstor García Canclini, *Hybrid Cultures: Strategies for Entering and Leaving Modernity*, trans. Christopher L. Chiappari and Silvia L. López (Minneapolis: University of Minnesota Press, 1995), 107–44, especially page 143.

7. Francisco Alencar, *História da sociedade brasileira* (Rio de Janeiro: Livro Técnico, 1981), 133.

8. Andrade left a vast literature on music, the most important are: *Ensaio sobre a música brasileira* (São Paulo: Livraria Martins, 1962 [1928]), *Aspectos da música brasileira* (São Paulo: Livraria Martins, 1965), *Modinhas imperiais* (São Paulo: Casa Chirato, 1930), and *Pequena história da música,* 9th ed. (Belo Horizonte: Editora Itatiaia Limitada, 1987 [1942]).

9. For an analysis of Andrade's ideas in *Ensaio,* see Christopher Dunn, "The Relics of Brazil: Modernity and Nationality in the Tropicalia Movement" (Ph.D. diss., Brown University, 1996), 56–58.

10. Canclini, *Hybrid Cultures,* 75.

11. Bernardo Illari's writings on South American colonial music are exemplary in that they deal with European music as one of the mediators between the various local subcultures. See his "No hay lugar para ellos: los indígenas en la capilla musical de La Plata," *Anuario* (Sucre, 1997): 73–108; and "Les hacen lugar? Y como? La representación del indio en dos villancicos chuquisaqueños de 1718," *Data* 7 (1997): 165–96. Antonio Alexandre Bispo has pointed out the need to reassess the musical production of nineteenth-century Brazil, see "O século XIX na pesquisa histórico-musical brasileira: necessidade de sua reconsideração," *Latin American Music Review* 2/1 (Spring 1981): 130–42.

12. Kirsten Schultz, *Tropical Versailles: Empire, Monarchy, and the Portuguese Royal Court in Rio de Janeiro, 1808–1821* (New York: Routledge, 2001), 102.

13. Florencia Mallon, "The Promise and Dilemma of Subaltern Studies," *American Historical Review* 99/5 (1994): 1510–11.

14. Most recent works on the topic focus on literature; see Maria Elizabeth Chaves de Mello, *Lições de crítica: conceitos europeus, crítica literária e literatura crítica no Brasil do século XIX* (Niterói, RJ: Editora da Universidade Federal Fluminense, 1997); and França, *Literatura e sociedade no Rio de Janeiro oitocentista.* For a most interesting investigation of Rio de Janeiro intellectuals and the commemoration of Carnival see Leonardo Affonso de Miranda Pereira, *O carnaval das letras* (Rio de Janeiro: Coleção Biblioteca Carioca, 1994).

15. Mark Slobin, "Micromusics of the West," *Ethnomusicology* 36/1 (1992): 29.

16. Adam Krims addresses this "mythical representation" in relation to the contemporary spread of rap music outside the United States; see *Rap Music and the Poetics of Identity* (Cambridge, U.K.: Cambridge University Press, 2000), 157.

17. See Benjamin Orlove and Arnold Bauer, "Giving Importance to Imports," in *The Allure of the Foreign: Imported Goods in Postcolonial Latin America* (Ann Arbor: University of Michigan Press, 1997), 18.

18. The expression "cultural management," coined by Daryle Williams as "an institutionalized, administrative relationship between the state and

culture" can be optimally applied here, where the monarchical government attempted to control most forms of institutionalized cultural expressions; see *Culture Wars in Brazil: The First Vargas Regime, 1930–1954* (Durham, N.C. and London: Duke University Press, 2001), 26.

19. Kay Kaufman Shelemay, *Soundscapes* (New York: W. W. Norton, 2001), 268.

20. William Rowe and Vivian Schelling, *Memory and Modernity: Popular Culture in Latin America* (London and New York: Verso, 1991), 9.

21. Jeffrey Needell defines the Carioca elite in terms of numbers and occupation; see *A Tropical Belle Époque: Elite Culture and Society in Turn-of-the-Century Rio de Janeiro* (Cambridge: Cambridge University Press, 1987), 237–42.

22. That is not always the case when the issue is "Otherness." As musicology opens its doors to culturally sensitive readings of the canon itself, it also begins to embrace repertories belonging to a generic Other—that is, a body of music implicitly different from the mainstream European art music, emanating from different cultures, geographically distant from the centers of economic power and/or historically removed from the canonic repertory.

23. Until very recently, few libraries in Brazil had updated cataloguing systems for the thousands of nineteenth- and early twentieth-century sheet music publications in their holdings. Usually, individual publications were grouped by genre (dance, song, and so on), by composer, or by date, and were tied together in like piles. Needless to say, they were sometimes impossible to retrieve.

24. Leo Treitler, "Gender and Other Dualities of Music History," in *Musicology and Difference: Gender and Sexuality in Music Scholarship*, ed. Ruth A. Solie (Berkeley: University of California Press, 1993), 23.

25. This is also true for studies of European-style music in other parts of Latin America. Speaking from a time when ethnocentrism often went unquestioned in academic discourse, Charles Seeger notes, "Like all colonial music, the history of the fine art of music in Mexico has been for the most part stumbling, mongrel, epigonic, and inept. Only a few works and those very recent, can stand beside the best works of the big world, except to disadvantage"; see Charles Seeger, review of *The Music in Mexico* by Robert Stevenson, *Notes*, X/2 (March 1953): 270.

26. Ulf Hannerz, *Cultural Complexity: Studies in the Social Organization of Meaning* (New York: Columbia University Press, 1992), 265.

27. For the history and analysis of the political implications of the Portuguese royal family transfer to Brazil, see E. Bradford Burns, *A History of Brazil* (New York: Columbia University Press, 1993), 112; see also Leslie Bethell, "The Independence of Brazil," in *Brazil: Empire and Republic 1822–1930,* ed. Leslie Bethell (Cambridge: Cambridge University Press, 1989), 14–19.

28. Schultz, *Tropical Versailles*, 15.

29. Schultz, *Tropical Versailles*, 80–87. See also the chapter "Cultural Management before 1930," in Williams, *Cultural Wars in Brazil*, 27–51.

30. For a history of printing in Brazil see Juarez Bahia, *Jornal, história e técnica: história da imprensa brasileira,* 4th ed. (São Paulo: Ática, 1990).

31. Richard M. Morse, "Cities and Society in Nineteenth-Century Latin America: Brazil," in *The Urban Development of Latin America*, ed. Richard Morse, Michael Conniff, and John Webel (Stanford, Calif.: Stanford University Press, 1971), 288.

32. The comparison between the Sun King's palace in France and D. João VI's residence in Rio de Janeiro is explored in the introduction of Schultz's *Tropical Versailles.*

33. Ayres de Andrade, *Francisco Manuel da Silva e seu tempo: 1808–1865, uma fase do passado musical do Rio de Janeiro à luz de novos documentos*, vol. 1 (Rio de Janeiro: Edições Tempo Brasileiro, 1967), 27.

34. For a description of the Theatro São João, see J. Galante de Sousa, *O teatro no Brasil* (Rio de Janeiro: MEC, Instituto Nacional do Livro, 1960), 286.

35. Roderick J. Barman, *Citizen Emperor: Pedro II and the Making of Brazil 1825–1891* (Stanford, Calif.: Stanford University Press, 1999), 4.

36. Bethell, "The Independence of Brazil," 40–42.

37. Barman, *Citizen Emperor,* 9.

38. For descriptions of the customs and fashions of mid-nineteenth-century Brazilian society see Gilberto Freire, *Vida social no Brasil nos meados do século XIX* (Recife: Instituto Joaquim Nabuco, 1964); see also his *Inglêses no Brasil: aspectos da influência britânica sôbre a vida, a paisagem e a cultura brasileira* (Rio de Janeiro: José Olympio, 1948). For the "Europeanization" of Brazilian cities see Richard Graham, "The Urban Style," in *Britain and the Onset of Modernization in Brazil: 1850–1914* (Cambridge: Cambridge University Press, 1968), 112–24.

39. Williams, *Cultural Wars in Brazil,* 28.

40. Burns, *A History of Brazil*, 117. Pedro I's *Marcha Nacional do Brazil*, a *Souvenir filial* (Divertimento para piano) is included in Christian Müller's 1837 catalogue, which lists the pieces for sale in his establishment in Rio de Janeiro.

41. Cristina Magaldi, "A disseminação da música de Mozart no Brasil (séc. XIX)," *Revista brasileira de música* 19 (1991): 15–32.

42. Richard Graham, "The Onset of Modernization in Brazil," in *Britain and the Onset of Modernization in Brazil*, 23–50.

43. Francisco Manuel da Silva was one of the most important musicians at midcentury Brazil. He studied with José Maurício Nunes Garcia (1767–1830), Marcos Portugal, and Sigismund Neukomm in Rio de Janeiro. In 1823 he was appointed percussionist and later cellist of the royal chapel and in 1841, on the death of Simão Portugal, he assumed the position of chapel master. Silva founded the imperial conservatory, was a member of

the Academia de Música e Ópera Nacional (1857), the author of a large number of sacred compositions, and wrote the music for the National Anthem. For a full-length biography see Andrade, *Francisco Manuel da Silva e seu tempo*, 2 vols.

44. For a list of Brazilian musicians who received financial support from the emperor see Guilherme Auler, *Os bolsistas do imperador* (Petrópolis: Tribuna de Petrópolis, 1956), 54–60. See also Maria Alice Volpe, "Compositores românticos brasileiros: estudos na Europa," *Revista brasileira de música* 21 (1994–1995): 51–76.

45. In 1872, the time of the first census, 21 percent of the capital's population was Portuguese; see June E. Hahner, *Poverty and Politics: The Urban Poor in Brazil, 1870–1920* (Albuquerque: University of New Mexico Press, 1986), 47. After Rio de Janeiro, the other major urban centers in 1875 were Salvador and Recife, each with about 100,000 inhabitants; see Richard Graham, "1850–1875," in *Brazil: Empire and Republic, 1822–1930*, 135. For general information on Brazilian population and immigration see also Thomas William Merrick and Douglas Graham, *Population and Economic Development in Brazil, 1808 to the Present* (Baltimore: Johns Hopkins University Press, 1979).

46. Barman, *Citizen Emperor*, 163.

47. João da Cruz Costa, *History of Ideas in Brazil: The Development of Philosophy in Brazil and the Evolution of National History*, trans. Suzette Macedo (Berkeley and Los Angeles: University of California Press, 1964), 58.

48. Georges Raeders, *Dom Pedro II e os sábios franceses* (Rio de Janeiro: Atlantica Editora, 1944).

49. Rev. Daniel Parish Kidder, *Sketches of Residence and Travels in Brazil* (Philadelphia: Sorin & Ball, 1845), 115.

50. For the importance of French literary ideas on nineteen-century Brazilian intellectuals and writers see Maria Elizabeth Chaves de Mello, *Lições de crítica*; see also Needell, *A Tropical Belle Époque*, 178–233.

51. Adolfo Morales de Los Rios Filho, *O Rio de Janeiro imperial* (Rio de Janeiro: Editora Noite, 1945), 240. Kidder compares the Rua do Ouvidor with the Palais Royal in Paris; see *Sketches of Residence and Travels in Brazil*, 74.

52. Adèle Toussaint-Samson, *A Parisian in Brazil; the Travel Account of a Frenchwoman in Nineteenth-century Rio de Janeiro*, trans. Emma Toussaint (Wilmington, Del.: Scholarly Resources, 2001), 35.

53. For an excellent study on the problems of sanitation and hygiene among Rio de Janeiro poor during the nineteenth century, see Sidney Chalhoub, *Cidade febril: cortiços e epidemias na corte imperial* (São Paulo: Companhia das Letra, 1996).

54. Needell, *A Tropical Belle Époque*, 22.

55. Toussaint-Samson, *A Parisian in Brazil*, xii.

56. Barman, *Citizen Emperor*, 157.

57. Toussaint-Samson, *A Parisian in Brazil*, 44.

58. *Capoeira* is an Afro-Brazilian fight, apparently of Bantu derivation, which has been converted into a dance/game with a specific choreography and music. In nineteenth-century Rio de Janeiro, *capoeiras* performed in squares and other open public areas where they displayed the rigor of their movements in fighting and dancing, sometimes causing great public disturbance. Capoeiras were indiscriminately prosecuted and punished almost daily by the imperial police. See Carlos Eugênio Líbano Soares, *A negrada instituição: os capoeiras na corte imperial, 1850–1890* (Rio de Janeiro: Access Editora, 1999).

59. Roberto Schwarz, *Ao vencedor as batatas* (São Paulo: Duas Cidades, 1977), 22.

60. Viotti da Costa, "Brazil: 1870–1889," in *Brazil: Empire and Republic, 1822–1930*, 182.

61. Richard Graham, "1850–1875," in *Brazil: Empire and Republic, 1822–1930*, 155.

62. Needell, *A Tropical Belle Époque*, 8.

Chapter 1

Imperial Rio de Janeiro Musical Milieu

VIA PARIS

"We have everything to equal the [balls] of the Grand Opéra in Paris," proudly announced the managers of a prominent Rio de Janeiro theater when advertising the music for a masquerade ball during the 1866 Carnival season.[1] Cariocas expected no less, as the music they admired and enjoyed was often validated by its Parisian provenance. Advertisements for operas, balls, concerts, and sheet music were frequently spiced up with catchy headlines that assured the music had been "also performed in Paris." Managers of local venues and musicians at large did not simply reach out to local residents with operas or vaudevilles, concerts or balls, but rather catered to the local public with "the best operas as [they are] presented in the Théatre Italien [in Paris]" and "the best vaudevilles of the Palais Royal and the Variétés [in Paris]." Cariocas's musical preferences depended largely on this Parisian connection, which served as an initial point of reference to the music they eventually would adopt as their own.

But while the simulation of a Parisian performance enhanced the cachet of the imported repertory, the music circulating in Rio de Janeiro was not exclusively French. Paris served as a filter where a wide variety of European musical genres and styles were selected before they traveled to the Brazilian capital. All kinds of musical fads enjoyed by the Parisian bourgeoisie at different points in the nineteenth century—from Italian opera to parlor songs in the vernacular, from German symphonic and chamber music to "exotic"

1

Spanish dances performed at theatrical intermissions—were sooner or later echoed in Rio de Janeiro theaters, concert halls, and private salons. No matter the provenance of the music, however, it was imperative that it arrive in Rio de Janeiro via Paris, for the local preference for French, Italian, or German music at different times during the century was closely tied to the predilections of Parisians.

Cariocas particularly inherited the Parisian preference for opera, and were enthralled by operettas and other Parisian music theater fashions, which they enjoyed in Rio de Janeiro theaters with names that recalled their Parisian counterparts, such as Theatro Alcazar Lyrique (modeled on L'Alcazar) and Theatro Gymnasio Dramatico (modeled on Théâtre du Gymnase Dramatique). They followed with equal attentiveness the repertory of the Théâtre-Italien, the Opéra, the Opéra-Comique, and the Théâtre des Bouffes Parisiens through accounts from Paris, which appeared frequently in local newspapers and magazines. The local elite, versed in the French language, also read about premieres and other Parisian performances directly from French publications that were widely available. Their knowledge of the repertory acquired through readings would eventually grow into truthful appreciation, for they were lucky enough also to have the chance to experience the music at home. During the First Empire (under Pedro I), operas by Rossini and the popular vaudevilles from Eugène Scribe (1791–1861), the two Parisian favorites during the first half of the century, were available in imperial Rio de Janeiro after a time lag of some five to ten years.[2] Rossini's *Aureliano in Palmira* (1813), for example, was heard in Rio de Janeiro in 1820; *Tancredi* (1813) and *La Cenerentola* (1817) in 1821. As the commercial, political, and cultural connections with France intensified during the Second Empire (under Pedro II), more Parisian musical successes became available more quickly. Verdi's *Ernani* (1843), for example, was presented in Rio de Janeiro only three years after its Italian premiere, and a new Parisian fad, Offenbach's *La belle Hélène* (1864), was presented to Cariocas on June 26, 1866, only eighteen months after its Parisian premiere.[3] By the 1880s, Cariocas had to wait no more than a few months to attend at home an operatic presentation that had achieved success in Paris. If nothing could be done about the geographical distance separating Cariocas from European capitals, the time distance between Paris and Rio de Janeiro musical premieres gradually diminished as the century progressed and Cariocas were kept au courant with Parisian successes.

The musical connection between imperial Rio de Janeiro and the French capital was particularly strong in the 1860s, 1870s, and 1880s. The growth of a more cosmopolitan city during the last decades of the monarchical regime prompted a larger number of Cariocas to seek frantically all the pleasures of urbane European life by diversifying their local musical choices. To diversify meant, of course, to create local counterparts to about every Parisian musical institution. Thus, in 1858, only three years after Jacques Offenbach (1829–1880) inaugurated his Théâtre des Bouffes-Parisiens, Rio de Janeiro replied with Cafés concertos and the Folies Parisiennes held at the large and luxurious Paraiso Hall.[4] Another enterprise in a similar vein was attempted by the Dutch immigrant André Gravenstein (1816–1869) who, from 1862 to 1869, provided residents of imperial Rio de Janeiro with local *bailes à Musard*, popular balls modeled on Philippe Musard's (1793–1859) fashionable masquerade balls of the 1830s held at the Théâtre des Variétés and at the Opéra in Paris. Musard's orchestra was well known for its loud and brassy sound and the balls were all the rage among Parisians and foreign visitors, who particularly craved the audacious finales that included gallops, cancans, and occasional police intervention.[5] In Rio de Janeiro, the balls were held at the Pavilhão Fluminense, the remodeled Paraiso Hall, now an even larger ballroom with capacity for some 1,500 dancers, and illuminated by 402 lights distributed among 13 crystal chandeliers and 68 sconces on its lateral walls. Gravenstein's programs in the 1860s included just the right variety of dances likely to be found in Musard's balls, from quadrilles and schottisches to polkas and waltzes. In the 1870s and 1880s, Cariocas enjoyed the Eldorado, an imitation of the Alcazar d'eté in the Champs-Elysées in Paris,[6] where they could listen to Gravenstein's orchestra while dining in a lavish garden.

More intimate and selective were the concert rooms Salão Arthur Napoleão & Miguez (1879) and Salão Bevilacqua (1880), which were direct replicas of the two famous Parisian concert halls owned by piano manufacturers Salle Pleyel (1830–1927) and Salle Herz (1842–1860?).[7] As in Paris, these local concert rooms were owned by musicians involved in piano sales as well as music printing, and who were well-respected individuals in the local musical business. Like the Parisians Camille Pleyel and Henri Herz, Alfredo Bevilacqua (1846–1927) and Arthur Napoleão (1843–1925) were also performers and composers and therefore well acquainted with the issues involved in the promotion of concerts. Their salons, colocated with their shops, were of much smaller dimensions than the Parisian Salle Pleyel or Herz, accommodating only chamber music and solo concerts, but according to a contemporary description, the Salão Bevilacqua was "beautiful, with good acoustics, ventilated, accommodating 250 to 300 people."[8] These Rio de Janeiro salons, like their Parisian counterparts, constantly welcomed an impressive stream of prominent performers and offered opportunities for new talent. They offered small-scale events open to the public, although always with a select circle in attendance. The concert of the Cuban violinist José White (1836–1918) and the pianist Arthur Napoleão on December 30, 1879, at the Salão Napoleão & Miguez, for instance, gathered "a vast number of very distinguished ladies, state ministers, prominent musicians, and other meritorious individuals."[9]

Local and foreign entrepreneurs also saw it fashionable, and potentially profitable, to transplant to imperial Rio de Janeiro Parisian musical institutions that offered concerts en masse and introduced the Viennese classics to the Parisian bourgeoisie. The main model was the Parisian Concerts Populaires (1861–1884) directed by Jules Étienne Pasdeloup (1819–1887). Pasdeloup's popular concerts introduced "established masterpieces and distinguished soloists to a larger, less affluent, (and presumably less cultured) audience" with low admission fees.[10] He installed his 101-member orchestra at the Cirque Napoléon (Boulevard de Filles-du Calvare), later called the Cirque d'hiver and now known as Place Pasdeloup, an enormous hall that seated about 5,000 and offered Parisians concerts every Sunday of the year.

The first Brazilian counterpart appeared in 1862, an initiative by the Italian immigrants Tiago Henrique Canongia and Angelo Carrero Canongia. Not as pretentious as the Parisian Concerts Populaires, Canongia and Carrero's first concert was presented at the hall of the Pavilhão Fluminense and one month later at the small Theatro Gymnasio Dramatico.[11] Their endeavor soon proved unprofitable and failed to survive long enough to have an impact on local musical life. The reason for the failure might have been Cariocas's unconditional devotion to the theater and the operatic repertory, but it also might have reflected the difficulty in gathering a sufficient number of local musicians capable of performing a more demanding repertory.

It was not until 1870 that Cariocas could enjoy a more faithful counterpart to Pasdeloup's popular concerts, this time in an enterprise put together by the Italian singer Carlotta Patti (1835–1889), the French pianist Théodore Ritter (1841–1886), and the Spanish violinist Pablo Sarasate (1844–1908).[12] The concerts were announced in the local newspaper *Jornal do commercio* on July 21, 1870, as Concertos Patti de Música Clássica (Patti's Concerts of Classical Music) and later simply as Concertos Populares (Popular Concerts). Without the grandeur of Pasdeloup's Parisian concerts, Patti's series took place at a local theater and ran for only six consecutive Thursdays. According to the organizers, the enterprise was a response to "suggestions of several Brazilian dilettanti," and had "the collaboration of a local orchestra of professional musicians."[13] Their aim was to replicate Pasdeloup's "musical temple" and to follow the French conductor by also introducing Brazilians to "the beauties that are found in symphonies by Mozart, Haydn, and Beethoven."[14] Unfortunately, Patti, Ritter, and Sarasate's performances, although reasonably successful, also failed to impress the local public. The difficulties were tremendous: first, there were complaints that the tickets were too expensive, at least for a series titled Popular Concerts; second, Patti and her companions were able to gather no more than fifty musicians for their orchestra, which could not offer Cariocas the same grandiose effects as Pasdeloup's ensemble in Paris; and finally, Cariocas were not interested in the repertory, which required more attention and deference than they were willing to give. In the end, the concerts turned out to be ephemeral events, and once Patti and her companions left Rio de Janeiro in August 1870, the local enthusiasm for the Concertos Populares died out. Three years later, André Gravenstein (son) made another attempt to replicate the Parisian concerts with his Concertos-Promenade but, unlike his father's popular bailes à Musard, the series lasted only a single season.[15]

Parisian enterprises devoted to chamber music from the Viennese classics took until the 1880s to be viable in imperial Rio de Janeiro, but they ultimately inspired local counterparts. Nonetheless, the adoption of "the classics," as opposed to opera, was an artificial trend that at first served no other cause than to fulfill Cariocas's earnest attempts to follow all Parisian musical fashions. But eventually, in the 1880s, the music found a following among the local elite, serving as a tool to boost their image of themselves as Europeans.

BRILLIANT IMMIGRANTS

Foreign musicians were mostly responsible for bringing imported music to Rio de Janeiro. Few who crossed the Atlantic searching for better opportunities failed; the majority found in Rio de Janeiro ideal conditions to launch a musical career. Continuing to arrive until late in the century, the immigrants were mostly Portuguese, Italians, French, and Germans with not only astute eyes (and ears) for music, but also a business sense that reflected their clear understanding of the needs of Rio de Janeiro residents to use music as a means to stand on equal footing with Europeans. A glance through the classified sections of midcentury Rio de Janeiro newspapers reveals a wide variety of immigrants offering their services as music teachers, performers, arrangers, and music copyists. Middle- and upper-class families regularly hired them to provide music for balls, background music for social gatherings, or private music lessons for their children. Copying and arranging music were also very profitable occupations for immigrants, considering that by midcentury the local publishing business alone could not meet the large demand for piano music or reductions for small ensembles. It is fair to say that immigrants dictated the music fashion in the imperial capital, for they occupied leading positions in the theater and in the music business at large. They also monopolized music teaching and prepared the musical careers of several native composers. In 1855, among the five teachers at the imperial conservatory were two Italians, Gioacchino Giannini (1817–1860) and Giovanni Scaramelli (d. 1857), and one Argentinean, Demetrio Rivero (1822–1889).

European immigrant musicians enjoyed the respect of Rio de Janeiro's aristocracy, and some were even granted imperial honors. Giannini, for instance, who arrived in the Brazilian capital in 1846 as the director of an Italian company, was appointed music director at the Theatro São Pedro de Alcantara two years later. Giannini prepared the musical careers of prominent native composers such as Antônio Carlos Gomes (1836–1896) and Henrique Alves de Mesquita (1830–1906), and in 1860 he held the privileged position of chapel master. A particularly successful story is that of the Portuguese virtuoso-pianist Arthur Napoleão, who, after performing several times in the Brazilian capital, settled there in 1869. Ten years later Napoleão had become not only one of the most respected individuals in Rio de Janeiro's musical life but also a successful businessman. He owned a large music-publishing house, a shop selling sheet music and instruments, and a salon hosting chamber and solo concerts that drew a select society. Napoleão performed extensively in private musical societies and, as a teacher, influenced a generation of local pianists.[16] He was presented with the imperial honorary insignia *Ordem da Rosa*, and managed to maintain his position as a leading figure within Rio de Janeiro's musical sphere after the proclamation of the republic in 1889.[17]

Immigrants dominated the local music business by providing Cariocas with music from Paris in the format of sheet music publications. As early as 1827, the French J. Crémière was announcing in a local newspaper that his shop had a deal with a Parisian merchant to regularly provide Cariocas with "new music" from Paris.[18] Ten years later, the Danish Johann Christian Müller started a Music Lending Library in Rio de Janeiro, offering music for sale and rental through quarterly, semestral, and annual subscriptions—an enterprise that, according to Müller, followed "European practice."[19] Müller's shop offered more than French music, but the provenance of the majority of the 1,584 pieces listed in his 1837 catalogue is unmistakable: it includes a conspicuous majority of composers active in Paris, and most of the pieces have French titles or are French translations of Italian operas. In 1871, the catalogue of music dealers Narciso & Arthur Napoleão still exhibited a wide majority of pieces with Parisian provenance, including transcriptions and arrangements of operatic hits for piano and small ensembles, and popular music for the dance hall.[20]

European immigrants also ventured into the local music publishing industry, which they found a particularly prosperous business. The Frenchman Pierre Laforge, who arrived in Brazil in 1816, pioneered the business, establishing his *estamparia de musica* (music publishing house) in the capital about 1834. He was followed by the German J. B. Klier, in Rio de Janeiro since at least 1828, who opened his own publishing house by 1836. The Italian Filippone started his publishing house in the 1840s, joining the Milanese singer Antonio Tornaghi in 1855 to form the firm Filippone & Tornaghi. Their business was so successful it permitted them to have distributors in other states and to export their publications to Buenos Aires. The Portuguese Raphael Coelho Machado (1814–1887), who reached Brazil in 1838, continued publishing from the mid-1840s until 1869, when his firm was sold to Narciso José Pinto Braga (d. 1889). Arriving in Brazil from Genoa in

1835, Isidoro Bevilacqua (1813–1897) opened a music shop with Milliet-Chesnay in 1846.[21]

These individuals transplanted to Rio de Janeiro the commerce of music, which had already reached an advanced stage in Paris and London. Those sectors of European music that did not cross the Atlantic in live performances, or took a long time to make it to the stages of the Brazilian capital, were rapidly replicated in Rio de Janeiro in sheet music, usually for piano, either published locally or imported. Piano reductions of operas, arrangements of arias for voice and piano, piano variations and fantasias of popular operatic tunes, and piano reductions of European ballroom dances were all welcome alternatives to Carioca amateurs, who could easily replicate the music popular in Paris in the comfort of their homes in Rio de Janeiro.

THE MAGIC MIRROR

If piano publications were abundant, so were pianos. Here, too, the parallel with Paris is inescapable. While the French critic Henri Blanchard maintained in 1839 that there were "enough pianists in Paris to hold a congress,"[22] the Brazilian Manoel de Araújo Porto Alegre (1806–1879) characterized Rio de Janeiro of the Second Empire as "the city of pianos."[23] As such, the imperial capital was an extremely profitable market for piano dealers and manufacturers, usually immigrants who made Europe's best pianos available in the city. The English Broadwood and the French Érard were the first to be imported.[24] By 1837, pianos of six, six-and-a-half, and seven octaves were available in Rio de Janeiro from French and English firms such as Érard, Broadwood, Small, Bruce, Clementi, Stoddart, Sannini, Wilkinson, Ruesch & Simonson, and Butcher & Comp. U.S. Chickering pianos were introduced in 1869 by the North American virtuoso Louis Moreau Gottschalk (1829–1869). Local piano manufacturers started competing with the English and French in 1837, when the Brazilian firm of immigrants Schmidt & Baguet announced their own pianos.[25] The competition intensified in 1845 when a U.S. manufacturer introduced a piano known especially for its "durability in tropical climates";[26] two years later, the Frenchman Henri Herz authorized a shop for the sale of his pianos in Rio de Janeiro, offering Cariocas a piano "made especially for Brazil" and "suitable to the Brazilian climate."[27] By 1854, other brands, such as Pleyel and Collard & Collard had distributors in Rio de Janeiro competing with three local piano manufacturers. According to Raphel Coelho Machado, English and French pianos were preferred over the German, Portuguese, and American, while Brazilian pianos were regarded as fragile due to the inferior wood used in their fabrication.[28]

In 1856, Rio de Janeiro had sixteen music shops that relied heavily on piano sales to turn a profit. To put this in a local perspective, by midcentury the city boasted no more than seven shops selling decorative items and twenty book dealers.[29] The buying and selling of pianos, as well as piano maintenance, remained profitable businesses until the turn of the twentieth century. It was not uncommon for amateurs, mostly women, to learn the art of piano tuning and general maintenance of the instrument. Extending his music business in the Brazilian capital, in 1838 the Dutch Müller advertised a course on piano tuning considered "very useful for music students."[30] In the 1840s, Raphael Coelho Machado issued his *Methodo de afinar piano* (Method for Piano Tuning), a guide which would attract few buyers in the twentieth century, but which reached three editions in nineteenth-century Rio de Janeiro (1843, 1845, 1849).

To be sure, the piano was by no means the only European instrument widely available; wind and string instruments were also sold at local music shops as early as 1837, alongside "Brazilian instruments of modern invention" such as *zabumbas* (bass drums), *pratos* (cymbals), triangles, *pandeiros* (membranophone similar to a tambourine), and *violas* (a folk instrument of the guitar family with five double courses).[31] Nor was the piano the only instrument used to transmit and re-create European culture through music. Harps, accordions, and especially guitars were widely available and shared with the piano the preferences of Carioca middle class for outdoor performances. But no instrument embodied such a deep sense of urbane European modernity and technological advancement as did the piano. The instrument was not simply a means of music making, but a sophisticated machine capable of producing awe-inspiring sounds worthy of "advanced cultures." Above all, the piano was a piece of furniture embodying the icon of power. Exhibiting a piano in a living room was an indication of one's acquaintance with, and admiration for, European music, through which one would gain considerable social status. Since the price of a piano was prohibitive for most Cariocas, the ownership of a piano was also a tangible sign of affluence. Contemporary data show that early in the century, fortepianos were sold in Rio de Janeiro for a considerable amount, roughly equivalent to the price of one or two slaves.[32] Later, small upright pianos were more affordable and became an indispensable item in the homes of the middle class.

The piano, a European bourgeoisie domestic musical instrument, also delineated gender roles in the local society. As with European bourgeoisie women, most middle- and upper-class Carioca women were amateur pianists and/or singers. Playing the piano was a necessary skill that attested to the female's domesticity as well as to her level of education. These two attributes were deemed essential in the female's upbringing, for they played a role in the game of attracting and holding men of high rank. But the instrument served women in many other ways. According to Brazilian novelist José de Alencar (1829–1877), "the piano was for the woman what the cigar is for the man, a friend for all times, and an alert confidant."[33] Most significant, knowing how to play the piano also attested to the woman's acquaintance with imported music and permitted her partaking in a much desired, male-dominated European world. Welcomed only in the boxes of the opera house and allowed at limited performances at the comic theater, women were also barred from participating, both as audience and as performers, from most events of musical societies ruled solely by men.[34] It was thus through the piano that most Carioca women had full access to the music imported from Europe, a back door access but nonetheless an access that was ultimately the key to a male world otherwise closed to them.

Perhaps the most important, and often overlooked, aspect of the piano dominance in Rio de Janeiro is the effect it had on the local perception of the music coming from overseas. The piano was the medium through which those living in peripheral areas were first exposed to the fashionable, European repertory, since the instrument permitted everyone around the world to experience orchestral scores, choral works, and operas by European composers through reductions and arrangements. Like no other musical instrument, the piano made possible the early globalization of music. Translating this into cultural politics, the instrument helped put European music and European culture in the center of musical and cultural production in remote areas. From the vantage point of the European music industry, the instrument was key in the early stages of music commercialization, for it helped boost the sales of European music beyond Europe. From the vantage point of those far from European centers, the piano was a most valuable tool for it allowed access to nearly every European musical fashion. The U.S. composer Arthur Farwell (1872–1952) offered an extraordinary description of this quality of the instrument:

> One's piano is a kind of magic mirror, which is capable of reflecting to one the whole musical world from classic times to the present, and throughout all lands. The tone of the orchestral instruments may not be there, vocal tone may not be there, or the sound of the chorus; but there is the melody, there is the harmony, and there is the rhythm—the three tangible factors that make up music. The soul is there, too, if we can get it out. Through our piano we can get into touch, more or less intimate, with everything from a Greek scale or a two-step, to Beethoven's Ninth Symphony, or a tone poem of Strauss. In short, we can take the whole world of music into our lives through our piano.[35]

If Cariocas took full advantage of this "magic mirror," they did so mostly without searching for the "soul" of the music. Piano reductions and arrangements were sometimes the only versions of imported operas and orchestral works Cariocas ever heard. The orchestral delicacies in *Il Barbieri di Seviglia's* overture, or the orchestral colors of Beethoven's symphonies, had little significance to those who absorbed the music solely through piano arrangements. To most Cariocas, and to most residents in urban areas in Latin America, the symbolism attached to the music imported from Europe, its association with modernity and power, was embodied through the music's melodic, harmonic, and rhythmic configurations—elements that could be retained (to a certain extent) in arrangements and facilitated versions; and these three "tangible factors" of music were understood when confined to the piano's timbre. Apparently, factors such as the music's originality and authenticity in performance were not critical issues for Cariocas. Piano reductions of operatic overtures and facilitated versions of popular arias could be so altered in printed arrangements and in piano performances that the imaginary original loomed as exotic in relation to them. It was one thing to hear Bellini's popular "Casta Diva" from *Norma* performed by professionals on stage at the opera house, and quite another to experience it in an informal, family performance, where younger and older sisters enjoyed a facilitated arrangement for voice and piano. This was particularly true for those who had never heard the staged opera. "Originality" and "authenticity" were in this case indeed irrelevant, for there was no "original" or "authentic" to serve as a point of reference.

As the main medium through which European music was absorbed into the local milieu, the piano offered Cariocas not only the opportunity to play the music and imagine that they were somewhere else, but also to improvise upon it. Farwell also noted that, "It requires only that one puts the music on his piano rack and play it, or, at least, play at it."[36] Not concerned with matters of authenticity, Cariocas used the piano to literally "play with" the music, and to modify and re-create it according to their tastes. Raphael Coelho Machado observed that one of the advantages the piano offered Cariocas was that it allowed for arias, duets, and choruses from operas to be "varied and transformed."[37] The piano thus offered a unique opportunity for a wider public to create an informal relationship with the music, a relationship that was less acceptable in a more formal setting such as a staged presentation or a concert.

THE THEATER

For Cariocas with means, the piano was a necessary item, one that permitted individual access to a fantasized European world as well as to the local upper-class society. Although not a portable instrument, it was small enough to fit in a corner of the living room to fulfill the social and musical needs of the family. Thus, while the piano was an indication of social status, gender roles, and musical preferences, it provided a means of cultural expression that was, for the most part, a private one. At the other extreme lay the theater, a shared space where novel, imported ideas and fashions, and plenty of music coming from Europe, were introduced to Cariocas. Unlike the piano, with which one could display individual musical preferences, the theater offered spectators less power of arbitration. The theater's symbolic role of dominance and permanence—displayed in sumptuous buildings constructed with generous aid from powerful individuals—was also reflected in managers' and impresarios' choice of repertory, mostly European music, which was primarily devised to please their patrons. As in other newly formed cities in Latin America, Rio de Janeiro theaters were glaring symbols that marked the presence of urbane European culture and, as Judith A. Weiss notes, were designed to draw crowds to hear "hegemonic messages repeated in new ways."[38]

In a practice that went back to Portugal, Rio de Janeiro's most luxurious theaters indeed served as a bridge between the monarchs and the people. All important courtly festivities such as birthdays, anniversaries, and political events were commemorated with theatrical or musical presentations. The transfer of power from João VI to his son Pedro I marked one such event, when the local aristocracy celebrated at the opera house with a gala performance of Rossini's *Cenerentola*.[39] Pedro II's birthdays were also regularly commemorated at the opera house: in 1853, his twenty-eighth birthday was observed with a gala performance of Verdi's *Nabucodonosor*.[40] The monarchs' and the aristocracy's frequent appearances at the opera house and at the theater served, among other things, to strengthen their roles as local perpetrators of European culture.

The theater was also vital in the early stages of the commercialization of entertainment, which involved the direct sale of tickets to the public. If, on the one hand, theaters were a testimonial to the monarchy's preeminence and power, on the other they were characterized by a distinctive social inclusiveness. This ambiguous position, as Weiss points out, also "led [the theater] to embrace systems of signs . . . not restricted to the hegemonic classes, in order to include audiences outside the small, restricted groups of patrons and other authorities."[41] In the nineteenth-century Brazilian capital, theater managers and musical directors played an important role in accommodating the status quo and the monarchical life to the rationality of an emergent bourgeois consumership. Significantly, and perhaps more than in other nineteenth-century Latin American cities, the stages of imperial Rio de Janeiro served as sites of informal political, social, and cultural arbitration, in which music, with its inherent potential for subjectivity, played a major role.[42]

Throughout the century, theaters were built, rebuilt, and replaced in the Brazilian capital, in a sequence of events hard to reconstruct completely. Fire was a constant threat and repeatedly burned down the city's most coveted theaters, taking with it valuable records.[43] Nevertheless, other primary sources and writings published in local newspapers and magazines make it clear that the theater was central to music making, and that European music was an integral part of the spectacle. In fact, in imperial Rio de Janeiro all musical activities were in one way or another linked to the theater. Local musicians found employment chiefly in theater orchestras; composers devoted themselves almost entirely to the composition of operas, operettas, or incidental music for plays, or short songs and dances to be performed as *intermezzi* or at the end of theatrical presentations;

and the singer occupied a central place in nearly every musical event. Moreover, professional musicians working in the theater monopolized music teaching. This was evident as early as 1841, when Brazilian composer Francisco Manuel da Silva set forth the early documents for the creation of the Imperial Conservatory of Music, stating that the chief goal of the conservatory was to prepare musicians able to fulfill positions at the theater and at the opera house.[44]

The largest and most luxurious theaters hosted operas and plays that regularly included European music. During D. João VI's government, opera was presented at the lavish Theatro São João, the largest theater in the city with a capacity of up to 1,200 spectators.[45] When the Theatro São João caught fire in 1824, it was replaced by the Theatro São Pedro de Alcantara. Inaugurated on April 16, 1827, with the performance of Rossini's *La Cenerentola*, the new theater accommodated some 1,100 spectators and remained the largest and most luxurious theater in Rio de Janeiro until midcentury. Destroyed by fire and rebuilt several times, the São Pedro de Alcantara continued to be active after the proclamation of the republic in 1889.

Figure 1.1.   Praça da Constituição in 1846, with the Theatro São Pedro de Alcantara in the background. Lithography published in the periodical *Ostensor Brazileiro* (Rio de Janeiro, 1846). Biblioteca Nacional, Rio de Janeiro.

When the Theatro São Pedro de Alcantara caught fire in August 1851, Cariocas were left without a theater big enough to host opera companies. While the imperial government put forward immediate plans to rebuild the São Pedro de Alcantara, it also introduced measures to build a provisory theater specifically for operatic presentations. Despite the suggestions of some that the plans for the new theater should follow those of Italian theaters so that Brazilians could brag to "possess a European opera house," limited financial resources resulted in a modest and inadequate building that left much to be desired in terms of architecture, decoration, and stage function.[46] Despite its shortcomings, by the time of its inauguration on March 25, 1852, the Theatro Provisorio (Provisory theater) was the largest in the city, with a total capacity of 1,326. The orchestra section (measuring 27 meters to the proscenium and 22 meters at its widest point) seated 830 male spectators in 514 seats and 316 benches. Women with their escorts were accommodated in the four tiers of pinewood boxes—thirty boxes in the two lower tiers, thirty-two boxes in the upper two tiers. The neoclassical exterior, without elaborate decoration, contrasted with the interior walls, which were painted rose and decorated with medallions honoring Auber, Donizetti, Verdi, and Meyerbeer, with Rossini occupying the central position.[47] Despite its precarious architecture, the provisory building was soon promoted to the status of a permanent opera house. In 1854, after the Theatro São Pedro de Alcantara was rebuilt and fully functional, the Theatro Provisorio was renamed Theatro Lyrico Fluminense and became the only theater to present operas on a regular basis. In 1865, it was remodeled to include new French tapestries and wallpaper, gas illumination, and new paintings on the ceiling.[48] Described by a local resident as "the first [theater] of its kind in the capital,"[49] the Theatro Lyrico Fluminense remained the main venue for operatic and dance companies hired in Europe for some twenty years.

When the Theatro Lyrico Fluminense closed its doors on April 30, 1875, Rio de Janeiro's audiences were finally presented with a new opera house, one that symbolized the zenith of the monarchy. Inaugurated February 19, 1871, the Theatro D. Pedro II was acclaimed not only for its good acoustics and for being the largest opera house in Rio de Janeiro, seating 1,400 people,[50] but also because it was conveniently located close to fashionable shopping and cafés. As is common in transferences of power, with the proclamation of the republic in 1889 the theater was renamed Theatro

Figure 1-2.　Theatro Provisorio in *Semana illustrada* (April 27, 1862). Young Research Library, UCLA.

Lyrico and it remained the center of musical life in the capital until 1934, when it was demolished.

Despite the splendor of these theaters and their stature among Rio de Janeiro's well-to-do, the São Pedro de Alcantara, the Theatro Provisorio (Theatro Lyrico Fluminense), and the Theatro D. Pedro II were not the only stages to gather crowds nor the only venues for the performance of European music. On the contrary, small, privately managed theaters regularly presented European music at more affordable prices. They numbered between two and five during the last decades of the Second Empire (1860s to 1880s), and accommodated from 400 to 800 people each. Members of the Carioca elite did not eschew being also habitués of these theaters, although they were more than willing to pay for the most expensive seats. Nonetheless, these venues were domains of the Carioca bourgeoisie and newly formed middle-class—made up of students, businessmen, intellectuals, and bureaucrats—who could enjoy the theater as sheer entertainment, rather than as a symbol of status.

These smaller theaters served as the main vehicles for the dissemination of new, imported ideas, since there was less direct government supervision and the powerful presence of the local aristocracy was diluted by a more socially mixed audience. Their stages were also particularly important in the popularization of music. In a city where 50 percent of the population was illiterate and a standard book edition of 1,000 copies could take five years to disappear from the shelves of bookshops, sheet-music editions circulated with a meager 100 copies.[51] Conversely, it could take less than twelve months for a show with 100 presentations in a theater with 500 seats to reach some 50,000 people (more than 20 percent of the city's population in 1872). Thus, not fundamentally different from today's mass media, the nineteenth-century theater was largely responsible for introducing novel musical genres and styles to massive numbers of people. Even if one takes into consideration the local practice of attending the same show numerous times, the number of people likely to have absorbed ideas and heard music in the theater was staggering. In Rio de Janeiro, theater managers took full advantage of such a popular venue, not only by providing local audiences with the latest musical fashions from Europe, but also by exploring ways in which these trends could be profitably adapted and incorporated into the local social and economic system to fulfill the demands of all sectors of the local social scale.

Smaller theaters were hardly praised for their architecture and decoration, least of all for their stages' technical suitability and acoustics. At midcentury, one commentator described the 480-seat theater São Januário (1838–1862) as having "no architecture whatsoever . . . imagine a house with five windows and as many doors in the form of an arc on the bottom. And nothing else."[52] The attraction of the Theatro São Januário and other small theaters like it lay less in their luxury than in the lighter repertory that contrasted with the music performed at the opera house. Another attractive attribute was the informal, flexible way in which music was presented; depending on the availability and technical capabilities of the performers and on the stage resources, in smaller venues European music was often rearranged, transformed, translated, paraphrased, and parodied. Especially in the 1870s and 1880s, as a result of political and social tribulations, the repertory in these small theaters was also shaped by the need to reach a wider audience whose affinities for the opera house and deference to the monarch were in sharp decline.

The informal and flexible manner in which music was presented, however, did not in any way undermine the local preference for musical fashions from Paris. Similarly to the opera house, managers of smaller venues relied on the Parisian success of a play as the hook to Cariocas. Actor João Caetano (1808–1863), manager of the Theatro São Januário in the 1840s, regularly brought in French companies to present vaudevilles and comedies by Scribe. The connection with Paris was enough to allow Caetano to advertise a company as Théâtre Français and later as Théâtre de Varieté (1856); subscription information appeared in newspapers in both Portuguese and French.[53] Early in 1847, the managers of the Theatro São Francisco (1846–1855) advertised a play by Varnet as being also "presented in Paris in the Palais-Royal [theater], where it has been received with the most deserved applause."[54] During the intermission, Rio de Janeiro audiences heard original music composed especially for the occasion by the conductor of the theater's orchestra, the Argentinean Demetrio Rivero; later that year, the Theatro São Francisco hosted a French lyric company that presented the French version of Donizetti's *La favorite*.[55]

All these attempts to offer Cariocas more and more pieces from Paris seemed futile when, in 1859, the Theatro Alcazar Lyrique arrived on the scene. No other venue fulfilled Cariocas's Parisian fantasy as well, and as much, as the Alcazar. The small theater was situated at the Rua da Valla, near enough to the fashionable Rua do Ouvidor to prompt novelist and critic Machado de Assis to refer to it as "a *departement* from France at the Rua do Ouvidor."[56] The Parisian model was here patent: in addition to its name, the theater had a French manager, Joseph Arnaud, who frequently hired singers and actors directly from Paris to present Cariocas with the latest musical fashions, vaudevilles and comic operas, operettas, and musical revues. It was Arnaud who first introduced staged versions of Offenbach's operettas to Cariocas, fueling the local passion for blending theater, music, and satire. Eight years after the theater's opening, the influential Rio de Janeiro French-language periodical *Ba-ta-clan* reported on the success of the Alcazar Lyrique in transplanting Offenbach's Parisian theater to the other side of the Atlantic:

> To implant in Rio de Janeiro the Théâtre des Bouffes Parisiens in a way that allows a reasonable comparison between the little jewel

box of a theater on Rua Urugayana [Alcazar] and the theater in the Passage Choiseul [Théâtre des Bouffes Parisiens]—that is the task that the management of the theater has given itself and, through perseverance, has succeeded in accomplishing. The theater is always filled . . . all of Offenbach's great successes and the best vaudevilles of the Palais Royal and the Variétés attract a crowd that comes to applaud Mademoiselles Aimée, Delmary, Madame Bourgeois, Messieurs Marchand, Urbain, etc., etc., all the top-flight artists that the administration of the French theater has been able to draw away from the foremost French stages.[57]

In almost two decades of its existence, no other public venue received as much attention from the local media as did the Theatro Alcazar Lyrique. Chronicled in the reports of visitors from abroad, as well as in the daily pages of local newspapers, the Alcazar was the center of attention for anyone drawn to the city's nightlife. A special column in the *Jornal do commercio* titled "*Noites do Alcazar*" (Nights in the Alcazar) informed audiences of the latest activities in the French theater, including the hire of French artists. Described as "a suffocating hole" by a foreign visitor, the architecture and lack of decoration never stopped members of the local *haute monde* from jamming the doors every night. So strong was the magnetism the Alcazar exerted over Cariocas that it remained one of the most glaring memories of imperial Rio de Janeiro: "In my youth, the Alcazar Lyrique Française was the favorite theater for all of the citizens of the best *fluminense* [from the state of Rio de Janeiro] society. In the orchestra chairs of that elegant theater, one saw almost daily the same persons, all of the elite."[58]

The audience, made up of writers, intellectuals, aristocrats, administrators, and students, was also predominantly white and male. For most, the Alcazar's main attraction was not the music, but the parade of female French singers, whose legs, more than voices, were topics of passionate discussions in local newspapers. Public reproaches from the Alcazar's opponents also permeated the daily news. Aligning himself with Carioca wives, prominent writer Joaquim Manuel de Macedo (1820–1882) described the theater as "a poisonous French plant that came to infiltrate and disseminate in Rio de Janeiro," with the exhibition of "half naked women, [who] corrupt our costumes and incite immorality."[59]

Figure 1.3. "Uma noite no Alcazar" (A Night at the Alcazar). *A vida fluminense* (August 15, 1868). Young Research Library, UCLA.

Figure 1.4. "Alcazar." *A vida fluminense* (August 1868). Young Research Library, UCLA.

The opposition was never too persuasive, however. During the 1860s and 1870s, there was hardly any competition for the Alcazar, with the exception, perhaps, of the Theatro Gymnasio Dramatico. Opened in 1855 as the remodeled Theatro São Januário, the repertory of the Gymnasio was distinctively modeled on the dramatic repertory of the Parisian Gymnase, particularly on Scribe's comedies and "novel" French realist plays.[60] Although the stage was small for opera companies, the Gymnasio offered Cariocas plenty of arrangements and adaptations of Parisian musical successes. The theater was particularly small with only 256 orchestra seats, in addition to three tiers of boxes and a large space beside the orchestra seats reserved for "standing listeners," who bought low-priced tickets.[61] But among the theater's mixed audience, one could easily find members of the local aristocracy, and even occasionally stumble on the monarch himself, who mingled with the "happy masses" at the Gymnasio to enjoy "plays from the most fashionable theaters in Paris."[62] And unlike the Alcazar, the managers of the popular *teatrinho* (small theater), as it was called,[63] guaranteed an inclusive audience by reserving the second tier of boxes especially "to families," who had private access to their seats through two lateral entrances.[64] In 1858, the Gymnasio was remodeled to receive more comfortable chairs and a long-awaited "big fan," which apparently solved the theater's uninviting lack of ventilation.[65]

The 1850s and 1860s were the heydays of the Theatro Gymnasio, which captivated the local audience with comedies ornate with music, short vaudevilles, operettas, and zarzuelas. The managers were able to organize shows that appealed to the preferences of the Carioca public at large, and that contrasted with the program of the opera house. While the Theatro Lyrico Fluminense (Provisorio) presented Verdi's *Il trovatore*, the Gymnasio opened its doors on April 12, 1855, with a play by Brazilian Joaquim Manoel de Macedo, *O primo da California*, "adorned with music by Sr. Demetrio Rivero." "The Gymnasio is going very well, indeed," noted the critic of the *Jornal do commercio*, because the managers regularly "bring to the public delicious compositions by Scribe."[66]

In the early 1870s, the Theatro Phenix Dramatica (1868–1888) took the place of the Gymnasio as the main stage for comedies, parodies and burlesques, opéra-comiques, operettas, and revues. It also hosted a wide variety of European novelties, such as the first presentation of the phonograph to Cariocas in 1879.[67] Several other theaters, although presenting mostly plays, also hosted musical presentations on a regular basis. The Theatro São Luis opened its doors on January 1, 1870, under the management of the Portuguese immigrant Furtado Coelho (1831–1900), with the Brazilian composer Henrique Alves de Mesquita as music director. The São Luiz was apparently slightly larger than the Gymnasio Dramatico: the orchestra section contained 294 numbered seats and benches along the lateral walls accommodating thirty-two more spectators. The thirty-four boxes were arrayed in two tiers, and two imperial boxes located at the right side of the stage were garnished with a private entrance and sitting room. According to contemporary commentators, the stage of the São Luiz was particularly esteemed for its acoustics and modern equipment, which permitted easier movement of the curtains, and the gas lighting provided "excellent illumination for the required scenic effects."[68] The Theatro São Luiz hosted smaller theatrical companies and presented mostly short plays with musical accompaniment. But it also brought to Cariocas several Spanish zarzuelas and other comic numbers that included music on a regular basis.

In 1872, the Theatro Gymnasio Dramatico closed its doors. The building was remodeled and reopened on January 18, 1873, as the Theatro Alhambra. The short-lived Alhambra reflected the need of the times to supply Rio de Janeiro's growing middle class with light and affordable entertainment. To accommodate a mixed public, the managers of the Alhambra eliminated the division of boxes and transformed it into a gallery open to everyone, where the audience was permitted to wear hats and to smoke in the halls and lobby. With a mission to offer cheap entertainment to families, the Alhambra's repertory ranged from gymnastics and comedies to concerts and operettas "in any language."[69] The same fate befell the Theatro Alcazar Lyrique, which was remodeled in 1881 and reopened as Café Cantante, with a new theater décor including tables that allowed for drinks and food to be served between musical numbers.[70]

CONCERTS

Although smaller in scale, the entrepreneurship of music in imperial Rio de Janeiro was similar in essence to that of most European capitals.[71] Following the English "academies" and the French *academie*, theater managers often organized *academias* (concerts) for the benefit

Figure 1.5.   Theatro São Luis. *A vida fluminense* (January 16, 1870). Young Research Library, UCLA.

of a company musician or charity institution, and impresarios included at least one such benefit night in every leading singer's contract.[72] Musicians would also organize academias themselves, in
which case they were in charge of general organizational matters such
as room reservation, advertisement, and ticket sales. All these events
involved the participation of several artists, as solo recitals were not
widespread in Rio de Janeiro until late in the century. But whether a
large benefit event or an independently organized concert, when presented in the theater, academias were regularly interspersed within an
operatic act or parts of a play. Even celebrity virtuosos who visited the
capital, such as Louis Moreau Gottschalk and Sigismund Thalberg
(1812–1871), performed in introductions and intermezzos of plays, or
shared the stage with the whole cast of the lyric theater. The concert
of the luminary Portuguese pianist Arthur Napoleão at the Theatro
Lyrico Fluminense on July 6, 1866, followed the tradition:

Theatro Lyrico Fluminense: Friday, July 6, 1866
Concert by ARTHUR NAPOLEÃO
And Mr. Vasques, artist from the Theatro Gymnasio, in one of his best
comic scenes.
Grand fantasy over motives from the opera *Luiza Miller*, composed and
performed by Arthur Napoleão
Play in four acts, *Heloiza Paranquet* from the Theatro Gymnasio
In the intermission between the second and third act Fantasia-Concerto
over motives from the opera *Africana* by Meyerbeer, for piano and large
orchestra, composed and performed by ARTHUR NAPOLEÃO.
After the play *Heloiza Paranquet*, will be presented the Grand Caprice over
the waltz and duet from the opera *Faust* composed and performed by
Arthur Napoleão.[73]

Even when academias were offered independently from theatrical
presentations or when they took place in smaller concert halls, the
repertory remained a heterogeneous blend of operatic excerpts,
dances from operettas, and virtuoso instrumental solo numbers de-
rivative of operatic airs. Thus, until the 1880s, when the symphonic
and chamber music of the classical tradition started to gradually appear in concert programs, for Cariocas there was virtually no difference between the music they enjoyed at the theater and the music
they heard in other venues.[74]

It would be misleading, however, to offer a portrayal of music
making in imperial Rio de Janeiro as a sole domain of the theater. A

large number of ballrooms coexisted with the local stages, while outdoor events such as parades on holy days, military occasions, and during Carnival season, offered Cariocas a busy musical schedule throughout the year.[75] During the Second Empire, Carioca elite were also entertained in the salons of private musical societies, or "clubs," by far the most important organizations for concert promotion in imperial Rio de Janeiro. Some musical societies were small neighborhood associations; others were so luxurious that they matched the splendor of the opera house. Here, more than in any other elite venue, European music served as the utmost symbol of Europeaness, "civilization," and power.

But music was just a bonus that these exclusive organizations offered wealthy Cariocas. Several types of activities other than music were held in their salons—the agenda sometimes being more social and political than musical in nature. For example, the Club das Laranjeiras, open from 6 p.m. to midnight, made available to its members, in addition to a concert hall and a ballroom, special rooms for billiards, fencing, card games, and dinner, as well as a reading room with all the national and leading European newspapers. However, by far the most enticing benefit these societies offered their members was the feeling that one was not in Rio de Janeiro, but at the Cercle des Amis de l'Art in Paris. Thus, like other musical organizations discussed in this chapter, Rio de Janeiro private societies were replicas of Parisian institutions. And since the French private societies were in turn modeled on the English, Cariocas's selective musical societies were third-hand copies.[76] Those who took as a task to organize and lead these societies in Rio de Janeiro did not need to travel to France to experience first-hand the Parisian clubs before replicating them on the other side of the Atlantic. They could easily find inspiration and guidance in printed literature such as Pierre François Clodomir's *Traité théorique et pratique de l'organization des sociétés musicales* (Theoretical and Practical Treatise on the Organization of Musical Societies), which was for sale in the 1870s at a local bookstore.[77]

As with other private institutions, the organization and success of musical societies depended on the support of wealthy patrons. Usually ruled by a membership system, private musical societies were managed by a board of directors consisting of aristocrats and *nouveaux riches*. Members were also carefully chosen from among the cream of the local elite, and certain memberships often guaranteed social status. To complete a select assembly, local leading composers and performers were habitués at musical events in these organizations, mingling easily with wealthy amateur performers. The most prestigious societies hired a musical director, who was in charge of concert organization, rehearsals, and programming. For example, in the late 1860s, the prestige of the Club Fluminense, or "The club," as Cariocas called it, was partially the result of cellist Casimiro Lúcio de Souza Pitanga's lead as music director. Pitanga, who was hired as the club's director in 1865, started sponsoring weekly concerts, events "not devoted to dancing, but to music appreciation and social conversations." Members had the opportunity to attend balls that were well liked for their "liveliness and animation," as well as concerts, which were more "proper by nature for spiritual entertainment and sociability."[78] Even so, long programs further prolonged by lengthy intermissions made these "music-only" events more social gatherings that could last until well after one in the morning.[79]

Cariocas also welcomed private societies devoted solely to music. As early as August 24, 1835, the Brazilian capital gave birth to a philharmonic society, directed by Francisco Manuel da Silva. As was customary, a distinguished board of directors comprising members of the aristocracy, coupled with the direction of professional musicians of some prominence, helped thrust the philharmonic to the highest rank among Rio de Janeiro societies. In 1861, the Sociedade Campezina had "no competitors in Rio de Janeiro" in the business of concert promotion. The Campezina's concerts, offered at the larger salon of the Pavilhão Fluminense, were worthy of "select spectators of fine social backgrounds."[80] The young opera composer Antônio Carlos Gomes was among the composers who frequently attended the society, even dedicating his second opera *Joana de Flandres* (1863) to the Campezina.[81] Another Sociedade Philarmonica Fluminense, active in the 1870s and early 1880s, provided Cariocas with "music only" events. Its success and endurance in the local musical milieu was the result of two crucial ingredients: it boasted several aristocrats on its board of directors, and it was attended by a high number of professional musicians, such as the Italian violinist Luigi Elena (d. 1879), and the native-born composer and conductor Leopoldo Miguez (1850–1902).

Each society had sufficient capital to produce *saraus*, or concerts, on a regular basis—weekly, biweekly, or monthly, and most maintained their own halls for balls and chamber concerts. When a gala night was needed, the most affluent societies often rented larger concert halls and enlarged orchestras and choruses were put together to produce memorable musical events. During the Second Empire, the largest and most prominent concert hall available was the Cassino Fluminense. Inaugurated September 8, 1860, the hall of the Cassino hosted balls and concerts attended and cherished by leading members of Rio de Janeiro society.[82] In 1883, the German immigrant Carl von Kozeritz described the hall of the Cassino Fluminense as:

> the largest, most beautiful and luxurious hall in South America . . . the room is very lofty and in a beautiful style; several columns support the gallery; the decoration is the richest imaginable with heavy curtains, golden drapery, golden ornaments throughout the room, a sumptuous chandelier with 200 lights lit by gas, and gigantic mirrors multiplying the size of the room—everything grandiose and luxurious.[83]

The large salon of the Cassino Fluminense could accommodate 3,000 people and was "almost as large as the Kensington Town Hall [in London]," observed a foreign visitor.[84] Because the stage could hold larger ensembles, the Cassino Fluminense outranked all others as the preferred venue for gala concerts. In a concert organized by Arthur Napoleão and Leopoldo Miguez on September 10, 1882, the stage of the Cassino held an orchestra of eighty musicians and a choir of eighty singers.

Such large ensembles were far from customary, however. Rio de Janeiro, with a limited number of professional orchestra musicians, could not supply performers for all its music societies. Assembling a fifty-member orchestra was no easy task, even in the theater or the opera house. And only for very special events were musical societies' directors capable of gathering sixty or seventy players. More often than not, Cariocas heard operatic overtures, parts of symphonies, and other orchestral works with very reduced ensembles, which were not much different from those accompanying singers in chamber concerts.

TOO MUCH TO DO

Despite Cariocas's growing complaints that the city lacked the entertainment options available in Paris, the harsh reality was that, on occasion, Rio de Janeiro had more musical events to offer than audience to attend them, or musicians to perform. To solve the problem, it was common practice to coordinate concerts and theatrical presentations in such a way that the audience could attend several events in the same evening. As early as 1838, the musical gatherings of the Sociedade Philarmonica, for instance, deferred to the program at the major theater: "The monthly meeting will be held today, April 30; in case there is theater, it is transferred to tomorrow, May 1."[85] Such arrangements continued being made throughout the century to guarantee attendance at scheduled events. Even successful public enterprises had to be coordinated among themselves; for instance, Gravenstein opened the doors of the Pavilhão Fluminense for his bailes à Musard at ten o'clock, but the ball started at eleven, "soon after the program of the Alcazar has ended."[86]

In the 1880s, even private societies suffered from the lack of an audience. Usually, the events were held on Saturday nights, since the dancing could last until early morning. Lavish complaints in newspapers about simultaneous attractions on Saturdays did not prevent music societies from continuing the practice. When the Club Beethoven started its activities on Mondays, a local magazine highly praised the decision:

> Every society organizes their *partidas* [balls] on Saturdays . . . every club gives their *saraus* [concerts] on Saturdays . . . The attendance would be better if the elegant audience of Rio de Janeiro did not have to choose between the Club Mozart and the Congresso Brasileiro. . . . The Club Beethoven started by giving a good example, organizing concerts on Mondays and, I am sure, they are proud of their decision. The attendance was never so large.[87]

Fierce competition for public remained a concern for theater managers and directors of musical societies alike throughout the century. Strategies for gathering an audience could include the offering of cheaper seats, the occasional opening of exclusive, private halls to women and families, but the most successful tactic remained to appeal to Cariocas with European-level performances, Parisian singers, and wonderful, cultivated European music.

NOTES

1. *Jornal do commercio*, February 9, 1866.
2. For the predilection for Scribe's works in Paris see William G. Atwood, *The Parisian Worlds of Frédéric Chopin* (New Haven, Conn.: Yale University Press, 1999), 205–6 and 271–73.

3. *Jornal do commercio*, June 26, 1866.

4. Inaugurated in 1846 as the Tivoly, the hall was renamed Paraiso in 1850. Located at the Campo da Acclamação nº 9, it was the largest ballroom in town, and was occasionally also used for concerts. See Francisco Marques dos Santos, "A sociedade Fluminense em 1852," *Estudos brasileiros* 18 (May/June 1941): 229–30.

5. Atwood, *The Parisian Worlds of Frédéric Chopin,* 183.

6. *Jornal do commercio*, August 4, 1888.

7. The Salle Pleyel was located at Rue Cadet nº 9 (1830–1839) and Rue Rochechouart (1839–1927), and the Salle Herz was located at the Rue de la Victoire 9e. See Nigel Simeone, *Paris: A Musical Gazetteer* (New Haven, Conn.: Yale University Press, 2000), 189 and 195.

8. *Revista illustrada*, September 4, 1880.

9. *Revista musical e de bellas artes*, Ano II, nº 1 (January 3, 1880), 6.

10. Jeffrey Cooper, *The Rise of Instrumental Music and Concert Series in Paris 1828–1871* (Ann Arbor, Mich.: UMI Research Press, 1983), 46–51; see also Elisabeth Bernard, "Jules Pasdeloup et les Concerts Populaires," *Revue de musicologie* 57/2 (1971): 150–78.

11. Announcements for these popular concerts appear in the *Jornal do commercio* of June 13 and 18, 1862.

12. Carlotta Patti was the sister of the famous Adelina Patti (1843–1919). The French pianist Théodore Ritter claimed to have studied with Franz Liszt. He wrote two operas and several piano pieces, some of which were published in Rio de Janeiro. The Spanish violinist and composer Pablo Sarasate studied at the Paris Conservatory where he was a pupil of Jean Delphin Alard. He toured extensively throughout Europe, North and South America, South Africa, and the Orient. Composers such as Max Bruch, Dvorák, Lalo, Saint-Saëns, and Wienawski composed pieces for him.

13. *Jornal do commercio*, July 21, 1870.

14. *Jornal do commercio*, July 21, 1870.

15. Gravenstein's Concertos-Promenade were announced in the *Jornal do commercio* of May 1873.

16. Among Napoleão's distinguished pupils was the Brazilian conductor and composer Francisca [Chiquinha] Gonzaga (1847–1935).

17. For biographical information on Arthur Napoleão see Sanches Frias, *Arthur Napoleão: resenha commemorative da sua vida pessoal e artística* (Lisbon: n.p., 1913); see also Luiz heitor Corrêa de Azevedo, "Arthur Napoléon 1843–1925; Un pianiste porguais au Brésil," *Arquivos do centro cultural Português*, vol. 3 (Paris: Fundação Calouste Gulbenkian, 1971), 572–602. Azevedos's biography is based on Napoleão's autobiography, published in the *Correio da manhã* (Rio de Janeiro) September 4, 1925. This autobiography came out in *Revista brasileira de musica* 3 (1962), 4–6 (1963). An early biography of Napoleão came out in the *Dwight's Journal of Music,* January 1, 1859.

18. See Ayres de Andrade, *Francisco Manuel da Silva e seu tempo*, vol. 1 (Rio de Janeiro, Ediçóes Tempo Brasileiro, 1967), 134.

19. *Catálogo da biblioteca musical de J. C. Müller e H. E. Heinen: fornecedores de musica de sua magestade* (Rio de Janeiro: Typographia Imp. e Const. de J. Villeneuve e Cª, 1837), 6. This rare catalogue is housed at the Biblioteca Nacional in Rio de Janeiro. For a facsimile see Cristina Magaldi, "Concert Life in Rio de Janeiro, 1837–1900" (Ph.D. diss., University of California at Los Angeles, 1994), 407–68. As early as 1784, William Napier started a Music Lending Library in London; see Laura Alyson McLamore, "Symphonic Conventions in London's Concert Rooms, ca. 1755–1790" (Ph.D. diss., University of California at Los Angeles, 1991), 258–59.

20. See *Catálogo das musicas impressas no imperial estabelecimento de pianos e musicas de Narciso & Arthur Napoleão* (Rio de Janeiro: Imprensa Nacional, 1871). This catalogue is extant at the Biblioteca Nacional in Rio de Janeiro.

21. Mercedes Reis Pequeno, "Brazilian music publishers." *Inter-American Music Review* 9 (1988): 91–104.

22. *Revue et gazzette musicale*, 1839, 221; quoted in Charles Russell Suttoni, "Piano and Opera: A Study of the Piano Fantasies Written on Opera Themes in the Romantic Era" (Ph.D. diss., New York University, 1973), 18.

23. Edinha Diniz, *Chiquinha Gonzaga: uma história de vida* (Rio de Janeiro: Editora Codecri, 1984), 31.

24. According to Carlos Penteado de Rezende, pianos Érard were being sold in Brazil as early as 1810; see his "Notas para uma história do piano no Brasil, séc. XIX," *Revista brasileira de cultura* 2/6 (1970): 27. Francisco Curt Lange reports that Broadwood pianos were already in Brazil by the time of the arrival of the royal family in 1808; see "Vida y muerte de Louis Moreau Gottschalk en Rio de Janeiro (1869)," *Revista de estudios musicales* 2/4 (1950): 76.

25. According to the data provided by Eulalia M. L. Lobo, there might have been piano manufacturers in Rio de Janeiro before that date; see *História do Rio de Janeiro*, vol. 1 (Rio de Janeiro: IBMC, 1978), 120 and 181.

26. *Jornal do commercio*, July 22, 1845.

27. *Jornal do commercio*, September 21, 1847. Hertz's piano shop was located at Rua do Rosario n. 94.

28. Raphael Coelho Machado, *Methodo de afinar piano,* 3rd ed. rev. (Rio de Janeiro: Typ. Francesa, 1849 [1843]), 15.

29. Lobo, *História do Rio de Janeiro*, vol. 1, 206.

30. *Jornal do commercio*, February 1, 1838.

31. Zabumba is a double-headed drum played with a beater and used in popular Brazilian bands, especially in musical groups from the Brazilian Northeast. Viola and guitar players (*violeiros* and *guitarreiros*) were actually registered professionals in 1856 and 1857; see Lobo, *História do Rio de Janeiro*, vol. 1, 182.

32. At mid-century, fortepianos went between 300$000 and 1:500$000; at R$1,800; see Paulo Rogério de Faria, "O pianismo do concerto no Rio de

Janeiro, no século XIX" (Master's thesis, Universidade Federal do Rio de Janeiro, Escola de Música, 1996), 29. To offer an idea of prices in nineteenth-century Brazil, in 1850 the prices for orchestra seats at the opera house, 2$000 (réis) and 1$000 was equivalent to U$1.00 and U$0.50 respectively (1:000$000=U$500); see C. H. Haring, *Empire in Brazil* (Cambridge, Mass.: Harvard University Press, 1958), 107.

33. Aleilton Santana da Fonseca, "Enredo romântico, música ao fundo" (Master's thesis, Universidade Federal da Paraiba, 1992), 130.

34. For the restrictions on women in theatrical presentations see Míriam Moreira Leite, *A Condição feminina no Rio de Janeiro* (São Paulo: HUCITEC, Instituto Nacional do Livro, 1984), 169–70. For the barring of women from the Club Beethoven see Cristina Magaldi, "Music for the Elite: Musical Societies in Imperial Rio de Janeiro," *Latin American Music Review* 16/1 (1995): 11.

35. Arthur Farwell, "Keeping in Touch with World's Musical Growth through the Piano," *Musical America*, November 5, 1910. For a discussion of the role of the piano in transporting people in time and space, as well as through social classes, see also James Parakilas et al., *Piano Roles: Three Hundred Years of Life with Pianos* (New Haven, Conn.: Yale University Press, 1999), 96.

36. Farwell, "Keeping in Touch with World's Musical Growth through the Piano."

37. Machado, *Methodo de afinar piano*, 11.

38. Judith A. Weiss, *Latin American Popular Theater: The First Five Centuries* (Albuquerque: University of New Mexico Press, 1993), 91–92.

39. Moreira de Azevedo, *O Rio de Janeiro*, vol. 2, 3rd ed. (Rio de Janeiro: Livraria Brasiliana Editora, 1969), 160.

40. Barman, *Citizen Emperor*, 136. The information is found in the *Jornal do commercio*, July 30 and December 3, 1853.

41. Weiss, *Latin American Popular Theater*, 91–92.

42. Décio de Almeida Prado, *João Caetano: o ator, o empresário, o repertório* (São Paulo: Editora Perspectiva, Editora da Universidade de São Paulo, 1972), 59.

43. Moreira de Azevedo, *O Rio de Janeiro*, 172.

44. See Renato de Almeida, *História da música brasileira* (Rio de Janeiro: F. Briguiet, 1926), 343.

45. These were modest dimensions compared with the standards for most contemporary Parisian theaters. But if one considers that, in the 1820s, Rio de Janeiro population was about 100,000, of which no more than 2 percent would attend the theater regularly, the size of the Theatro S. João was more than adequate.

46. For a valuable and well-documented history of the construction of the Theatro Provisorio see Eric Gordon, "A New Opera House: An Investigation

of Elite Values in Mid-Nineteenth-Century Rio de Janeiro," *Inter-American Institute for Musical Research Yearbook* 5 (1969): 49–66, especially 52. See, also, his "Opera and Society: Rio de Janeiro, 1851–1852" (Master's thesis, Tulane University, 1969).

47. Gordon, "A New Opera House," 56–58. The Theatro Provisorio had 230 more seats in the orchestra section than the Theatro São Pedro de Alcantara, which accommodated altogether around 1,100 spectators; see Sousa, *O teatro no Brasil*, 286.

48. *Jornal do commercio*, August 20, 1865.

49. *Jornal do commercio*, August 20, 1865

50. The Theatro D. Pedro II was located on the Largo da Carioca. See Lafayette Silva, *História do teatro brasileiro* (Rio de Janeiro: Serviço Gráfico do MEC, 1938), 55–56.

51. Laurence Hallewell, *O livro no Brasil* (São Paulo: Editora Universidade de São Paulo, 1982), 147–48. For the number of music prints see Mercedes Reis Pequeno, "Impressão musical," *Enciclopedia de musica brasileira* (Rio de Janeiro: Art Editora, 1977).

52. Gordon, "A New Opera House," 52.

53. See, for example, the advertisement for this theater in the *Jornal do commercio*, January 14, 1845. Scribe's vaudeville in one act *Quand L'amour s'en va* was performed at the Theatro São Januário on April 17, 1845. For the activities of João Caetano in these theaters, see Prado, *João Caetano*, 169.

54. *Jornal do commercio*, March 1, 1847.

55. *Jornal do commercio*, March 22 and July 10, 1847.

56. Joaquim Manuel de Macedo, "Memórias da Rua do Ouvidor," in João Roberto Faria, *Idéias teatrais: o século XIX no Brasil* (São Paulo: Perspectiva, FAPESP, 2001), 572.

57. *Ba-ta-clan*, June 1, 1867.

58. E. Mattoso, *Cousas do meu tempo* (Bordeaux: Gounouilhou, 1916), 285–87; quoted in Jeffrey Needell, *A Tropical Belle Époque: Elite Culture and Society in Turn-of-the-Century Rio de Janeiro* (Cambridge: Cambridge University Press, 1987), 165.

59. Joaquim Manuel de Macedo, "Memórias da Rua do Ouvidor," 572; quoted in Faria, *Idéias teatrais*, 572.

60. For the vogue of French realist play in Rio de Janeiro theaters see João Roberto Faria, *O teatro realista no Brasil* (São Paulo: Editora Perspectiva, 1993).

61. Faria mentions just the 256 seats, but the *Jornal do commercio* includes a description of the boxes. See *O teatro realista no Brasil*, 78.

62. *Diário do Rio de Janeiro*, December 14, 1855; quoted in Faria, *O teatro realista no Brasil*, 81.

63. *Jornal do commercio*, November 30, 1856.

64. *Jornal do commercio*, April 7, 1855.

65. *Jornal do commercio*, May 29, 1858.

66. *Jornal do commercio*, June 3, 1855.

67. The presentation of the phonograph was advertised in the *Jornal do commercio* of October 23, 1879.

68. *Jornal do commercio*, January 3, 1870.

69. *Jornal do commercio*, January 17, 1873.

70. The news of the remodeling of the Alcazar appears in the *Jornal do commercio* of June 13, 1881.

71. Atwood's description of the hurdles encountered by professional musicians in putting together their concerts in Paris could easily apply to imperial Rio de Janeiro; see *The Parisian Worlds of Frédéric Chopin*, 161–62.

72. One example of such a contract appears in *Jornal do commercio*, November 16, 1850. The Portuguese word *academia* is modeled on the English eighteenth-century term *academy,* used for chamber concerts with a miscellaneous program.

73. This concert advertisement came out in the *Jornal do commercio* of July 5, 1866.

74. The same can be said for the repertory of concerts in other Latin American cities such as Santiago and Buenos Aires; see Pereira Salas, *Historia de la música en Chile, 1850–1900* (Santiago: Publicaciones de la Universidad de Chile, 1957), 111; see also Vicente Gesualdo, *Historia de la música en Argentina*, vol. 2 (Buenos Aires: Editorial Beta, 1961), 142.

75. For a study of outdoor celebrations in nineteenth-century Rio de Janeiro see Martha Abreu, *Império do Divino: festas religiosas e cultura popular no Rio de Janeiro, 1830–1900* (Rio de Janeiro: Nova Fronteira and Fapesp, 1999).

76. For a discussion of the links between English and French private societies and "clubs" see Atwood, *The Parisian Worlds of Frédéric Chopin*, 152–54.

77. This work is listed in *Catálogo das musicas impresas no imperial estabelecimento de pianos e musicas de Narciso & Arthur Napoleão.*

78. *Jornal do commercio*, September 13, 1865.

79. *Revista popular*, October 10, 1861.

80. *Revista popular*, April 26, 1861.

81. *Jornal do commercio*, September 3, 1863.

82. The society Cassino Fluminense was created on October 4, 1845. In 1854 a building in the Rua do Passeio was bought to serve as a permanent hall. After remodeling, the salon was inaugurated in 1860; see Santos, "A sociedade Fluminense em 1852," 226–27. In 1900 the Cassino merged with the Club dos Diários, and today the building is used by the Automóvel Clube; see Needell, *A Tropical Belle Époque*, 70.

83. Carl von Kozeritz, *Imagens do Brasil*, trans. Afonso Arinos de Melo Franco (Belo Horizonte: Ed. Itatiaia; São Paulo: Ed. da Universidade de São Paulo, 1980), 215–16.

84. Quoted in Míriam Moreira Leite, *A condição feminina no Rio de Janeiro*, 146.

85. *Jornal do commercio*, April 30, 1838.

86. *Jornal do commercio*, May 5, 1866.

87. *Revista illustrada*, April 8, 1882.

Chapter 2

Embracing Opera

A TALE OF ISOLDES AND OTELLOS

The extent to which nineteenth-century European opera transformed and shaped the lives of those living in Latin America is a topic yet to be fully explored in music scholarship.[1] Nonetheless, it has been magnificently described in literature. The following excerpt from Gabriel Garcia Marquez's novel *Love in the Time of Cholera*, offers a most vivid assessment of how the European operatic craze was transplanted to peripheral areas of the New World:

The restoration of the Dramatic Theater . . . was the culmination of a spectacular civic campaign that involved every sector of the city in a multitudinous mobilization that many thought worthy of a better cause. In any event, the new Dramatic Theater was inaugurated when it still lacked seats or lights, and the audience had to bring their own chairs and their own lighting for the intermissions. The same protocols held sway as at the great performances in Europe, and the ladies used the occasion to show off their long dresses and their fur coats in the dog days of the Caribbean summer, but it was also necessary to authorize the admission of servants to carry the chairs and lamps and all the things to eat that were deemed necessary to survive the interminable programs. . . . The season opened with a French opera company whose novelty was a harp in the orchestra and whose unforgettable glory was the impeccable voice and dramatic talent of a Turkish soprano who sang barefoot and wore rings set with precious stones on her toes. After the first act the stage could barely be seen and the singers lost their voices because of the smoke from so many palm oil lamps, but the chronicles of the city were very careful to delete these minor inconveniences and to magnify the memorable events. Without a doubt it was Dr. Urbino's most contagious initiative, for opera fever infected the most surprising elements in the city and gave rise to a whole generation of Isoldes and Otellos and Aidas and Siegfrieds. But it never reached the extremes Dr. Urbino had hoped for, which was to see Italianizers and Wagnerians confronting each other with sticks and canes during the intermissions.[2]

Dr. Juvenal Urbino, one of the characters in Marquez's novel, is a Paris-educated native, whose efforts to bring opera to his home Caribbean country were transformed into an obsession. Although Marquez's description is sprinkled with a great deal of sarcasm, his portrayal summons well the topic explored in this chapter: a tale of Isoldes and Otellos, Aidas and Siegfrieds in the context of nineteenth-century Rio de Janeiro.

As in Dr. Urbino's Caribbean town, imperial Rio de Janeiro was captive in the international deluge of opera, a striking phenomenon that was a predecessor to twentieth-century globalization. As a major force in European colonialism, opera is said to have been more enduring than any military glory.[3] For opera was experienced, transmitted, and perceived as emblematic of European culture, embodying the idea of civilization, urban life, modernity, and financial and cultural power. Such an association, very real among those living in Paris and London, was transplanted to peripheral cities like Rio de Janeiro in a remarkably overstated fashion. Because Cariocas were geographically distant from European political and cultural centers, they thought it necessary to overstress their kinship with opera not only to warrant a certain social rank, but, above all, to assure their image as Europeans. Attending the opera house was primarily a symbolic act that revealed Cariocas's constant efforts to behave, feel, and be seen as "civilized," modern, and, ultimately, as Europeans. The efforts to bring opera so far away in a time when traveling across the ocean was no light undertaking, and the large sums expended on costly buildings and lavish productions all seemed miniscule tasks given the advantages opera provided some Cariocas in the end.

A PLACE TO SEE AND BE SEEN

"What people love most about the Opéra [in Paris] is not the music," observed an aristocrat Frenchman. It was the action going on in the audience, rather than the drama on stage that most interested opera-goers in Paris.[4] Cariocas felt the same. In 1855, the *Jornal do commer-cio*'s critic eagerly complained that,

> Our dilettanti go to the opera every night not knowing what they are about to hear. For them it is enough to have the theater's door open. They are like gluttons, who are only interested in eating and completely indifferent to the quality of the food that they are served. . . . [Our dilettanti] go to the theater to see and be seen . . . what they aspire is to be included in the exclusive group of the opera habitués.[5]

A night at the opera house was much more than a musical event: it indeed provided the best place to see and be seen, but it was also an opportunity for business meetings and romantic encounters. Machado de Assis perceptively observed in one of his novels that in imperial Rio de Janeiro the boxes in the opera house were themselves transformed into "a miniature stage."[6] And he was not talking in figurative terms. The architecture of Rio de Janeiro theaters was especially designed to provide everyone with ample visibility of the whole spectacle: on and off the stage. In 1878, a French visitor noted that the internal division of boxes in local theaters favored a larger sociability than in French theaters, since in the Brazilian capital,

> The boxes, like in Spanish theaters, are separated only by a guard-rail, and their fronts are lower than in our [French] theaters. . . . It is not necessary, like in our new Ópera in Paris, to hang to the chandeliers to see the dresses of the women in the boxes. . . . There are no galleries like in our theaters; just in the lower level, forming a circle around the orchestra. The accommodations are large enough to make it possible for one to leave [his/her] seat and come back without having to ask the neighbors to step onto their seats to offer the way.[7]

If the opera house's internal architecture was made to provide ample visibility of the off-stage action, it also allowed for unique patterns of socialization among the different sectors of the audience. The seating design in the theater and the internal dynamics of the audience in an operatic performance actually unveiled numerous facets of Rio de Janeiro's newly formed urban society. It also provided a bold sketch of the local social clichés, political factions, ethnical hierarchies, and gender roles.

While Cariocas experienced opera in different venues and in a wide array of formats that permitted ample variance of social perceptions, it is also true that the musical language of opera was primarily "the representation of elite fantasy on stage" and that the spectators in the opera house were "the manifestation of [Carioca] elite reality in the boxes."[8] Inside the opera house, Cariocas looked for more than enjoyable music; they expected to see and commingle with aristocrats, wealthy families, members of the government, and well-reputed intellectuals and artists. The presence of the monarch and his family would come as an occasional bonus to the already prominent *haute monde*. Thus, a ticket to the opera house was more than a pass to hear music: it provided access to elite circles. Representatives of the status quo gathered there several times a month to flaunt their privileged position. Their clothing, their actions and reactions, their companions, and their slightest movements were watched as if they were at center stage. And in many ways they were. The elite were not only an important sector of the opera's audience, but they were also the major characters in the off-stage plot. Their names appeared regularly in the social columns of daily newspapers, which included full reports of their garments, hairstyles, and behaviors at the previous night's operatic performance. Not-so-prominent and less-affluent individuals followed the same social protocols and behavioral patterns. But no matter where they focused their attention, the onstage performance or the off-stage action, their role in both was that of audience, never of player. The middle-class presence in operatic performances, copiously described in contemporary novels by Rio de Janeiro's authors,[9] went conspicuously unnoticed in contemporary newspapers' reports and visitors' comments. The off-stage action was motive for contemporary chronicles' interest insofar as it highlighted the top of the local social and political hierarchy, nothing more.

As with female characters in romantic novels, the women's role in the off-stage plot during an operatic performance unfolded quite predictably: women were displayed in the boxes as trophies for males' romantic conquests. Not welcome in the orchestra seats, their movements and actions inside the theater were quite restricted.[10] Women sat passively in the boxes and were admired as a deluxe part of the opera house's decor. A male's description of a night at the Theatro Lyrico serves to exemplify:

> Last Tuesday night the lyric company of the well-known impresario *cavaliere* Giovanni Sansone made its debut in the Theatro Lyrico, the theater being almost full. The most fine in beauty, talent, and elegance decorated the boxes, seats, and balconies. Like great and splendid

fleshy flowers, the seductive forms of the gentle ladies and damsels appeared, framed in the boxes, giving the theater the appearance of an enormous animated flowerbed.[11]

As "fleshy flowers" women had passive roles in the off-stage action, but they were parts nonetheless, both as audience and as characters. That was not the case with the black population. Their initial role was an active one, although not voluntary, since they provided the labor that helped erect most theaters in the city.[12] A few freed blacks were hired as performers in theater orchestras, supplementing the ensembles brought along with lyric companies.[13] Generally, however, they had no part in any of the actions going on inside the opera house. Nor were they formally part of any sector of the audience.[14] Blacks were there to provide logistics support to elite families. They were seen at operatic performances as bodyguards; they did not have assigned seats and remained in the corridors outside boxes waiting to serve, to bring food, and to provide other needs for their "masters." In an announcement for a masquerade ball at the Theatro São Pedro de Alcantara, for instance, elite families were allowed to bring with them "a servent," most probably a black or mulatto slave, provided that he or she did not leave that family's box.[15] One contemporary observer who lived near the Theatro São Januário reported that when families went to the theater, "No one stayed at home; the slave-girls took mats for the smaller children, the male slaves carried little chairs for the bigger ones, and even the cook with dishes of food wrapped in napkins, for snack during the intermission."[16]

At the lower end of the local social rank, blacks were neither invited nor allowed to take part in any of the actions. Nonetheless, albeit unnoticed, blacks were surely part of the off-stage plot, as necessary ghosts whose appearance as characters was dependent on the other spectators' wishes. Their ghostly presence in the opera house, nonetheless, completed the static picture of the local social and ethnic hierarchy. For those few interested in the action taking place on stage, there was surely a lot there to entertain them, too. And European music fit the scenery perfectly.

ITALIAN OPERA VIA PARIS

As in other spheres of the local literary, artistic, and musical life, in the opera house the model was Paris,[17] and it was the ambiance of

the luxurious Parisian Théâtre-Italien—presenting Italian opera—
that was first re-created by the elite in the Brazilian capital. Accordingly, until late in the nineteenth century, in imperial Rio de Janeiro,
opera meant primarily Italian opera.[18] An overwhelming number of
works by Italian composers made it to the city and Cariocas, following their Francophile tastes, welcomed the bel canto with amazing ease.

Transported boldly across the ocean throughout the nineteenth
century, the Italian operatic language landed on familiar shores.
Long before the arrival of the Portuguese monarchs in Rio de
Janeiro, Italian opera had invaded Brazil in response to the "Italian-
ization" of Portuguese musical life promoted by João V in the eighteenth century. The Italian language itself had indeed become the
lingua franca in the Portuguese court, where Italians dominated all
music activities.[19] As a result, Portuguese translations of Metastasian
dramas circulated widely in eighteenth-century Brazil,[20] and, as
early as 1767, the French navigator Louis Antoine de Bougainville
(1729–1811) reported the performances of Metastasio's works in Rio
de Janeiro. Other Italian works in vogue such as Domenico
Cimarosa's *L'Italiana in Londra* (1779) and Giuseppe Millico's *La pietà
d'amore* (1782) are also known to have been performed in Brazil before the arrival of the Portuguese court.[21]

In 1811, the Portuguese composer Marcos Portugal (1762–1830) arrived in Rio de Janeiro accompanied by a large corps of Italian
singers and was appointed director of music at the Theatro São João.
Admired in his own country chiefly as an Italian *opera seria* composer, when choosing the repertory for Rio de Janeiro's opera house,
Portugal also emphasized the Italian repertory, especially Rossini's
operas. Rio de Janeiro then held the privilege of being not only the
first New World city to see the performance of a complete Rossini
opera,[22] but also of initiating the Rossini "mania" which grew into a
kind of "universal musical idiom" in Latin American cities.[23] Beginning with *Aureliano in Palmira* (1813), performed on May 13, 1820,
Rossini's music reigned supreme in the capital for two decades. Between 1820 and 1824, Cariocas saw no fewer than twenty-one
Rossini operas, and from 1826 to 1832, the seasons consisted almost
exclusively of Rossini operas: in 1821 came *La Cenerentola* (1817),
Tancredi (1813), *Il barbiere di Siviglia* (1816), and *L'Italiana in Algeri*
(1813); in 1827, *La Pietra del Paragone* (1812); in 1828, *Adina* (1818) and
Otello (1816); in 1829, *Matilde di Shabran* (1821); and in 1830 *La gazza*

ladra (1817).[24] In 1828, Cariocas saw the premiere of a Donizetti opera, *L'ajo nell' imbarazzo* (1824).

Due to the political instability of the regency from 1831 to 1840, no single complete opera was staged in Rio de Janeiro, but the operatic frenzy returned on January 17, 1844, with the premiere of Bellini's *Norma* (1831). During the 1840s, a new wave of Italian operas by Donizetti and Bellini competed with Rossini's for Cariocas's appreciation. From 1844 to 1862, there were only three Rossini premieres in Rio de Janeiro—*La donna del lago* (1819) in 1844, *William Tell* (1829) in 1850, and *Mosé in Egito* (1818) in 1858—while in the same period *Cariocas* saw dozens of new operas by Bellini and Donizetti. Bellini's *I Capuletti ed I Montecchi* (1830) was presented in 1844, *I puritani* (1835) in 1845, *Beatrice di Tenda* (1833) in 1846, and *La sonnambula* (1831) in 1848. In 1844 alone six new operas by Donizetti made it to Rio de Janeiro: *Belisario* (1836) *L'elisir d'amore* (1832), *Anna Bolena* (1830), *Il furioso* (1833), *Torquato Tasso* (1833), and *Betly* (1836). Then, in 1847 came *La figlia del regimento* (1840), *Lucia de Lammermoor* (1835), and *La favorita* (1940); in 1848, *Linda di Chamounix* (1842); in 1849, *Parisina* (1833), *Marino Faliero* (1835) and *Maria de Rohan* (1843); in the following year *Roberto Devereux* (1837) and *Fausta* (1832); in 1851, *Maria de Rudenz* (1838); in 1853, *Poliuto* (1840) and *Don Pasquale* (1843); in 1856 *Maria Padilla* (1841); and *Dom Sébastien* (1843) received its Rio de Janeiro premiere in 1862.[25]

Cariocas first heard a Verdi opera in 1846, when *Ernani* (1843) was presented in Rio de Janeiro only three years after its Italian premiere. The following two decades were marked by the dominance of Verdi's music: in 1848 came *I Lombardi* (1842); in 1849, *I due Foscari* (1844); *Macbeth* (1847) was performed in 1852 at the opening of the Theatro Provisorio;[26] in the following year came *Luiza Miller* (1849), *Attila* (1846), and *Nabucodonosor* (1841), the latter was performed at a gala night commemorating Pedro II's birthday. *Il trovatore* (1852) was presented in 1854, only two years after its European premiere, followed by *La traviata* (1853) in 1855, *Rigoletto* (1851) in 1856, *Giovanna D'Arco* (1844) in 1860, *Un ballo in maschera* (1858) in 1862, and *Aroldo* (1857) in 1864. Cariocas heard Verdi's *Aida* (1870) for the first time in 1876.

By the end of the 1860s Rio de Janeiro had been flooded with Italian operatic hits, and the city's reputation as a privileged site for opera aficionados and a mecca for European lyric companies soon spread in Europe. Some Italian composers even praised Pedro II's support of opera by dedicating works to him: Giovanni Pacini, for example, dedicated his *Niccolò dei Lapi* (1857) to the emperor,[27] and Giuseppe Mercadante praised Brazil in his *Exulta, oh! Brasil* (1852).[28] The dedications came, of course, after works such as Pacini's *La regina di Cipro* (1846) and Mercadante's *Il Vascello de Gama* (1845) (announced in Portuguese as *O Naufrágio de Vasco da Gama*) were widely acclaimed in Rio de Janeiro. Cariocas particularly welcomed works by Mercadante, a composer "admired internationally for his instrumentation," according to the report of a local critic.[29]

However, in the second half of the century, the operatic frenzy started to wane. This is evident in the report of the same critic, who, along with his deference to Mercadante, also expressed a deep concern with the absence of novelty in the opera house. "If this opera [*Il Vascello de Gama*] does not appeal to the public," he warned, "there is not another equivalent work [available here]. . . . The music lover should . . . remember that Bellini's repertory is exhausted and that Donizetti's is almost there."[30] In reality, the Italian repertory was far from exhausted in imperial Rio de Janeiro, as it continued to be performed and somewhat admired until late in the century. Nonetheless, now competing with a wide variety of new musical options available in the city, the supremacy of the bel canto and the Carioca devotion to the opera house began to be challenged.

A LOCAL TRADITION

In the 1860s, premieres started to become more infrequent, and Cariocas began to accept the Italian repertory as part of an ongoing local tradition in no need of renewal. An Italian lyric company could get by in imperial Rio de Janeiro with "oldies" like *Il barbiere di Siviglia*, *Norma*, *Il pirata*, and other similar "European antiques," as a local commentator sarcastically put it.[31] The new Italian company that arrived in town in 1865 attempted to overcome this inertia when it promised "to present four new operas in a small period of two months"; a local critic observed blissfully that,

> Five or six [new operas] is the number that our theaters have seen in ten years. This company is capable of making this promise a reality, for these [new] operas are already in their repertory and with only a few rehearsals they will be able to present them; according to some, the im-

presario brought with the company all the attire and accessories needed for the mise en scène.[32]

Although Cariocas had surely heard more than six new operas in the last ten years, the chronicler was correct to point out the need to renew the operatic repertory. In 1866, the Italian conductor and impresario Bozoni attempted to do just that by offering local audiences "the most beautiful operas from the modern repertory"[33] in a subscription for fifteen operatic presentations at the Theatro Lyrico Fluminense (Provisorio). However, his endeavor proved unsuccessful, for by "modern" repertory Bozoni probably meant the seven operas by Verdi that Cariocas heard in a row during that season: *La traviata*, *Il trovatore*, *Un ballo in maschera*, *Rigoletto*, *La forza del destino*, *Aroldo*, and *Les Vêpres siciliennes* (1854), all of which were familiar to local audiences and had premiered in Europe eight to fifteen years earlier. To appeal more directly to Cariocas, Bozoni then managed to squeeze into the season three recent works by Brazilian composers: Antônio Carlos Gomes's *A noite do castelo* (1861) and *Joana de Flandres* (1863), and Henrique Alves de Mesquita's *O vagabundo* (1863).

Five years later an Italian company still offered Cariocas a season consisting of seven operas by Verdi presented alongside works by other Italian composers that ranged up to fifty years old.[34] Apparently, the high point of that season was the four operas by Meyerbeer, *Le prophète* (1849), *L'Africaine* (1865), *Les Huguenots* (1836), *Robert le diable* (1831), and Gounod's *Faust* (1859), which although decades old, had not yet dominated the local stages. True, some of Meyerbeer's earlier operas such as *Robert le diable* had been staged in Rio de Janeiro as early as 1848 and his tunes had circulated in piano arrangements since the early 1840s. But it took until the 1870s for Meyerbeer's works to make it into the "traditional," local operatic repertory and to share the local public's preference for the Italian masters. One can only speculate about the reason for the delay, but most probably it had to do with the length of the works and the lavish mise en scène needed to stage them, especially at a time when the musical options in the capital had diversified immensely, and when the monarchical government was having difficulties justifying large subsidies to operatic productions.

Still, foreign lyric companies continued to try new ways to appeal to Cariocas. In 1887, an Italian company advertised "an extensive repertory," and guaranteed a season in which "no work will be presented more than once."[35] In 1886, when the company of the Italian Claudio Rossi brought to the imperial capital new productions of *Aida*, *Les Huguenots*, and *Faust*, the local chronicles praised the performances, but the center of attention was a young Italian cellist with the company, Arturo Toscanini, who, at the last minute, successfully substituted for the principal conductor.[36] In 1888, another Italian lyric company directed by P. M. Musella offered sixteen operas to Cariocas, the newest works in their repertory being *Aida* and Amilcare Ponchielli's *La Gioconda* (1876). Musella enticed the local audiences with his company's lavish productions; the garments, he guaranteed, were provided by the Italian Casa Zamperoni, "the same shop that provided attires for companies operating in the theater S. Carlos in Naples, the Scala in Milan, and the Eden in Paris." He also emphasized that his company owned sixty complete scenarios "painted by the best scenographic artists in Italy," in addition to special stage machinery and "original" music bought directly from the Italian publishing houses Casa Ricordi & C. C. Fl Lucca.[37] All these novelties, Musella believed, were supposed to be more attractive to Cariocas than any new opera.

If clinging to the same old Italian repertory annoyed some local critics, it was hardly a local predicament, for in the neighboring Latin American countries operatic "oldies" also had quite a following. As John Roselli has observed, in the case of Spanish speaking countries the phenomenon was a predictable result of the Hispanic oligarchy conservatism.[38] The argument could easily also be applied to the elite in imperial Rio de Janeiro, who, in the last decades of the monarchy, desperately clung to Italian oldies as a way to demonstrate the continuing preeminence of their own worn down regime. Nonetheless, if Cariocas waited passively for a new opera to come, and if they were willing to go to the opera house to listen to the same works repeated several times during the same season, it was also because they were curbed by financial limitations. By repeating old works, one could reuse scenery and costumes. Moreover, there was also the possibility of saving money by supplementing the foreign casts with local performers, singers, and prima donnas who were more familiar with the popular old repertory. At a time when keeping the opera house operational was crucial in maintaining the status quo, the local elite was less interested in the novelty of the music and more preoccupied with keeping the old operatic tradition, which was cheaper than the new grand operas in vogue in Paris, but still "cultivated" and European.

During the final two decades of the empire, however, gathering a crowd to fill the opera house started to become a chronic problem. In the mid-1850s a local observer noted that "the boxes and orchestra seats of the Theatro Lyrico (Provisorio) are becoming unaccustomed to having spectators."[39] Two decades later the problem had surely escalated. According to a local critic, the endless repetition of the same old works was to blame for the lack of audience in the opera house. But the problem rested mostly in the diversification of entertainment options that started in the 1860s, putting Cariocas's devotion to the Italian bel canto and the opera house to the test. Managers of the competing Theatro Gymnasio enticed bored Italian opera fans by assuring that "in our repertory there are no cursing screams, neither poisonings nor daggers; instead our goal is to entertain by making people laugh."[40]

Apparently, the social glamour of the opera houses appealed more to well-to-do residents of imperial Rio de Janeiro than the operas that the buildings were made to host. While Cariocas were surely eager to be part of the exclusive group of opera aficionados that showed up every night at the opera house, one's real appreciation for an operatic performance was never under direct scrutiny. The Englishman John Codman, who visited Rio de Janeiro in 1865, denounced the locals' lack of "adequate taste for dramatic performances [and] love for the musical perfection in the representation."[41] Even the monarchs, who openly supported and subsidized opera companies, apparently lacked a truthful commitment to staged performances of operas. Prince Regent João VI, for example, was caught several times sleeping in the royal box during gala performances;[42] and Pedro II, who was well-known for his support and appreciation of the arts, was not entirely captivated by opera, at least not in his youthful years. In an 1844 letter, his sister Princess Francisca expressed her surprise by the news that Pedro II was enjoying the new Italian operatic company in town; "[even] you my Brother" she wrote, "who were always bored with music."[43]

It was perhaps not the music, but the level of the local performances that started to drive the public away from the opera house. According to some visitors, the skills of local and foreign singers left a lot to be desired. As early as 1829, the Frenchman Victor Jacquemont had reported that "in Rio de Janeiro [there is] a theater where a terrible Italian company and a horrible orchestra destroy three times a week the beautiful operas by Rossini."[44] Later, another visitor lamented that, "Italian operas are staged in a very special manner. For example, during my stay [in Rio de Janeiro], the opera *Tancredo* (sic) was staged, but I could hardly recognize it because it was maimed by a terrible orchestra."[45]

If the orchestras and singers lacked skill, additional operational and logistical problems certainly helped to impair the local appetite for the bel canto, at least as it was presented in the theater. Small venues with very small stages were obviously not exemplary hosts for operatic companies, but they did somehow manage to present operatic acts regularly. To be viable, the works had to be so cut and rearranged to fit the small orchestras and limited cast to the extent that to some the most popular operas were hardly recognizable. Furthermore, rather than complete operas, in these venues it was customary to put together parts of different works: for example, the first act of *La Cenerentola*, the third act of *Norma*, and the second act of *La fille du régiment* could be easily performed in the same night by the same cast, a combination that strained singers whose voices were required to quickly adapt to different technical demands. The lack of ventilation in most theaters and the extreme heat during the performances also caused numerous health problems in singers and audiences alike. And there were also concerns with the equipment; one foreign visitor noted that in Rio de Janeiro theaters the decoration was beautiful but "the stage machinery was in its infancy."[46]

Even when there was construction around or inside the hall, theaters remained operational. In 1824, for example, when the São Pedro de Alcantara was being reconstructed after a fire, one visitor recalled that an opera was put on, but the performance was particularly poor because the building was not fully finished, "with part of the roof and the front wall still lacking, which caused the voices of the singers to lose their intensity."[47] In the 1850s, the construction of the Theatro Provisorio was so faulty that apprehensions about the effect of its lack of proper acoustic on singers' voices, and the complaints about the annoying dust that the audience had to endure in the theater's interior were overridden by legitimate concerns about the building collapsing on top of a thousand spectators during the performance.[48] It was not until 1871, when the Theatro D. Pedro II was erected, that Rio de Janeiro could boast a theater with perfect conditions for operatic presentations. Even so, the theater, which was built to serve both as an opera house and a circus, had removable orchestra seats that could turn into a circus ring. According to Vivaldo Coaracy, it was only "by chance" that it turned out to be appropriate for operatic performances.[49]

While foreign visitors and members of the elite could not hide their uneasiness with the less-than-exemplary performances, the great majority of opera house habitués seemed a bit more tolerant, perhaps because they viewed the actual performance as just a part of the whole opera house spectacle. In 1862, even after the singers from a new Italian company received less than laudatory reviews from local critics, the audience continued to attend the opera house because, according to a local commentator, "the public is so eager for Italian singing, that it is willing to put up with the unfavorable merit of the artists."[50] The way they "put up with" the artists' lack of merit was by creating an imaginary aura of virtuosity around their names, to which Cariocas vowed unconditional loyalty. Some singers built such large followings after particularly good performances that even on their worst nights when their voices did not meet the audience's expectations, devoted Cariocas would still throw flowers and jewelry at their feet in gratitude for their performances. The Englishman John Codman noted that "the habitants of Rio de Janeiro are not preoccupied with political parties [that advocate] religion, abolition, or the rights of women . . . but they subscribe to the parties devoted to the [singers] Aimée and Lovato."[51]

There were many other entertaining acts that kept Cariocas's attention away from the poor performances. In introductions and intermissions managers and impresarios offered pantomimes and juggling acts, vernacular songs, and lots of solo dances. There were so many of these extra entertainments that a German visitor described operatic performances in Rio de Janeiro as "spurious acts, accompanied by all sorts of theatrical artifices without any value."[52] But for most, the dances were a given. "As in Paris," a Frenchmen noted, "the public here [in Rio de Janeiro] appreciate and applaud [dancers] enthusiastically . . . the organizers of the ballet presentations are French, from the Porte St. Martin Theater in Paris."[53] Unlike the skills of orchestra and singers, the ballet numbers were always the subject of praise by locals and foreigners alike to whom "the ballets are always performed with the highest skills and are deserving of the greatest praise."[54]

For those Cariocas for whom the extra entertainment was not worth the poorly staged performances of old Italian operas, there were other musical options. French vaudevilles, short comic operas, and operettas started to arrive in imperial Rio de Janeiro in the 1840s, and came to dominate the repertory of local small theaters in the second part of the century. For those not preoccupied with preserving the operatic tradition or with safeguarding the status quo but still wanting to keep up with Parisian musical fashions, the novelty was a given, for it was entertaining, French, and replete with European appeal.

COMPETING CRAZES

In the smaller Theatro São Januário, Eugène Scribe's vaudevilles and comedies were the first to compete with the Italian masters, but soon works by French composers of *opéras comiques* and *petits opéras* such as Adolphe Adam (1803–1856), Daniel Auber (1782–1871), François Adrien Boieldieu (1775–1834), and Ferdinand Hérold (1791–1833) also found local followings.[55] In 1846, a French lyric company contracted by the Brazilian manager and actor João Caetano premiered no fewer than seven French operas at the Theatro São Januário: Hérold's *Le pré aux clercs* (1832) was followed by Boieldieu's *La dame blanche* (1825) and *Le nouveau seigneur du village*, Auber's *L'ambassadrice* (1836), *Le domino noir* (1837), and *Concert à la cour* (1824). The season closed on December 26 with Hérold's *Zampa* (1831). In 1847, another collaboration between Scribe and Auber, *Les diamants de la couronne* (1841) appeared on the stages of the São Januário. These works, which were quite popular with Cariocas well into the 1860s, were usually performed (in French) by a French cast of singers.

Cariocas had a special place in their hearts (and ears) for Offenbach's operettas, which started to dominate the scene in 1859 with the opening of the Theatro Alcazar Lyrique. For almost two decades operettas shared with Italian bel canto the patronage of Rio de Janeiro's public. Starting with *Orphée aux enfers* (1858), which premiered in 1865, Offenbach's operettas were brought to Rio de Janeiro in an uninterrupted sequence: in 1866 came *Les Bavards* (1862), *Le chanson de fortunio* (1861), *La belle Hélène*, and *Daphnis et Chloé* (1860); *La grand duchesse de Gérolstein* (1867) and *La Périchole* (1868) came in 1870; and *La princesse de Trébizonde* (1869) in 1871. In the 1870s, Cariocas could also enjoy other operetta composers who were regularly featured in theaters such as the Gymnazio Dramatico and the Phenix

Dramatica. Hervé's (1825–1892) *Le petit Faust* (1869) and *Chilpéric* came in 1871; Alexander Charles Lecquoc's (1832–1918) *La fille de Mme Angot* (1872) and *La fleur de thé* (1868) premiered the following year. In 1875, only one year after its premiere in Europe, Lecquoc's *Giroflé-Girofla* (1874) was presented in Rio de Janeiro. The local newspapers were proud to note that the work, which was an "immense success in Europe," was destined also to become an "immense success in Rio de Janeiro."[56]

The third European music fad to appear in Rio de Janeiro's stages was not French, although it arrived via Paris. Early in the nineteenth century, Spanish immigrant composers such as Miguel Tonamorrel, Salvador Sarmiento, and Ramón Carnicer brought Spanish music and dance to the French capital, and predictably, a few years later Spanish music was also echoed in imperial Rio de Janeiro. Andalusian dances, which fascinated the French, also captivated the Brazilian public. *Polos*, *boleros*, and especially the *caxuxa* (or cachucha)[57] were being danced in Brazilian theaters as intermezzos in comic plays, farces, and *opéra-comique* as early as 1845. During the three decades from the 1830s to the 1850s, benefit performances invariably included Spanish numbers as attractions. Spanish *tonadillas*, short, comic acts sung in Spanish, served as intermezzos in the 1840s, while from the 1850s on the popular zarzuelas started to arrive in the capital directly from Spain. These comic works in Spanish, alternating spoken dialogue with songs, found quite a following among the general public probably because of the inclusion of popular and folk materials. Asenjo Barbieri's (1823–1894) popular zarzuela *Jugar con fuego* (1851), premiered in the capital in 1857, and later Joaquín Gaztambide's (1822–1870) *El barberillo de Lavapiés* (1874) and *Estrea de un artista* became local favorites in small venues like the Theatro Gymnasio and Theatro Phenix Dramatica.[58]

Finally, in the 1870s, Wagner's music and the Wagnerian myth entered the lives of Cariocas. The composer and piano virtuoso Louis Moreau Gottschalk first introduced a Wagner tune in a piano fantasy on themes from *Tannhäuser* (1845). The start was a grandiose one: the fantasy was presented at a concert in the Theatro Lyrico (Provisorio) on October 5 and 7, 1869, with no fewer than two orchestras and thirty-one pianists.[59] In the following year, Carlotta Patti featured an orchestral version of the *Rienzi* (1840) overture in one of her Concertos Populares. The "new" work was introduced as "a beautiful composition that provoked a truthful revolution in Europe. [Wagner's work] is today recognized everywhere as the superior [music] school; it defeated its enemies, and has been proclaimed victorious everywhere."[60]

Cariocas tried dutifully also to engage in the European buzz that surrounded Wagner's name and his music. Always alert to the trends in Europe, earlier in 1857 Pedro II had made a frustrated attempt to commission a Wagner opera, probably *Tristan und Isolde* (1857–1859), to be performed in Rio de Janeiro. The emperor continued his pursuit of Wagner and his music, and in 1876, he finally visited Bayreuth for the premiere of the Ring cycle.[61]

On September 19, 1883, an Italian company premiered *Lohengrin* in the imperial capital. Proud of not having napped during the presentation himself, a commentator noted that Wagner's melodies bored the audience, who applauded the first act, but were generally "cold" toward the rest of the work. The local newspapers did not spare harsh criticisms of the opera, pointing out candidly that, "As a musical conception, *Lohengrin* is deplorable." Another newspaper critic mockingly pointed out that, "There is nothing new in Wagner's music, since here [in Rio de Janeiro] we are already tired of orchestral dissonances."[62]

In truth, apart from a few Wagner devotees, Rio de Janeiro audiences did not immediately succumb to the Wagner spell. They were too busy enjoying operettas and bel canto "oldies" to notice anything really captivating in Wagner's music. Moreover, Rio de Janeiro's small orchestras probably could not produce the same effect in the performance of Wagner's works that European orchestras could. Finally, the unfamiliarity with the German language made it difficult even for the local elite to enjoy Wagner's works. Nonetheless, once European criticism started to resonate in Rio de Janeiro, local critics became supporters of Wagner and began to forecast the defeat of the Italian repertory and to question the local bel canto operatic tradition.

PAYING FOR OPERA

With its port connected to Europe via regular steamship lines by mid-century, imperial Rio de Janeiro was the starting point of the South American circuit ventured by European impresarios, conductors, and singers.[63] The decision to leave Europe in search of New World audiences and the courage to undertake a long and strenuous trip seemed to pay off in the end, as more and more immigrant musicians arrived on Latin American shores as the century progressed. John Roselli has conjectured that Italian impresarios and singers left Europe because of the end of European circuits that allowed modest singers to perform in a network of small towns; some were driven out by war or revolution, or by the changing economy in Europe.[64] Most singers who ventured to South America had had some experience with comic operas in small theaters in Italy; a few could boast small parts in middle-size and large theaters; others left no trace of a previous singing career in Europe.[65] Whatever their professional experience, all of them traveled to South America in the hopes of gaining prominence, and most with the expectation of higher incomes. Imperial Rio de Janeiro was especially attractive in this regard, for the city housed an imperial court and an aristocracy willing to pay for opera, an element lacking in other Latin American capitals.

As in Italy, Rio de Janeiro theaters and opera houses, although built and managed by private enterprise, regularly received government subsidies and other incentives that helped keep them profitable. Imperial aid was extensive and could come in the form of leases for the land and payment of contractors to erect theaters, tax exemptions for imported materials needed in construction and decoration, and allocation of governmental funds from lotteries to cover operational and maintenance costs. Theater managers could also count on money obtained through an association of *acionistas* (shareholders), who were eminent, moneyed individuals with prestige within the local society. In return for their investment in the construction of the Theatro Provisorio, for example, shareholders were entitled to permanent seats, with the location in the theater varying according to the number of shares held. They were also automatically part of an inspectorate that oversaw the construction plan and made sure that it went according to the government contract.[66]

The government, which actually owned the building of the Theatro Provisorio, also had a strong hand in the local workings of operatic companies hired in Europe, and sometimes even in the direct employment of singers and instrumentalists. Contracts signed between the imperial government and foreign impresarios were considered official business and were published in local newspapers for the knowledge of the general public, who were expected to informally supervise the companies' practical workings during the performances.

"The promises made publicly [by the impresario] to subscribers and the general public [are regarded by the government] as if they are written contracts, which should be enforced by the local authorities," reported the *Jornal do commercio* in 1850. These contracts were usually extended documents that regulated almost every aspect of opera making in the city and as such they offer a remarkable insight into the extent to which the monarchical government intervened in the local business of opera.

The contract signed in 1850 between the minister of the empire and an impresario willing to act in the Theatro São Pedro de Alcantara serves as an example. According to the document published on November 16, 1850, in the *Jornal do commercio*, the impresario had to report regularly to a commission made up of prominent individuals appointed by the government, who would supervise the company's finances. The impresario, who was promised a sizable amount by the imperial government, could receive the money only after presenting receipts for all monthly expenses. As further measures of budget control, the imperial government established such particulars as the number of operatic presentations (eight to twelve a month), the prices of tickets, and the number of benefit and gala concerts. The contract also established the number of hires to be made in Europe: in this case, the impresario was expected to bring to Rio de Janeiro a lyric company made up of twelve soloists and twenty singers, plus a technician and two painters. It was also established that the soloists should "have worked as first role in any of the theaters from London and Paris, or in Italian theaters such as the Scala in Milan, the S. Carlos in Naples, or the Fenice in Venice."[67] Artists were not to be contracted for more than two years and the impresario was required to present a new opera every month, although this last requirement was not always met. Finally, before the premiere of any new opera, the impresario had to apply for special approval by a commission nominated by the imperial government. The commission was in charge of inspecting the final rehearsal to ensure that the work was staged with the proper mise en scène and that it followed "the habits of the place and time in which the action takes place."[68]

Given the large sums allocated to operatic companies throughout Pedro II's government, these tight contracts were viewed as indispensable, especially considering that imperial subsidies were not unconditionally well received by the majority. In fact, government support of foreign operatic companies was always grounds for contestation among political factions. In 1865, for instance, when an Italian company did not honor its contract with the government and left town without presenting the promised operas and without paying the contracted artists, a fierce debate emerged in the local newspapers about the validity of government subsidies for operatic presentations.

To some, the argument for subsidy was quite obvious: Why not follow Europeans and pay for "civilization" and "culture"? In support of the government, a habitué of the opera house declared in a daily newspaper that "the audience, without any reason, forgets that to hear these celebrity singers the government has to give a small subvention, in the same way it is done in Europe. It has long been accepted that the lyric companies cannot maintain themselves with the theater revenues alone, and that the growing civilization justifies the subsidy from the state."[69]

As with several members of the local elite, this anonymous writer assumed that opera was a primary need of the majority and that it more than justified the expense. But the issue was obviously not quite so straightforward. The high cost of presenting fully staged, complete operas was a financial burden not to be taken lightly, especially considering that, in reality, one production was usually performed no more than five or six times a season, if that, and benefited a meager percentage of the city's population.

Consequently, criticisms of the government's policy of subsidizing foreign operatic companies were not in short supply. Reacting to the large sums paid by the government to an Italian Lyric company, for example, a critic noted,

> Nobody [among us] ignore the fabulous amounts of money that we [Brazilians] have spent in the presentation of Italian opera in our theaters. It is also quite clear that the only result of these sacrifices has been a chain of scandals that started in 1851, when the ill-fated Theatro Provisorio was built. The minister of the government himself, who signed the contract with the recent lyric company, knows [better than anyone else] the impossibility of the government subsidizing the lyric theater. But, in devious ways, everything can be obtained from the government. . . . Under the excuse of the development of our lyric theater, the government gave some 200$000 [*réis*] to help the last company, which left us with sad memories.[70]

The "chain of scandals" mentioned by the chronicler started when large sums of money were paid by the government to an inexperienced contractor who built the Theatro Provisorio with considerable structural defects that continually threatened the regular operation of the building.[71] In 1865, similar scandals and the continuing condemnation of imperial government policies led to the temporary closure of two large theaters, the São Pedro de Alcantara and the Lyrico (Provisorio).[72] And yet, in the midst of inflammatory debates, subsidies continued to be granted. Managers and impresarios were particularly engaged in the discussion, arguing that governmental subsidies were needed because ticket sales alone were not enough to cover the costs of operatic productions. Whether or not that was the case, the issue ultimately reached the audience, who relentlessly asked: why is it that the larger the subsidy the higher the ticket prices? For a majority of theater-goers, it was neither the government nor theater managers, but the audience that in the end paid for the costly operatic productions.

Despite the controversy, contemporary reports do not seem to indicate that ticket prices for an operatic presentation were exorbitant or prohibitive, at least not for the 2 percent of the city's population who attended such events. If, on the one hand, in 1878 the Frenchman Gaston Lemay complained that he had to pay "an incredible number of *milréis*" to get an orchestra seat to hear *Faust* at the Theatro D. Pedro II,[73] on the other hand, in 1884 Machado de Assis reported that the ticket for an orchestra seat at the opera house went for an amount he considered "excellent, moderate, and realistic."[74] In fact, a comparison of ticket prices at local theaters, including the opera house, shows that all venues offered relatively inexpensive low-end tickets, which permitted the regular attendance of students and single males. At the high end, it was a different story. First- and second-class boxes in the opera house were about 30 percent to 50 percent more expensive than the boxes in other venues, although those willing to buy subscriptions for a whole season in the opera house could receive as much as a 20 percent discount.[75]

If the relationship between governmental subsidies and ticket prices at the opera house remained a relevant issue for the less affluent, it was apparently not simply an issue of money, since for them the ticket prices were worth the privilege of being part of the exclusive group of the opera house habitués. The intimidating nature that the pomposity of the opera house exerted over those aspiring to climb the social ladder was more likely to scare them away than the tickets. At a higher level, the debate lay not in ticket prices, but in the questionable use of public money to sustain a form of entertainment exploited by the status quo, particularly after the 1870s, at a time when the monarchical regime was having severe budget problems. And in this case, the only viable argument seemed to be the emphasis on the European nature of the music, which, although expensive, embodied the promise of fulfilling the monarchy's aspirations to transform the country into a European-like nation and, accordingly, a more "civilized" society. In the end, the issue of subsidies to foreign lyric companies turned into a casual battle between political factions, a battle that was ultimately resolved in the boxes of the opera house alongside not so civilized discussions about the performances of beloved prima donnas.

OPERATIC SUBCULTURE

While the debate about governmental subsidies for opera productions reflects the elite's perception of the music as a compelling tool for indoctrinating European values and for exerting social and political control by directly managing the local culture, it provides but a glimpse of the extent to which operatic music reached those living in imperial Rio de Janeiro. The exclusive, elite character of opera was largely dependent on the restricted context of the opera house, and indeed on the manner in which the music was presented in private social gatherings and small concert venues. However, operatic music spread well beyond these selective circles, and was performed in various, less sophisticated contexts and formats that permitted a much wider spectrum of social perceptions. Outside the opera house, operatic music could exist simultaneously on several social strata and embodied meanings that had less to do with asserting elite values than with fashion, "Europeaness," and cosmopolitan life.[76] In informal contexts such as in the homes of the newly formed bourgeoisie, in ballrooms, in street parades during Carnival, and in the streets performed by troubadours, European operatic music reached a larger number of Cariocas, and became a significant cultural phenomenon in the wider context of the monarchical Rio de Janeiro society.

While the discussion of the fading local operatic tradition and the lack of audience in the opera house permeated the editorials of daily newspapers, beyond the opera house Cariocas's love for bel canto was far from exhausted. The local kinship for opera and other genres of music theater continued to grow well into the twentieth century, as famous tunes from Verdi and Offenbach moved from number-one hits in the catalogues of sheet music publications to become hits in radio shows. The reason opera and related music theater genres enticed large numbers of Cariocas outside elite circles lay in the wide social contexts in which the music could be performed and enjoyed, in the endless possibilities of its performance practices, and, above all, in the nature of the music itself.

Operas, operettas, zarzuelas, and other products of musical theater were not perceived as finished, unalterable works of art, as Lawrence Levine rightly points out.[77] They were easily adapted to new performance circumstances, mixed with different genres and embellished according to new preferences, and were transformed according to the tastes of different territories, stimulating burlesques and parodies.[78] As in other urban centers, arias in Rio de Janeiro were replaced by local songs or more popular arias from other operas, while operatic reminiscences appeared disguised in other musical genres such as dances, hymns, and religious compositions. It was also common practice in local theaters to present operatic tunes as intermezzos during plays and mingled with comedies; the play *A inquisição de Roma* presented at the theater Lyrico Fluminense on June 30, 1866, for example, closed with the comedy *Um casamento pelo Jornal do commercio* (A Wedding through the *Jornal do commercio*) "ornate with music from the opera *Norma* and the operetta *Orphée aux enfers*."[79] It was precisely this flexibility that made the nineteenth-century operatic repertory so accessible and appealing to a wider audience in urban centers like Rio de Janeiro. Rather than appropriating an imported music that required authenticity in performance, Cariocas wholeheartedly adopted operas and operettas because indirectly they could participate in the performative aspects of the music by mixing, interpolating, and re-creating, at their will, the music arriving from overseas.

In a cosmopolitan city like Rio de Janeiro it was mostly through sheet music publications that close, individual, and creative contact with the music first occurred. Local music dealers explored the local market fully, both by boosting the importation of sheet music from Paris and by investing in local publications. These publications appeared in a wide variety of formats—from elaborate fantasies over operatic tunes, to reductions for voice and piano, to simplified versions for the dilettanti. Often they matched the current repertory performed in the opera house. For instance, Rossini's music, which crowded Rio de Janeiro stages in the 1820s and 1830s, prevailed in the 1837 catalogue of imported sheet music available at the Dutch Müller's music establishment. In the 1850s, bel canto masters Bellini and Donizetti, then in vogue in local theaters, dominated the catalogues of sheet music available in the city.[80] In general, however, imported sheet music reflected the vogue in Paris and anticipated the music to appear in Rio de Janeiro theaters. Reductions and arrangements of Auber's operas, for instance, reached their peak popularity in the capital much earlier than the stage production of his operas, which started in 1846. Also, Müller's 1837 catalogue listed reductions and excerpts of a few operas by Donizetti and Bellini that had to wait ten to fifteen years before being premiered in Brazilian theaters. It was thus in sheet music format that some operas were first introduced to the public so that when the operas finally reached the local stages their most coveted tunes had long been admired.

Periodical publications containing music, rather than literary material, were common alternatives for middle-class amateurs and dilettanti in general. At midcentury, the most important and longest lasting music periodical containing music was *O Brasil musical* (Musical Brazil) published between 1848 and 1870 by the Casa de Filippone e Cia, later Filippone & Tornaghi.[81] Eventually including more than 500 pieces, *O Brasil musical* came out twice a month in alternate issues, with works for voice and piano in even numbers, and for piano solo in odd numbers. More than any other publication of its kind, *O Brasil musical* concentrated on the music performed at the theater; tunes from operas and operettas came out regularly as simplified excerpts and reductions for piano and piano and voice, as well as in the format of fantasies and variations on operatic themes aimed at more advanced performers. A large number of pieces were direct reprints of French and English publications of works by composers established in Paris such as P. Musard, Franz Hünter (1792–1878), and H. Herz; it also included technically demanding pieces by other virtuoso pianists such as Alexandre-Édouard Goria (1823–1860), Ferdinand Beyer (1803–1863), Eugene Ketterer (1831–1870), Ignace Leybach (1817–1891), Émile Prudent (1817–1863), and Rosellen (1811–1874). Also favorites in *O Brasil musical* were pieces by the virtuoso pianist Sigismund Thalberg, whose music remained among the best selling in Rio de Janeiro for more than two decades after his visit to the capital in 1855.[82] In the 1860s, works by Joseph Ascher (1829–1869), a Dutch Jewish composer resident in Paris, led the publication of pieces for piano in *O Brasil musical.* Ascher's output, like that of his contemporaries Goria and Thalberg, was largely dependent on popular operatic themes, the arias by Donizetti, Bellini, and Verdi being the most favored.

To Cariocas, it was not at all bizarre that the bulk of the pieces in a periodical titled *Musical Brazil* were works based on European opera by artists whose careers were centered in Paris.[83] But the local element was not altogether absent, since this famous periodical also included works by immigrant composers, such as the Italians Antônio Tornaghi and Ercole Pinzarrone (1826–1924), who provided the local market with homemade operatic reductions, arrangements, fantasies, and variations modeled directly on the imported pieces. Given that a great number of Cariocas were first introduced to popular operatic tunes through these kinds of reductions, arrangements, fantasies, and variations, these composers were largely responsible for paving the way and creating a taste for certain operas in the imperial capital.

Outside the theaters, bel canto and songs and dances from operettas and zarzuelas pervaded the life of Cariocas at many more levels. While operatic tunes served as themes for variations and fantasies that were regularly performed in local concert rooms by virtuoso pianists and violinists from abroad, the splendor of the opera house was also transplanted to small, private circles and family gatherings in piano reductions and other arrangements and performed mostly by amateurs. Reductions of arias and simplified arrangements in inexpensive sheet music publications for piano, flute, or violin, were especially good alternatives for those who could not afford a ticket to the opera house. Thus, in new *roupage*, operatic music lost its elitist character and infiltrated all strata of the local society. To cite a few examples: tunes from Verdi's *Il trovatore,* which after being performed several times in the local opera house, became hits in the opera's parody *O capadócio* (1872) performed in the Theatro Gymnasio; tunes from the opera later dominated the "pop charts" of local publishers disguised as dances and facilitated versions for piano, flute, and guitar.[84] Themes from Offenbach's *Orphée aux enfers* eventually became popular enough outside the theater that they were transmitted orally throughout the country, ultimately mingling with local folklore in Brazil's most remote regions.[85]

Independent from the operas and operettas to which they originally belonged, estranged from the plots that once gave them particular meanings, and reworked enough that their final form only remotely recalled something that once belonged to prima donnas, operatic derivatives had a life of their own, embodying a whole new set of local symbols and associations. They created an operatic subculture outside the European realm with unbounded ramifications. Excellent examples of this operatic subculture are operatic reminiscences that appeared disguised as dances with titles such as *Quadrilhe Anna Bolena*, *Polka Barbe Bleu*, *Waltz Roberto o diabo*, *Mazurka Manon Lescaut*, or *Schottisch Marco Visconti*.[86] These pieces were digested as "the music of the day" and not as a local tradition that depended on associations with the opera house and elite culture. If, in this case, the appealing factor still rested in the music's provenance, in its Europeaness, it was not so much for the subliminal idea of power and control, as for the association with fashionable, urbane life. And as an additional benefit, the music could be recreated and manipulated enough to fit perfectly in the local context as an integral part of the local culture.

NOTES

1. John Roselli's study on the opera business in South America is exemplary; see his "The Opera Business and the Italian Immigrant Community in Latin America 1820–1930: the Example of Buenos Aires," *Past and Present* 127 (May 1990): 155–82. For general works on opera in other Latin American countries see José Ignácio Perdomo Escobar, *La ópera en Colombia* (Bogotá: Litografía Arco, 1979); Olavarria y Ferrari, *Reseña histórica del teatro en México*, 3rd ed. (Mexico City: Editorial Porrúa, 1961); Pereira Salas, *Los orígenes del arte musical en Chile* (Santiago: Universidad de Chile, 1941); and Vicente Gesualdo's *Historia de la música en Argentina* (Buenos Aires: Editorial Beta, 1961).

2. Gabriel García Márquez, *Love in the Time of Cholera*, trans. Edith Grossman (New York: Penguin, 1989), 44.

3. John Dizikes, *Opera in America: a Cultural History* (New Haven, Conn.: Yale University Press, 1993), 14.

4. According to Atwood, Honoré Balzac typically sat with his back to the stage to watch the action in the audience; see *The Parisian Worlds of Frédéric Chopin* (New Haven: Yale University Press, 1999), 192 and 190.

5. *Jornal do commercio*, April 11, 1855.

6. Machado de Assis, *Memórias póstumas de Brás Cubas*; quoted in Miécio Táti, *O mundo de Machado de Assis* (Rio de Janeiro: Secretaria Municipal de Cultura, Turismo e Esportes, 1991), 152. For the presence of Rio de Janeiro's aristocracy in the Theatro Provisorio, see also Eric Gordon, "A New Opera House: An Investigation of Elite Values in Mid-Nineteenth-Century Rio de Janeiro," *Inter-American Institute for Musical Research Yearbook* 5 (1969): 49–66.

7. Gaston Lemay (1878), quoted in Míriam Moreira Leite, *A Condição feminina no Rio de Janeiro* (São Paulo: HUCITEC, Instituto Nacional do Livro, 1984), 173.

8. Jeffrey Needell, *A Tropical Belle Époque: Elite Culture and Society in Turn-of-the-Century Rio de Janeiro* (Cambridge: Cambridge University Press, 1987), 79.

9. Aleilton Santanna da Fonseca provides an analysis of the role of opera in the local society according to nineteenth-century Brazilian novelists; see "Enredo romântico, música ao fundo" (Master's thesis, Universidade Federal da Paraíba, 1992).

10. Leite, *A condição feminina no Rio de Janeiro*, 169–70.

11. Quoted in Needell, *A Tropical Belle Époque*, 78.

12. According to Gordon, documents show that at least a hundred "Africans" were sent by the government to aid the contractor in the construction of the Theatro Provisorio. See "A New Opera House," 60.

13. Freed blacks were often employed as performers in theater and ball orchestras and performed the music required by the local elite, mostly European imports. During the celebrations of his coronation, Pedro II freed twenty slaves, eighteen instrumentalists and two singers, who performed at the ceremonies; see Roderick J. Barman, *Citizen Emperor: Pedro II and the Making of Brazil 1825–91* (Stanford, Calif.: Stanford University Press, 1999), 85. A few Afro-Brazilians reached fame as composers, as was the case with José Maurício Nunes Garcia, a mulatto hired by João VI to direct the royal chapel. However, Afro-Brazilians rarely took part as members of the audience in the musical events of the white middle and upper classes.

14. Jurandir Malerba reported on an incident at a local theater during the Regency, when a black woman was taken into police custody for being drunk at the theater and for disrupting the audience. It is not clear, however, whether the woman was accompanying a white family, as was customary, or whether she was part of the audience. See *A corte no exílio: civilização e poder no Brasil às vésperas da independência (1808 a 1821)* (São Paulo: Companhia das Letras, 2000), 139–40.

15. *Jornal do commercio*, February 4, 1847.

16. José Vieira da Fazenda, "Antiqualhas e memórias do Rio de Janeiro," *Revista do instituto histórico e geográfico brasileiro*, t. 93, v. 147 (1923), 85–86; see also Gordon, "A New Opera House," 52.

17. James Harding's analysis of music and society in nineteenth-century France highlights the special appeal of opera to Parisian audiences; see

"Paris: Opera Reigns Supreme," in *Music and Society: The Late Romantic Era*, ed. Jim Samson (Upper Saddle River, N.J.: Prentice Hall, 1991), 106.

18. Roselli notices that in nineteenth-century Argentina opera also meant Italian opera; see, "The Opera Business," 155.

19. Aware of their appeal in the Portuguese court, Italian composers such as Niccolò Piccinni (1728–1800) and Niccolò Jommelli (1714–1794) dedicated operas to the Portuguese rulers in an attempt to gain their patronage. Jommelli was especially popular in Lisbon. In 1760 D. José offered him a pension to produce an opera every year for the Portuguese court. In the nineteenth century Gaetano Donizetti dedicated his opera *Dom Sébastien* (1843) to Queen D. Maria II. See Manuel Carlos de Brito, *Estudos de história da música em Portugal* (Lisbon: Imprensa Universitária, Editorial estampa, 1989), 109–22; see also his *Crónicas da vida musical portuguesa* (Lisbon: Imprensa Nacional, Casa da Moeda, 1990), 22.

20. João Carneiro da Silva's *Composições dramaticas do Abbade Pedro Metastasio* (Lisbon: Simão Thaddeo Ferrera, 1783) includes Portuguese translations of Metastasio's works. For a complete list of Metastasio works performed in Brazil in the eighteenth century, see J. Galante de Sousa, *O teatro no Brasil* (Rio de Janeiro: MEC, Instituto Nacional do Livro, 1960), 123–37.

21. See Sousa, *O teatro no Brasil*, 113; see also Ayres de Andrade, *Francisco Manuel da Silva e seu tempo*, vol. 1 (Rio de Janeiro: Ediçoés Tempo Brasileiro, 1967), 67.

22. According to Juan Andrés Sala, the first complete opera performed in Buenos Aires was *Il barbiere di Siviglia* on September 27, 1825, followed by *La Cenerentola* on May 4, 1826, and *L'inganno felice* on June 8 of the same year; see "Actividad musical en Buenos Aires antes de la inauguración del actual teatro Colón," in *La historia del teatro Colón 1908–1968*, ed. Roberto Caamaño (Buenos Aires: Editorial Cinetea, 1963), 21–23. Chile had to wait until 1830 for the premiere of *Il barbiere di Siviglia*, *L'Italiana in Algeri*, *L'inganno felice*, *Edoardo e Cristina*, *La Cenerentola*, and *La gazza ladra*; see Pereira Salas, *Los orígenes del arte musical en Chile*, 119–20. In Colombia, a complete Rossini opera was first performed in 1848; see José Ignácio Perdomo Escobar, *La ópera en Colombia*, 12. In Mexico, Manuel Garcia's (1775–1832) company performed a Rossini opera, *Il barbiere di Siviglia*, for the first time on June 29, 1827; see Olavarria y Ferrari, *Reseña histórica del teatro en México*, vol. 1, 231.

23. The Chilean magazine *El album* reported the following commentary of a performance of *Il barbiere di Siviglia*: "Rossini's music is a universal idiom because it is understood by everyone, because it excites our senses and evokes passion to its limits"; see Pereira Salas, *Historia de la música en Chile 1850–1900*, 64–65.

24. Ayres de Andrade, *Francisco Manuel da Silva e seu tempo*, vol. 1, 115–16.

25. See Andrade, *Francisco Manuel da Silva e seu tempo*, vol. 1, 197.

26. The Theatro Provisorio had opened earlier with a masked ball on February 21; see Gordon, "A New Opera House," 56–59.

27. According to Ayres de Andrade, the first attempt to perform the work in Brazil was in 1857 by the singer Rosina Laborde, but it did not reach stage performance; see Ayres de Andrade, *Francisco Manuel da Silva e seu tempo,* vol. 2, 59.

28. "Exulta, oh! Brasil . . . Imno a 3 voci con cori a grande orchestra composto sulle parole dell'Exmo. Commendatore Sig. José Gonçalves de Magalhães, dedicato a S. M. Don Pedro 2 do Imperatore del Brasile dal Cav. Maestro Saverio Mercadante, Diretore del R. Conservatorio Musicale di Napoli, 1852." The manuscript is housed in the Biblioteca Alberto Nepomuceno at the Music School of the Federal University in Rio de Janeiro. Mercadante's *Exulta, oh! Brasil* was recorded in the collection *Música na côrte brasileira*, vol. 4 (Angel Album N° 3-CBX 413).

29. *Jornal do commercio*, July 3, 1850.

30. *Jornal do commercio*, July 3, 1850.

31. *Jornal do commercio*, October 8, 1865.

32. *Jornal do commercio*, October 8, 1865.

33. *Jornal do commercio*, February 19, 1863.

34. Rossini's *Guiglerme Tell* and *Moysés* were followed by Halévy's *La Juive* (1835), Auber's *La muette de Portici* (1828), Mercadante's *La vestale* (1840) and *Il bravo* (1839), Flotow's *Martha* (1847), Bellini's *Norma*, and Pacini's *Saffo* (1840); *Jornal do commercio*, March 22, 1871.

35. *Jornal do commercio*, October 14, 1887.

36. *Jornal do commercio*, August 7, 1886.

37. *Jornal do commercio*, August 2, 1888.

38. Roselli, "The Opera Business," 170.

39. *Jornal do commercio*, May 16 1854.

40. *Jornal do commercio*, May 20, 1855.

41. John Codman (1865), quoted in Leite, *A condição feminina no Rio de Janeiro*, 173.

42. Max Fleiuss, *Paginas de historia* (Rio de Janeiro: Imprensa Nacional, 1924), 425.

43. Barman, *Citizen Emperor*, 100.

44. Fleiuss, *Paginas de historia*, 438.

45. Th. von Leithold, quoted in Leite, *A condição feminina no Rio de Janeiro*, 121.

46. E. Th. Böesche (1825), quoted in Leite, *A condição feminina no Rio de Janeiro*, 171.

47. Carl Schelichthorst (1824), quoted in Leite, *A condição feminina no Rio de Janeiro*, 122.

48. Sousa, *Teatro no Brasil*, 360; and Gordon, "A New Opera House," 55, 57, and 61. A picture of the Provisorio theatre with comments on the precariousness of the building was published in *Semana illustrada* of April 27, 1862; the picture is reproduced in Francisco Curt Lange, "Vida y muerte de Louis Moreau Gottschalk en Rio de Janeiro," *Revista de estudios musicales* 2/5–6 (1950–1951): 155.

49. Vivaldo Coaracy, *Memórias da cidade do Rio de Janeiro* (Rio de Janeiro: Livraria José Olympio, 1965), 140–41.

50. *Jornal do commercio*, May 3, 1862.

51. John Codman (1865), quoted in Leite, *A condição feminina no Rio de Janeiro*, 172.

52. E. Th. Böesche (1825), quoted in Leite, *A condição feminina no Rio de Janeiro*, 171.

53. Th. von Leithold, quoted in Leite, *A condição feminina no Rio de Janeiro*, 121.

54. E. Th. Böesche (1825), quoted in Leite, *A condição feminina no Rio de Janeiro*, 171.

55. These works were announced in the *Jornal do commercio* from September to December of 1846.

56. *Jornal do commercio*, February 14, 1875.

57. A triple-meter dance from Andalusia, related to the *fandango*, the *cachucha* was used in Fanny Elssler's ballet *Le diable boiteux* (1836). In Rio de Janeiro the *cachucha* was danced at theaters since the early 1830s; see Mercedes Reis Pequeno, ed., "1770–1970: Exposição Beethoven no Rio de Janeiro" (Rio de Janeiro: Divisão de Publicação Biblioteca Nacional, Seção de Música e Arquivo Sonoro, 1970), 1.

58. *A estreia de um artista* was performed in the Theatro Gymnasio Dramatico on July 17, 1857. In the same year, *La estrea de un artista* was performed in Chile and Buenos Aires; see Pereira Salas, *Historia de la música en Chile, 1850–1900,* 51. Barbieri's *Jugar con fuego* was produced in Rio de Janeiro on August 31, 1857, at the Theatro São Januario.

59. Lange, "Vida y muerte de Luis Moreau Gottschalk en Rio de Janeiro (1869)," 120; see also Robert Stevenson, "Gottschalk Programs Wagner," *Inter-American Music Review* 2 (Spring–Summer 1983), 84.

60. *Jornal do commercio*, July 29, 1870.

61. Robert Stevenson, "Wagner's Latin American Outreach (to 1900)," *Inter-American Music Review* 2 (Spring–Summer 1983), 63–83.

62. Carl von Koseritz, *Imagens do Brasil* (São Paulo: Ed. da Universidade de São Paulo, 1980), 205–6.

63. For the circuits of foreign opera companies in Latin America see John Roselli, "The Opera Business," 165–66.

64. Roselli, "The Opera Business," 162.

65. Roselli, "The Opera Business," 163–64.

66. Gordon, "A New Opera House," 53.

67. *Jornal do commercio*, November 16, 1850.

68. *Jornal do commercio*, November 16, 1850.

69. *Jornal do commercio*, October 8, 1865

70. *Jornal do commercio*, January 6 and 7, 1865.

71. For a complete report on the problems faced by the government in the construction of the Theatro Provisorio, see Gordon, "A New Opera House," 51–63.

72. John Codman (1865), cited in Leite, *A condição feminina no Rio de Janeiro*, 173.

73. Leite, *A condição feminina no Rio de Janeiro*, 173.

74. Miécio Táti, *O mundo de Machado de Assis*, 159.

75. First and second-class boxes in the opera house went for 30$000 and 25$000, respectively; see *Jornal do commercio*, May 12, 1871.

76. Michael Broyles discusses the nineteenth-century view of different musical styles cutting across the tastes of various social strata; see *Music of the Highest Class* (New Haven, Conn.:: Yale University Press, 1992), 277.

77. Lawrence Levine, *Hibrow/Lowbrow: The Emergence of Cultural Hierarchy in America* (Cambridge, Mass.: Harvard University Press, 1988), 90–92.

78. In the United States, Rossini's *La gazza ladra* was transformed into *The Cat's in the Larder*; see Levine, *Hibrow/Lowbrow,* 92. In Brazil, Offenbach's operettas constantly inspired parodies: *La duchesse de Gérolstein* was transformed into *A baroneza de Cayapó*, *Orphée aux enfers* into *Orpheo na roça* and *Orpheo na cidade*, *La vie parisienne* into *A vida no Rio de Janeiro*; see *Jornal do commmercio*, January 4, 1870. Verdi's *Il trovatore* was transformed into *O capadocio*; see *Jornal do commercio*, July 4, 1872.

79. *Jornal do commercio*, June 30, 1866.

80. Mercedes Reis Pequeno, "Brazilian Music Publishers," *Inter-American Music Review* 9 (1988): 91–104; also "Impressão musical Enciclopédia de musica brasileira (Rio de Janeiro: Art Editora, 1977)."

81. For information on the Casa de Filippone e Cia, see Pequeno, "Impressão musical no Brasil," 353.

82. For the impact of Thalberg's visit to Rio de Janeiro see Ayres de Andrade, "Um rival de Liszt no Rio de Janeiro," *Revista brasileira de música* I/I (1962): 27–50.

83. Most of these pianist-composers were French or spent part or all of their careers in Paris. The German-born Henri Herz moved to Paris when he was a child. Franz Hünter spent most of his active career there. For an anthology of virtuoso production in nineteenth-century Paris see Jeffrey Kallberg's *Piano Music of the Parisian Virtuosos 1810–1860* (New York: Garland, 1993).

84. The 1871 catalogue of Narciso and Arthur Napoleão listed no fewer than seventeen pieces inspired by tunes from *Il trovatore*.

85. Manuel Vicente Ribeiro Veiga Jr. shows that the folk song from the state of Bahia "Negro Gege quando morre" derives from Offenbach's *Orphée aux enfers* see "Toward a Brazilian Ethnomusicology: Amerindian Phases" (Ph.D. diss., University of California at Los Angeles, 1981), 254–60.

86. A large number of these works are listed in the 1871 catalogue of Narcisa and Arthur Napoleão.

Chapter 3

Music for the Elite

A SPECIAL MYSTIQUE

The music stemming from the theater, along with its derivatives, was understood in the Brazilian capital as the "music of the day" and referred to by Cariocas as *música moderna* (modern music). It directly followed Parisian fashions and was readily imported to the imperial capital in large numbers, enjoying a wide appeal until the turn of the twentieth century. More than an artificially adopted fad, música moderna was one of the preferred forms of entertainment and was, in its various forms, accessible to large numbers of Cariocas.

By contrast, very few in the imperial capital could claim acquaintance with or inclination toward *música clássica* (classical music), understood in nineteenth-century Brazil generically as "works of the past," but specifically as the music by composers such as Haydn, Mozart, and Beethoven, and by early romantics such as Schumann and Mendelssohn. Early attempts to introduce música clássica in Rio de Janeiro were limited to courtly circles during Pedro I's reign,[1] or to societies of German immigrants. In 1854, for example, the German descendent Christiano Stockmeyer organized a concert for the benefit of the German Association of Rio de Janeiro, the *Sängerbund* society. Advertised as *concerto clássico* (classical concert), the concert featured works by Mozart, Beethoven, Schubert, and Mendelssohn, composers who were then virtually unknown to the general public. Nonetheless, the program was carefully put together according to the local taste and included operatic excerpts, variations, and fantasies rather than large-scale works. Thus, Stockmeyer succeeded in

both paying homage to German "classics" and enticing local music
lovers with operatic numbers.

Theatro São Pedro de Alcantara, October 7, 1854, Christiano Stockmeyer, music director[2]

Overture from *Zauberflöte*	Mozart
Piano Concerto in C Minor	Beethoven
A capella (Die Kapelle)	Kreutzer
"Des Lagers Abschied"	Mendelssohn
Elegia for Violin and Piano	Ernst
Aria "Robin des Bois" from *Der Freischütz*	Weber
Overture from *Der Wasserträger*	Cherubini
Variation *Le tre Nozze*	Alary
Concerto in B Minor for Violin	Beriot
Fantasia *Les Huguenots*	Thalberg
Three romances: *ErlKönig*	Schubert
Serenade	Schubert
Chorus from *Der Freischütz*	Weber

Despite such isolated attempts, in the second part of the century
residents of Rio de Janeiro continued to enjoy a vast repertory of
música moderna, mostly operatic derivatives, which did not fit the
Germanic concept of "high art." Música clássica began to make a
presence in Rio de Janeiro concert halls in the late 1870, only after
French audiences started to sanction German composers in concert
series devoted to Viennese classical and German romantic music,
such as Société Alard-Franchomme (?1847–?1872). Société des
Dernières Quatuors de Beethoven (1851), and Société des Quatuors
de Mendelssohn (Quatuor Armingaud, 1856–1867). Carioca elite became particularly captivated by the classical repertory's "aura of respectability," which contrasted with the popular, cheap arrangements of operatic music that circulated widely and rather
indiscriminately. But it was the German classical canon's embodying
"special mystique" that appealed the most,[3] an attribute that had little to do with the music, but rather with the music's connotations of
edification and progress, sophistication and preeminence. As with
the music itself, the connotations attached to the repertory were imported and arrived third-hand in Rio de Janeiro from Germany via
Paris. Like the elite groups in Paris, elite Cariocas embraced música
clássica as a powerful tool to distinguish themselves from the less af-

fluent and seemingly less cultured. But in imperial Rio de Janeiro the music also served to boost their feeling of belonging to an imagined European "elevated culture."

This imagined "mystique" of música clássica served the local elite particularly in the 1870s and 1880s, when the country was mired in political and economic problems that immediately followed the end of the Paraguayan War. It was during these decades that the Republican Party started to gain political voice, that the institution of slavery began to be regarded with contempt by the population at large, and that the general discontentment with the status quo conspicuously took a front seat in the political arena. More than ever, the imperial government strived for validation and support, and above all, for cohesion among its ruling members.[4] Within a troubled social, political, and economic scenario, música clássica became a crucial tool that helped shape the local elite's identity, guaranteeing them a position not only of social distinction but of cultural superiority. Engaging in the music of the German classical cannon was a symbolic act of self-confidence and calculated self-favoritism. Thus, it was by no means fashion alone that made the Carioca elite open the doors of their exclusive concert halls to música clássica, and certainly not a truthful appreciation for the music, but the candid belief, learned second-hand from Parisians, that German classical music embodied some kind of elevated code that could be accessible only to some.

The Italian singer Carlotta Patti was one of the first to introduce música clássica to Rio de Janeiro audiences as a repertory that deserved special deference. If Patti's 1870 *Concertos Populares* were modeled on Pasdeloup's *Parisian Concerts Populaires*, they deviated considerably from Pasdeloup's idea of entertainment for the masses. Because Rio de Janeiro lacked a large hall similar to the one in Paris, Patti presented her concert series in a small, closed theater and emphasized "classical" symphonies by German composers as the main attraction to a select circle of Cariocas. To persuade the audience to welcome the new repertory, Patti felt compelled to advertise her concert series in the local newspaper with a long explanatory text that identified the "new" música clássica with intellectual and musical progress and unparallel artistic value, while not leaving out the music's previous validation by audiences in Paris:

> The city of Rio de Janeiro, which has appreciated this century's great lyric artists and soloists, still does not know very well nor praise very

much the beauties that are found in symphonies by Mozart, Haydn, Beethoven, Mendelssohn, Litolff, etc.

At Paris, for more than ten years, every Sunday in the winter 5,000 people from all social classes have gathered at the Cirque Napoléon, under the direction of Mr. Pasdeloup [to admire] the true beauty of musical art. . . . Why is it that the brilliant teachers of our orchestras and players do not gather in societies and awaken . . . the desire of enjoying the same [repertory] of their brothers in France, Germany, England?

The time for [instrumental] fantasies has gone . . . let us now give room to the true, divine masters, applauded and adored on the other side of the equator. The time has now arrived for intellectual and musical progress in Brazil.[5]

Patti's advertisement also included excerpts from an article explaining the musical characteristics of the symphony, written by "an authority in the genre," Hector Berlioz, and which had been published in the *Journal du dèbats* almost forty years earlier.[6]

In spite of such an authoritative introduction, Patti soon realized that to succeed in Rio de Janeiro she needed to compromise. Thus, in keeping with the spirit of "popular" concerts, she entrusted the orchestra to Gravenstein, the son of the well-known director of the popular bailes à Musard. She also conceded in offering Cariocas a program that blended Beethoven and Auber, Mendelssohn and Rossini. Following is the program for Patti's *Concertos Populares*, July 25, 1870, with orchestra director André Gravenstein.[7]

Rossini	Overture to *Semiramide*
Verdi/Vieuxtemps	*Nabucco* Fantasy for Violin
Mendelssohn	Piano Concerto in G Minor
Beethoven	Pastoral Symphony
Donizetti/Artôt	Scene from *Lucia de Lammermoor*
J. S. Bach	Gavotte and Musette for Piano
Ritter	*Les courriers*
Auber	L'éclat de rire for Soprano
Auber	*Fra Diavolo*, Overture

However, even with the inclusion of tunes from *Semiramide* and *Fra diavolo*, Patti's enterprise was not immediately successful. The daily newspapers declined commenting on música clássica or the performances in the Concertos de Populares. Instead, the critic from the

Jornal do commercio focused his commentaries on the local spectators' reaction to the erudite music. Reporting on the second concert of the series, he noted that the audience listened to Ritter's performance of Mendelssohn's *Rondo capriccioso* with "a religious silence"; but he also pointed out rather ironically that Cariocas proudly "endured" classical music, a music that in the mind of several was "synonymous with boring," he concluded.[8]

If the public could not immediately applaud the "divine [German] masters" in public concerts, in private musical societies, ruled by the privileged few, música clássica eventually found a following. Not that the local elite could profess a deep appreciation for or an understanding of classical music, which was presented out of its original context and for the most part with very limited resources. In fact, even those in the most exclusive elite circles found the music less than appealing and by no means entertaining. The acceptance of the classical canon relied solely on the music's European glamour and powerful "mystique" that allowed for its consumption as a symbolic act of superiority.

Thus, seeking higher status, several private musical societies were named after musical celebrities from the German classical and romantic traditions: a Club Mozart was founded in 1867, a Club Beethoven and a Club Schubert were founded in 1882, followed in 1883 by a Club Ricardo [sic] Wagner.[9] Among these, the Club Mozart and the Club Beethoven deserve special mention, since these societies regularly hosted the city's most prestigious and affluent individuals; even the monarch and his family made occasional appearances in their salons. The societies' names, Mozart and Beethoven, symbolized their preeminence and guaranteed their respectability. But by far the most significant aspect concerning the dominance of these clubs in imperial Rio de Janeiro was the dilemma that emerged in their halls between música clássica and música moderna. Notwithstanding the fact that both music styles had European provenance and that the dilemma about them was in itself imported, the arguments pro and contra música clássica and música moderna, and by association pro and contra harmony and melody, symphony and opera, had a particular local significance. For the issue took the shape of a local battle that translated the social and cultural conflicts of the local elite and emergent bourgeoisie in the last two decades of the monarchical regime.

CLUB MOZART

Established in 1867, the Club Mozart reached its apogee in the 1870s. According to its 1868 statutes, the main purpose of the club was "the cultivation and development of vocal and instrumental music,"[10] though, as with other private societies in Rio de Janeiro, the Club Mozart was also intended to be a gathering place for the privileged few. The statutes stipulated that membership in the club required applicants to demonstrate "good conduct and a decent position in society."[11] Applications were submitted through another member and were judged by a board of directors consisting of aristocrats, prominent politicians, intellectuals, and artists.[12] In several ways, these regulations and social credentials were less restrictive than other private Rio de Janeiro societies, since the Club Mozart offered membership to "individuals of both sexes without distinction of nationality."[13] The club also encouraged professional and amateur musicians and other individuals whose "positions in the society could help in the development of the club" to participate in the musical events, even if nonmembers.[14]

What most differentiated the Club Mozart from other similar elite institutions was the emphasis on music. Rather than being the usual male gathering place, where cards, billiards, and European politics served as the main attractions, the Club Mozart also favored musical activities. Accordingly, the club maintained a music library, with a librarian and an archivist, and eventually organized a music school where members could take lessons on various instruments.[15] Thus, the club offered its members the opportunity to get acquainted with the music of various European composers, and to transform themselves from mere dilettantes into true music connoisseurs. The focus on music gave the club its aura of authority, and the use of Mozart's name allowed this private society to become imperial Rio de Janeiro's utmost musical institution. In 1870, two years after its foundation, the Club Mozart had 400 members, of whom 150 were professional and amateur musicians.[16] The club sponsored chamber music concerts every other week, in addition to four annual gala concerts with orchestra, events that were frequently honored by the presence of the royal family. The club also hosted the most prominent singers and performers to visit Rio de Janeiro, including the North American pianist and composer Louis Moreau Gottschalk.

Figure 3.1. "A gala concert at the Club Mozart." *A vida fluminense* (December 26, 1870). Young Research Library, UCLA.

Interestingly enough, despite being named after the "illustrious" Mozart, the club did not emphasize Mozart's music or the music of any of the Viennese masters. The programs organized by the club's directors did not differ in essence from programs put together by smaller neighborhood associations, or from benefit concerts presented at the theater that included voice numbers, operatic derivatives, and short pieces for piano, violin, or flute. Furthermore, the events sponsored by the Club Mozart were coveted not only for the music performed by amateurs, but also for the lively balls lasting until dawn.[17] In fact, according to the statutes, the music director was expected to organize "attractive and accessible" programs that did not go beyond "the unavoidable limits imposed on the music performed at meetings of this kind."[18]

The limits were several. To start, the small dimensions of the club's salon required concerts of an intimate nature. The new *salão* (hall) of the Club Mozart inaugurated on July 14, 1881, for instance, measured 10 by 8 meters, being linked to another room by an aisle

27 meters long. Despite a contemporary's comment that the illumination of the room was excellent and the decoration showed "good taste,"[19] the reduced dimensions of the concert hall led the music director to emphasize works that required reduced forces. Furthermore, only in gala concerts or other special circumstances was the music director able to count on a large number of professional musicians to perform more complex, large-scale compositions. Amateur performers were habitués at the club, where they showed off their musical proficiency to other affluent individuals as well as to their friends and relatives. But the most compelling limitation against the inclusion of Mozart's music stemmed from the public's preference for short pieces and operatic derivatives, from their expectation to hear catchy, popular melodies that were entertaining, and that did not require from the listener a critical effort or any kind of aesthetic contemplation.

Thus, in the 1870s, programs sponsored by the Club Mozart usually began with an operatic overture performed by a small group, followed by vocal numbers—the music of Rossini, Bellini, Donizetti, and Verdi predominating—and character pieces for piano or piano duet written by foreign virtuoso pianists such as Joseph Ascher, Émile Prudent, and Alexander Goria, composers very familiar to a large number of Cariocas since their music circulated locally in sheet music or periodicals. The following program from June 14, 1879, exemplifies a typical concert at the Club Mozart.[20]

Auber	Overture *Zanetta*
Verdi	Aria from *Il finto Stanislao*
Meyer	*Carnaval marche*
Moderati	*Il primo baccio*, Romance for Bariton
Kalliwoda	Grand Fantasy for Clarinet
Palloni	"Noi ci amavamo tanto!" Romance for Soprano
Verdi/Ricordi	Quartet from *Rigoletto* (for two violins, cello, and piano)
Weber	*Oberon*, Barcarolle for Soprano
Verdi	Duet from *Nabucco*
Meyerbeer/Stasny	Potpourri for Orchestra

Programs for special events were more elaborate and usually featured two parts, each opening with an orchestral operatic overture.

However, performed by a small orchestra or a chamber string group, they rarely included music by the "master" Mozart. Members of the club profited from the authority and special mystique embodied in the composer's name, without having to endure a music that was perceived as difficult and uninteresting. In the salons of the club, members could gaudily pretend to have a connection to the classics, while at the same time continue to enjoy their preferred popular operatic tunes.

However, by the 1880s, this uncompromising and comfortable position no longer functioned as an effective delimiter of social boundaries. Similar competing clubs sprawled all over the city to welcome the growing middle class who also aspired to visibility in the high ranks of the local social scale.[21] And since the social functions of the Club Mozart and its musical events favoring gaudy entertainment were no longer the domain of an exclusive group, the club started to lose its selective clientele, as well as its privileged position as a musical institution. In the 1880s, the Club Mozart's activities had declined sharply, and it was ultimately dissolved before the proclamation of the republic in 1889.

CLUB BEETHOVEN

On January 9, 1882, twenty-eight prominent members of Rio de Janeiro society gathered with violinist, composer, and conductor Robert Kinsman Benjamin (1853–1927) to write the Club Beethoven's first statutes.[22] At the time of the first concert on February 4, the club had 56 members, and after one year of activities it had grown to 222 members. In 1884, the Club Beethoven was a well-established society with 485 members, a number that remained relatively constant throughout the decade. In the 1880s, taking the place of the Club Mozart, the most significant musical events in imperial Rio de Janeiro were entrusted to the directors of the Club Beethoven. Considered an enterprise "never paralleled by any society of its kind in South America," the club's reputation as the foremost musical society in the imperial capital echoed beyond the country's borders, reaching other cities in Latin America and Europe.[23]

The Club Beethoven operated with a membership system similar to that of the Club Mozart, requiring members to have a distinguished position in the local society, and functioned with similar categories of contributors, participants, benefactors, and honorary members. The added category of "visitor"—aimed at those individuals who spent short periods of time in Rio de Janeiro—particularly benefited "diplomatic emissaries, as well as officials of warships anchored at the port of Rio de Janeiro."[24] More than the Club Mozart, the Club Beethoven was a closed society, ready to admit as members only the cream of Rio de Janeiro social, political, and intellectual society. According to its statutes, the club's purpose was "to provide the *men* of our society with a meeting point where they can enjoy all the advantages of the most important European clubs and, at the same time, offer our members the music of the best school, interpreted by outstanding performers of Rio de Janeiro."[25]

The association between the "music of the best school," the European world, selectiveness and superiority, and male dominance could not be more flagrant. Women were not admitted into the club's salons before 1888, not even as singers, being invited only to the annual symphonic concerts and to special events. *"Pas de femme,"* commented a local critic with a typical Carioca/Parisian irony, yet adding that "the founders of the Club Beethoven are too rigorous, since women and gambling are the two lungs sustaining Rio de Janeiro's clubs."[26] Accordingly, chess and billiards competitions were among the several male-related activities that took place in the salons of the Club Beethoven and that also set it apart as the most coveted of the Carioca (male) *haute monde*.

Given that music promotion was among the main purposes of the society, the directors of the Club Beethoven were also committed to maintaining the highest standards in its musical meetings. In 1883, the Club Beethoven's new building located at the Rua da Glória nº 62 included not only chess, billiards, and fencing rooms, dinners, buffets, but also a concert room with a Grand piano Érard and a music library.[27] In addition, in their leisure hours members could enjoy a reading room that boasted eighty leading European newspapers and magazines, including current European music periodicals such as the English *Monthly Musical* and *Musical World*, the German *Neue Musik-Zeitung*, the French *L'art musicale*, the Italian *Gazzetta musicale*, and the Spanish *El mundo artístico*.[28] The club also maintained a string quartet, consisting of the violinists Vincenzo Cernicchiaro (1858–1928) and Kinsman Benjamin, the violinist Luis Gravenstein, and the cellist J. Cerrone.[29] Starting in 1886, the club maintained a music school directed toward the "cultivation of high music," offering courses in music initiation, harmony, counterpoint, piano, flute, clarinet, oboe, violin, viola, cello, bass, horn and other wind instruments, ensembles, and composition.[30]

The biweekly chamber concerts held at the Club Beethoven's concert hall were among the city's most coveted musical events. In its first year of existence, the Club Beethoven sponsored no fewer than 136 of these concerts. Starting regularly at eight p.m., members usually gathered socially in the main salon for the customary chat before the concert and waited for the sound of the trumpets, which pompously announced the beginning of the music program.[31] Once the event started, the etiquette required that no late seating or talking be allowed. And there was a musical reason for the requirement. Sticking to the idea of offering its members "the music of the best school, interpreted by outstanding performers," the club indeed gathered the best professional performers available in Rio de Janeiro, musicians who demanded the audience's full attention and deference. Unlike the Club Mozart, few amateurs had the chance to take part in the Club Beethoven's concerts, a characteristic that helped maintain the club's "European standards."

By far the Club Beethoven's most distinctive characteristic was its commitment to *música clássica*. Nowhere else in imperial Rio de Janeiro, not even in the boxes of the opera house, was a specific repertory so tightly linked with exclusiveness, superiority, European culture, and male dominance. There was no room for popular arias and lively balls, for distractions with female displays or socialization during the performances, only for pieces by Mozart, Haydn, Beethoven, Schumann, Mendelssohn, and so on—works that required high standards from both performers and listeners, and that were to be respectfully gazed at as art. Schubert's songs, performed by a male, were favorites, especially "Le Voyageur" (*Der Wanderer*). Excerpts from Wagner's *Tannhäuser* were also occasionally heard at the club's concert hall alongside pieces by Schubert, Haydn, and Mendelssohn, works, which, despite their stylistic differences, were nonetheless perceived as shining representatives of *música clássica*.

The penchant for classical music was particularly conspicuous in the Club Beethoven's gala concerts, featuring symphonic music, and in the extravagant Beethoven Festivals. These concerts, held at the larger room of the Cassino Fluminense, were great enterprises, sometimes involving the entire musical community of Rio de Janeiro. An orchestra put together especially for the events included professional musicians from the theater orchestra, teachers of the conservatory, and other performers, Club members and nonmembers. In the 1884 symphonic concert, the orchestra consisted of seventy-six musicians, which, although small for Parisian standards, was significantly larger than local orchestras, usually consisting of some fifty members. Also, for these special solemnities a special commission was charged with exceptionally admitting and "welcoming ladies," who were not exactly expected to partake in the male pleasures of música clássica, but to "cheer the hall with their brilliant toilettes."[32]

Presented to an audience of 3,000 people, the first symphonic concert took place on October 12, 1882, and assembled in the large room of the Cassino Fluminense "the elite of Rio de Janeiro . . . diplomats, senators, ministers, deputies, [and] prominent men." Although extremely high, the concert's expenses, collected from members' fees and the society funds, were considered justified by an enterprise that "marked the history of music in Rio de Janeiro." According to the club's president Albert Tootal, "It would be difficult to match the success of this event even in large European capitals, where there are many good performers available and the population is educated according to the classic school models."[33]

Usually, the symphonic concerts had three parts: the first opened with an orchestral overture (in 1882, Mendelssohn's *Fingal's Cave* overture; in 1883, Mozart's overture to *The Magic Flute*; in 1884, Schumann's overture *Genoveva*; and in 1885 Beethoven's *Leonora* overture n° 3); the second started with a Beethoven symphony (in 1882, Symphony n° 5; in 1883 Symphony n° 7; in 1884, Symphony n° 6; and in 1885, Symphony n° 3); and the third part ended with an effective orchestral piece (in 1882, Rubinstein's Suite *Feramors*; in 1883, Berlioz's "Valse des Sylphes" and "March Hongroise" from *Damnation de Faust*; in 1884, *Kaiser Marsch* by Wagner; and in 1885, Liszt-Muller, 2me. *Rhapsodie Hongroise* for orchestra). Although pieces for solo voice with orchestral accompaniment held some attraction, the organizers of symphonic concerts preferred to indulge the audience with romantic concertos for solo piano and violin.

Opened to a larger portion of Rio de Janeiro's population, these gala events did not demote the club's exclusiveness; on the contrary, they helped publicize the club as a powerful institution for the cultivation of "high culture." Because the majority that attended these large-scale concerts was not familiar with the music they were supposed to appreciate, the gala concerts sponsored by the Club Beethoven had a noteworthy didactic nature. To help introduce música clássica to an audience that rarely had the chance to listen to symphonic music, the directors of the club offered special printed programs—large booklets containing critical commentaries on each work as well as extended composers' biographies. These printed materials, available for purchase at local bookstores, not only helped advertise the club's luxurious events, but were, above all, a way to "educate" Cariocas, to get them also to aspire to música clássica and eventually become part of a "cultured" society.

Still, these attempts to indoctrinate the larger public did not pay off instantaneously. The local press, which regularly included the club's activities in its social columns, did not shun critical commentaries on the society members' explicit devotion to música clássica. At the time of the club's founding, for instance, a commentator announced that the new society was committed to the promotion of "good music"; but he had to stress to the reader his disappointment that "good music [according to the club's members] means classical music." In 1883, commenting on a concert at the Club Beethoven, a local chronicler offered a sarcastic comparison between his musical preferences and those of the club's members: "Concerning classical music, I confess I am a barbarian—in the opinion of those who have musical knowledge . . .—In my instance, the sensation produced by such a scientific music makes me feel like listening to it in the horizontal position, tasting a good Havana [cigar]."[34]

In the 1880s, the Club Beethoven organizers still faced a formidable competitor: "traditional" Italo-French opera and its derivatives. Offering flexibility in performance and accepting wide participation of dilettanti, operatic derivatives fulfilled a social function very different from música clássica. If música moderna was European, it was also an attractive form of entertainment that required no devotion to music as an object of aesthetic contemplation. Operas were considered music of "high level," but they were also entertaining; in fact, the music presented at the opera house and other theaters served as an effective mediator between high art and genuine entertainment, between serious (art) and popular music. Conversely, the concerts sponsored by the Club Beethoven were to be grandiose, exclusive, and enlightening, but not necessarily entertaining.

The nature of Club Beethoven's exclusiveness could not have existed apart from Rio de Janeiro's political momentum in the 1880s.

At a time when a substantial number of Cariocas no longer unconditionally supported the monarchy and when elite ideas and values
were subject to intense scrutiny, elite Cariocas felt compelled to
characterize themselves as distinct from the emerging middle class
and to further separate themselves not only by merely engaging in
European music, but in música clássica. Similarly to the habitués at
the opera house, members of the club attended concerts primarily as
a symbolic act, but in the exclusive club there were no cheap tickets,
discounts, or any kind of social mingling. In the Club Beethoven
música clássica was an effective tool to delimit social and cultural
boundaries.

Not coincidentally, in 1890, one year after the end of the monarchical regime, the Club Beethoven ceased its activities. The hall of the
club was sold to the music dealer Mr. Hetch, who continued to offer
concerts with a more varied repertory, was and open to the public.

A DREAM COMES TRUE

In the 1880s, while the Club Beethoven established itself as a private
and selective music society, other enterprises offering música clássica started to enter the public sphere. A reasonably successful endeavor of this kind was the Sociedade de Concertos Classicos (Classical Concerts Society), founded in 1883 by two immigrant
musicians, the Portuguese Arthur Napoleão and the Cuban José
White (1836–1918). Unlike the Club Beethoven, this music society
did not promote social activities, but rather was restricted to the organization of concerts for which tickets were offered to the general
public. Concerts organized by the society were devised as series and
sold by subscription. Nonetheless, these events could not be finan-
cially viable if revenues were solely derived from the small audience
attracted to música clássica. To survive in imperial Rio de Janeiro,
the organizers of the Sociedade de Concertos Clássicos still required
the financial and social support of the wealthy. This dependency on
patronage blurred the line between public and private enterprises, a
common trait in artistic events in the nineteenth-century Brazilian
capital, which nonetheless serves to exemplify the extent and nature
of the Carioca elite's management of cultural enterprises.

To succeed in their endeavor and to gain the financial support of
affluent patrons, the two organizers of the Sociedade de Concertos

Clássicos relied on their local and international reputations. The Portuguese virtuoso pianist Arthur Napoleão had an impeccable curriculum vitae, which included a long list of successful performances and acquaintances abroad. While a music student in Paris ten-year-old Napoleão met luminaries such as Herz, Ascher, Thalberg, Marmontel, and the young cellist Offenbach; Emperor Napoleon III saluted him in a concert directed by Auber. Before settling in Rio de Janeiro in 1868, he had performed in Paris and London and toured the United States, where he played in New York, New Orleans, Washington, Philadelphia, and Boston, receiving laudatory reviews from the respected *Dwight's Journal*. Napoleão also met Meyerbeer and Rossini while he was in Germany, and he played for Liszt at Weimar. In Rio de Janeiro, Napoleão was a well-established businessmen as well as a Maecenas, who had a hand in nearly every local musical event. He collaborated with the director of the Alcazar Lyrique, Arnaud, the theater director Furtado Coelho, and well-known local literary figures, such as Machado de Assis. In 1876, he was invited by Pedro II to direct the first performance of Verdi's *Requiem* in Rio de Janeiro. He was also a powerful contact for European musicians willing to perform in Rio de Janeiro.[35]

Napoleão's partner in the Sociedade de Concertos Clássicos was the Cuban violinist José White, whom Napoleão had met in the early 1860s in Havana. Before reaching the Brazilian capital in 1879, José White had toured the United States in 1875 and 1876, appearing with the New York Philharmonic Society and with the Brooklyn Philharmonic Society in performances that were highly praised by American critics.[36] From March 1877 to September 1879, White toured Latin America: starting at Caracas, he visited Lima, several cities in Chile, Buenos Aires, and Montevideo. Having studied in Paris with the renowned violinist J. D. Alard (1815–1888), White's international reputation preceded him in Rio de Janeiro as an "eminent violinist . . . one of the distinguished members of the Paris Conservatoire."[37] With such flawless credentials, White had ample access to aristocratic spheres and enjoyed imperial support from the time of his arrival, being readily appointed music teacher of Pedro II's sister, Princess Isabel, and her children.[38]

Using their international reputations and local influences in the organization of the Sociedade de Concertos Clássicos, Napoleão and White carefully put together a board of directors comprising an exceptional assortment of barons and counts—among them names highly respected, such as the Conde D'Eu (honorary president), who was the son-in-law of the emperor. The eminent board served not only with the generosity of their pockets, but also helped boost the society's credibility among the Carioca bourgeoisie, and, above all, convinced them to pay for subscriptions to hear música clássica.

Since White's arrival in Rio de Janeiro in 1879, he and Napoleão started to take action "improving" the local musical taste. Napoleão's review of a concert given by White, for example, emphasized the need for the local audiences to get acquainted with works by "classic" authors. Regarding White's performance of Bach's D-minor Chaconne, Napoleão noted that,

> Bach represents a tradition in art. Innovator and creator, he is the founder of a pleiad to which belong Haendel, Haydn, Mozart, and Beethoven, and a large number of composers after them. One needs a special faculty to appreciate the value of this piece. . . . The applause received by White [during the concert] should have double merit, since it came from an audience that, despite its innate taste for music, is not yet accustomed to hear daily and by the best artists, performances of the classic authors—as is the public of London, Paris, and Germany.[39]

To hearten the "special faculty" in Cariocas, which, according to Napoleão, was needed to appreciate the "classic authors," is what propelled the creation the Sociedade de Concertos Clássicos. Thus, the idea behind the Sociedade was not simply to foster exclusivity and delineate social boundaries, as was the case in the Club Beethoven, but its primary aim was of a didactic nature, and ultimately also one of indoctrination. The Sociedade aspired to "educate" Cariocas at large, teaching them not only how to respect but also how to fully appreciate the music of the classics. Implicit was the assumption that música clássica was a necessary tool to improve the local society by bringing it more closely in line with the European standards of "civilization."

According to contemporary reports, the first concert of the Sociedade de Concertos Clássicos, which took place on August 12, 1883, was a resounding success:

> Fortunately, the classical and popular concerts are now a reality; I come from the Escola da Gloria, where I heard the first concert [of the Sociedade de Concertos Classicos]. . . . The royal family was present. I noticed, with great pleasure, that the salon was crowded with a select au-

dience of Rio de Janeiro's society. Therefore, it is not a dream; the classic concerts are a reality.[40]

The commentator was correct: the classical concerts were a reality. Following the successful opening, concerts continued to be offered every spring, the best season for concerts because of the mild climate.[41] Instead of an evening event like those offered by private societies, the concerts of the Sociedade de Concertos Clássicos took place regularly on Sunday afternoons, at 2 p.m. in the Salão da Escola da Gloria, facilitating the attendance of entire families. The programs clearly emphasized German classical composers, but were also open to newer music and sometimes even to local composers whose compositions emulated the "classics." Mendelssohn's piano trios in D Minor and C Minor, Schumann's piano quartet in E flat, and Mozart's string quintets were favorites; Anton Rubinstein (1829–1894) and Joseph Raff (1822–1882) were generously included alongside Bach's Chaconne, which gave the chamber programs a historical touch.

In 1886, after three successful seasons of chamber music concerts, White ventured into the organization of large-scale events in the same manner as the Club Beethoven's annual symphonic presentation. The Sociedade de Concertos Clássicos's first Grand Concert, which took place on Monday, October 11, at the luxurious room of the Cassino Fluminense, was honored by the presence of the imperial family and the cream of Rio de Janeiro society. The program.[42] included music by the German classics, as well as by local composers:

Lucien Lambert Filho	Abertura Symphonica
Carlos de Mesquita	Preludio
· Beethoven	Fourth Symphony
Faulhaber	Reverie
Beethoven	Piano Concerto in E flat, "Emperor"
Weber	Aria from *Der Freischütz*
Mozart	"Voi che sapete" from *Le nozze di Figaro*
Weber	Symphonia *Oberon*

Apparently, this was the first time Rio de Janeiro audiences heard Beethoven's Fourth Symphony and the "Emperor" Concerto. Despite complaints about the small orchestra and problems with the woodwinds, local critics highlighted White's talents as a conductor who was able to get from the strings a "homogeneity in articulation and details of light-dark, which is an entirely new sound in the history of our orchestras!" Napoleão's performance of the "Emperor" concerto was considered the best of his career.[43]

As the music director, White was constantly at work to insure that the finest members of Rio de Janeiro society supported the concerts. But as didactic events, the concerts were also expected to reach out to those whose interests were not exactly centered on música clássica. Thus, White regularly announced his concerts in the entertainment section of daily newspapers, alongside the program of local theaters, in the hopes of attracting a larger audience. Moreover, unlike the policy of the Club Beethoven, the Sociedade de Concertos Clássicos's concerts were open to both sexes. Carioca women quickly flooded the society's concerts, not missing the chance to partake in the "paradise of classic music." For them, it was not simply the world of música clássica that they were being allowed to enter, but a far-reaching, male-oriented world, which had classical music as a symbolic point of reference. According to the review of the opening of the 1885 concert series, Carioca women's reaction to the music surprised even the most experienced (male) connoisseurs, for women not only marked their presence in the audience with elegant garments and elaborate hair styles, but they also demonstrated a true appreciation for the music:

> The concerts of this season opened yesterday with the social cream of Rio de Janeiro in attendance. Perhaps four-fifths of the audience were women—these unfortunates who were previously banished from the paradise of classic music. Yesterday, at the Gloria school, they heroically proved, without chattering or sleeping, that the old music of the masters can impress and move them.[44]

White's earnest efforts toward inclusiveness indeed had some results. He surely did attract the finest members of Rio de Janeiro society to his classical concerts, while managing to sell tickets to the public, keeping the educational nature in his programs, and enticing women to hear música clássica.

White also inspired other musicians to start similar enterprises. On August 1, 1886, the pianist Jeronymo Queiroz (1857–1936) and the violinist Vincenzo Cernicchiaro founded the Sociedade de Quartetos do Rio de Janeiro (Quartet Society of Rio de Janeiro). Sponsored by wealthy individuals such as eminent Viscount Alfredo d'Escragnolle Taunay (1843–1899), the Sociedade de Quartetos offered a few advantages over White's society, as it covered not only classical music but also a wider repertory "in which chamber music from all periods and styles are included."[45] Most likely, the idea was to parallel in Rio de Janeiro the Concerts Historiques, organized in the 1830s in Paris by François-Joseph Fétis (1784–1871), which exposed Parisians to sixteenth- and seventeenth-century composers.

In 1887, another competitor appeared on the scene: Carlos de Mesquita and his Sociedade de Concertos Populares (Society of Popular Concerts). Beginning on June 5, 1887, Mesquita's series of nine concerts offered at the Theatro São Pedro de Alcantara shared with White's society the attention of the public. Similar to White's events, Mesquita's concerts were devised as public enterprises, which nonetheless had the financial and honorary support of wealthy and influential individuals.[46] Furthermore, they were also marked by the need to reach out to a growing middle class with an educational flavor. Mesquita's intentions were both noble and innovative: unlike White's and Queiroz's chamber concerts, Mesquita's series were large-scale events that offered orchestral music to large numbers of people in the manner of Pasdeloup's Concerts Populaires in Paris. He also diversified the repertory, blending the classical and the historical, in the manner of Fétis's Concerts historiques, but also added a few local composers to his hybrid programs, unequivocally matching Camille Saint-Saëns's (1835–1921) Société Nationale de Musique. The parallel with the latter was unmistaken, since under Mesquita's direction a fifty-plus member orchestra introduced to Brazilian audiences the music of a large number of contemporary French composers such as Jules Massenet (1842–1912), Emmanuel Chabrier (1841–1894), and Saint-Saëns, as well as compositions of immigrant and Brazilian composers such as Arthur Napoleão, Francisco Braga (1868–1945), Alberto Nepomuceno (1864–1920), Abdon Milanez (1858–1927), Frederico Nascimento (1852–1924), and Leopoldo Miguez (1850–1902).[47] Local critics gladly supported his series, stressing that: "The popular concert embraces all music periods, all schools, all genres; it has two advantages [over the others]: the music education of the public and the creation of a trained orchestra, with a unified style . . . conducted for a long period by a talented and competent conductor . . . something not yet achieved in Rio de Janeiro."[48] This was the first series with symphonic music for the masses successful enough to deserve such praise. Other musicians continued in Mesquita's footsteps, bringing European symphonic music to the Carioca public in a gamut of styles.

During the last decade of the empire, the emphasis on music as a tool for the public's education remained at the forefront in these semipublic music enterprises. And to improve the musical taste continued to mean the privilege of música clássica over música moderna, although later in the century the definition of "classical music" became flexible enough to include both works that were centuries old and pieces by contemporary composers, local and European. Whether Carioca audiences at large were convinced of música clássica's appeal, other than its attractive association with European "civilization" and progress, is a question that remains. One popular poem titled "Observations of a patron of the Sociedade de Concertos Clássicos," extant at the National Library in Rio de Janeiro, offers a candid description of one spectator's attitude toward classical music in the 1880s: it stresses the glamour surrounding the society's concerts, the torment of having to listen to the music, and the general relief when the concert is over:

> The concert ended without incident
> Garments were being fixed
> Men offering their arm [to the ladies]
> Ladies exhibited their dresses
> And the public left whispering
> Praising Schubert, Haydn, and Mendelssohn
> But *in petto* think differently
> Everyone unanimously agreed
> The program's best parts
> Were the end, the beginning, and the
> intermission.[49]

While the author's satirical poem offers a straightforward picture of the locals' attitudes toward classical music, in the late 1880s, the prevalence of música clássica in concert programs was a fact. The concert organizers disregarded the general public's taste in favor of a minority of spectators who were supposedly able to enjoy the "true musical art."[50] Already in 1886, the *Jornal do commercio* reported that "the taste of our public is beginning to adapt to classical music, and we do not hesitate to attribute this change to the efforts of the Sociedade de Concertos Clássicos."[51] Strikingly, in the 1880s, música clássica was a novelty. Works by Haydn, Mozart, and Beethoven, as well as a wide range of other "compositions of the past," that ranged from 100 to 300 years old, emerged in imperial Rio de Janeiro as the "music of the day," a music that demanded respectability and deference from the audience, and that separated the European music available to Cariocas into clear-cut categories. In the 1880s, dichotomies such as high- and lowbrow, popular and serious, art and entertainment entered the vocabulary of local musicians and critics for good.

It was not a coincidence that the glamour of the imported music came under scrutiny in the 1870s and 1880s at the same time that the monarchy started to lose its grip on the political management of the local culture. As with the imported political and intellectual ideas in Rio de Janeiro, the choice of specific musical styles arriving from Europe became increasingly politically charged. While the operas presented at the opera house were deemed part of a local tradition claimed by the traditional status quo, música clássica represented the new society and was directly equated with progress, intellectual advancement, and "modernity." Audiences for different European musical styles overlapped, but their specific musical preferences, at different points, ultimately delineated their political choices.

IMPORTED MUSIC CRITICISM

The dilemma between música clássica and música moderna facing concert organizers and audiences in the last decade of the empire was a direct reflection of views imported from Europe. Paris, which had long exported ideas to Brazilian intellectuals, poets, and writers, also provided musical concepts to Brazilian music critics.[52] These concepts were promptly available in the music literature circulating in nineteenth-century Rio de Janeiro, which, as with the printed music, regularly arrived from Paris. Arthur Napoleão's musical establishment was up-to-date, offering Cariocas a wide range of music literature options: from biographical works to critical essays, the great majority were either in their original French, or French translations of German and Italian editions.[53]

Alexis Jacob Azevedo (1813–1875), a major contributor to the French periodical *Le ménestrel* (1833/34–1914), opens Napoleão's 1870s music catalogue with *Rossini et ses oeuvres*. Stendhal's

(1783–1842) *Vie de Rossini* (1824) and *Vies de Haydn, Mozart et Métastase* (1817) were still in vogue in Rio de Janeiro in the second half of the nineteenth century, as was Blaze de Bury's (Henri Blaze, Baron de Bury, 1813–1888) *Meyerbeer et son temps* (1865). Blaze de Bury, a contributor to the influential French periodical *Revue des deux mondes,* also published a biography of Rossini (1854) that circulated in Rio de Janeiro.[54]

French translations of the German Ferdinand Hiller's (1811–1885) writings were also widely available. A pupil of Hummel at Weimar, Hiller spent several years in Paris (1828–1835), where he became acquainted with Chopin, Liszt, and Berlioz. His *Lettres et souvenirs de Mendelssohn*, a French translation of his *Felix Mendelssohn-Bartholdy: Briefe und Erinnerungen* (1874), was for sale at Napoleão's establishment only six years after the first German edition. In the 1880s, French translations of the biographies of German composers such as Gluck, Mozart, Beethoven, Liszt, Weber, and Wagner by the German Carl Friedrich Ludwig Nohl[55] were also available to Cariocas, as were Lenz's *Beethoven et ses trois styles*, and French translations of Wagner's *Quatre poèmes d'opéras précédés d'une lettre sur la musique.*

The histories of music circulating in Rio de Janeiro also bore French provenance. Jacques Félix Alfred Clément (1822–1885), organist and choirmaster at the Sorbonne Church and director of sacred music at the Ste.-Chapelle du Palais, brought to light a number of thirteenth-century works by French composers in his music history writings.[56] His *Dictionnaire lyrique ou histoire des opéras* (1869–1881),[57] and *Les Musiciens célèbres depuis le XVIe siècle* (1868; 4th ed., 1887) headed the list of his works on sale at Napoleão's shop. Léon Escudier (1816–1881), owner of a music shop in Paris and editor of the music periodicals *La France musicale* (1837–1860) and *L'Art musical* (1860–1881), was co-author with his brother Marie-Pierre-Yves Escudier (1809–1880) of a large number of music history publications, three of which were available in Rio de Janeiro: *Mes souvenirs (Les Virtuoses)*, *Vie et aventures des cantatrices célèbres, précédées des musiciens de l'Empire, et suivies de la vie anecdotique de Paganini* (1856) and *Dictionnaire de musique, théorique et historique* (1854; 5th ed., 1872).[58] The music history writings of French Adolphe-Gustave Chouquet (1819–1886), custodian of the instrument collection at the Paris Conservatoire, such as his *Histoire de la musique dramatique en France depuis ses origines jusqu'à nos jours* (1873), took less than a decade to reach Brazil. Edouard Deldevez

(1817–1897), who taught at the Paris Conservatoire and was conductor of the Paris Opéra and the Société des Concerts du Conservatoire, published works on notation, orchestration, performance, history of music, and a history of the Société;[59] his *Curiosités musicales* (1873) was for sale in Rio de Janeiro in 1880. Théodore Lajarte (1826–1890), composer and writer, and archivist of the Paris Opéra (1873–1890), left a series of writings about the Opéra, one of which reached Brazil, *Bibliothèque musicale du théatre de l'opéra: Catalogue historique, chronologique, anecdotique* (1876–1878).

It was François-Joseph Fétis, however, whose music writings dominated the Brazilian market and consequently shaped the local ideas about music. The founder, editor, and music critic of the French periodical *Revue musicale* (1827–1835), Fétis was also composition teacher and librarian of the Paris Conservatoire before he left for Belgium in 1835. He left a notable body of music publications, all of which were available in Rio de Janeiro starting in 1859.[60] One of his works was popular enough in Brazil and Portugal as to deserve a Portuguese translation: José Ernesto de Almeida's (1807–1869) 1845 Portuguese edition of Fétis's *La musique mise à la portée de tout le monde* (1830; 3rd ed., 1847) came out as *A Musica ao alcance de todos* to which a dictionary of terms was later added.[61] Almeida's translation was sold in Rio de Janeiro as late as 1880 alongside the following works in French by Fétis: *Biographie universelle des musiciens* ("new edition," 9 vols.), *Histoire générale de la musique* (5 vols., 1869–1876), *Grand traité d'harmonie, Traité du chant en choeur* (1837), *Traité de l'accompagnement de la partition sur le piano ou orgue* (1829), and *Manuel des principes de musique* (1837; 2nd ed., 1864). When the Portuguese immigrant Raphael Coelho Machado published his *Diccionario musical* (Rio de Janeiro: Typ. Francesa, 1842, 1855, 1888, 1902, 1909), the first work of its kind written in Portuguese, the dictionary showed an unmistakable dependence on eighteenth- and early-nineteenth-century French writers,[62] particularly on the writings of Jean-Jacques Rousseau (1712–1778) and Fétis.

In the last decade of the monarchical regime, the strong influence of French writers could be directly seen in the short-lived but influential music periodical *Revista musical e de bellas artes (1879–1880),* another enterprise of the influential Arthur Napoleão. The *Revista* came out uninterruptedly every week during the year of 1879, fortnightly in the first five months of 1880, and again weekly from May through December 1880, containing both music and literary articles.

It included news from European theaters and concert halls, translations of French articles exploring technical advances such as the
metronome, diapason, and tuning systems, biographies of European
composers, and translations of writings by Berlioz and Liszt.[63] In the
pages of the *Revista*, Cariocas also read about positivism, which enjoyed powerful support from the Brazilian academia, and the latest
acoustic discoveries of the German Hermann L. F. von Helmholtz
(1820–1894), which came out in his *Die Lehre von den Tonempfindun-
gen als physiologische Grundlage für die Theorie der Musik* (1863).

It did not take long for the musical controversies occupying
French publications to surface in the *Revista*: issues that ranged from
German "classic" versus French "modern" music, theater versus instrumental music, melody as epitomized in Italian opera versus German harmony, Wagnerians and counter-Wagnerians, were brought
to the consideration of Carioca readers, even though most of the music discussed in the imported publications was still largely alien to
the local public. The growing Parisian interest in German music
around midcentury, gradually transplanted to Rio de Janeiro during
the 1870s and 1880s, was patent in the imported literature. Conse-
quentially, the local idealization of German music as "superior," the
emergence of private music clubs devoted to música clássica, the increasing number of quartets and symphonies from the classical
canon in concert programs, were all responses to the ideas found in
the French writings.

Émile Michel's "A musica na Allemanha" (Music in Germany),
translated into Portuguese from the *Revue des deux mondes*,[64] appeared
in thirteen consecutive issues of the *Revista*. The article offers a comparison between French and German musical life, particularly the elements that made the German a more "elevated culture." The author
pointed out, for instance, that in Germany applause between scenes
and acts of plays and operas was unusual, while at Paris singers usually interrupted their performances to receive "bravas" from the audience. The German singers, he says, "aspire to the more honored sat-
isfaction of expressing in full the composer's creation; keeping
themselves in the background, they make all the light focus on the
compositions."[65] Émile Michel also notices that the higher social con-
dition of performers in Germany greatly contrasted with their status
in France where, apart from an elite upper class, conditions of intellectual and moral culture were greatly inferior. In sum, the author
stresses that French musical societies "ought to mirror the German."

A different view was offered in "A musica instrumental" (Instrumental Music), a Portuguese translation of a French article that came out in the *Revista* of March 22, 1879. After praising the Paris Conservatoire and the virtuosos educated at that institution, the author refers to the cultivation of German music in France as "a German importation . . . which quickly displaces the French and Italians."[66] In defense of the Italian tradition, the author stresses that: "If Italians are superior in melody, this does not mean that they are weak in harmony; if that were true, they would not have reached such an important place in music; to defend this view it suffices to cite operas such as Moïse, Semiramide and William Tell, or to mention works by Mercadante, Verdi, etc."[67]

Yet another perspective comes to light in a French article translated to Portuguese as "A Symphonia" (The Symphony). The author, concerned with the subservience of the symphony to the opera, asks for governmental support for symphonic composers in France. Comparing the symphony to poetry, he contends that in Paris the symphony has a very select audience and is, for that reason, neglected by publishers who "Say that a romance and a song, even a page of opera, a melodious excerpt or a transcription for piano, talks more directly to the general public, while the symphony is only appreciated by a very small number of musical intellects."[68] Convinced that operas were purely seasonal compositions, forgotten with time, the author cites Haydn, famous for his symphonies but whose operas and romances were forgotten. Most composers, he adds, start writing symphonies, but soon are enticed by the "demon of the stage."

While Carioca musicians and writers read these debates with interest, some ideas in imported literature were directly channeled in the speech of a few local critics. That was the case with the French writings of Antoine-François Marmontel, a pianist and teacher at the Paris Conservatoire. Translations of his biographical essays on composers such as Rameau, Bach, Schubert, Schumann, and Mendelssohn appeared regularly in the *Revista*.[69] Although not a partisan of Schumann, Marmontel saw the composer as "one of the apostles of German music reforms and a forerunner of Wagner's new school." Schubert's *Lieder* earned Marmontel's unqualified praise,[70] while he considered Mendelssohn's *Songs without Words* the high point of his "very original" piano music.[71] Marmontel also criticizes the French audiences who did not receive Mendelssohn's music with deserved acclaim; a public, he says, who applauded "masterpieces" alongside "frivolous music."

Marmontel's teachings and ideas published in the *Revista* were particularly echoed in the influential writings of the Brazilian pianist and critic Oscar Guanabarino (1851–1937). Guanabarino's article "O professor de Piano" (The Piano Teacher), which came out serially in the *Revista* from March 27 to December 25, 1880, for example, was clearly modeled on Marmontel's piano teaching suggestions.[72] Although never in Paris, Guanabarino demonstrates his familiarity with the curriculum of the Paris Conservatoire, as he praises the same collections of progressive piano exercises advocated by Marmontel, particularly those by Clementi, Cramer, Moscheles, Czerny, Herz, Thalberg, and Bertini.

Guanabarino's writings also provide significant information about the local system of music education, the state of music in Rio de Janeiro, and, reflecting Marmontel's ideas, the controversies surrounding performances of *música clássica*. Claiming that the performance of classical music is a tool for achieving higher standards of musical taste, Guanabarino suggests that the public of Rio de Janeiro should learn to respect the music of "more educated cultures," giving up "futilities" in favor of "noble ideas." He berates the sheet music repertory, and deplores the unfamiliarity of the Brazilian public with any repertory other than opera, operettas, and dances.[73] In his article in the *Revista,* he cites a long list of European composers who deserved the attention of Carioca music connoisseurs, ranging from Orlando di Lasso, Nicolas Gombert, Arcadelt, Palestrina, Frescobaldi, Rameau, Scarlatti, Handel, and J. S. Bach, to "Beethoven and Mozart, [who] put the expression of sentiments and thought above the action of pleasing the ears."[74]

Not having studied abroad himself, Guanabarino's access to the repertory he describes and advocates was necessarily restricted. His personal knowledge of the "early" and "classical" music was acquired second-hand, through collections of piano reductions published in France and heavily edited by piano teachers of the Paris Conservatoire. Among them, Guanabarino cites his study of Jules Weiss's *Le jeune pianiste classique*, a collection of symphonies by Haydn, Mozart, and Beethoven arranged for piano; Le Couppey's *Les classiques du piano*, organized in order of difficulty;[75] and Amodée Méreaux's collection of keyboard classics, containing 200 pieces by clavecinists, from 1637 to 1790, arranged chronologically and including biographical and historical information. But the most cited by Guanabarino is Marmontel's *École classique du piano* and *Chefs-d'oeuvre classique pour le piano*, graded by difficulty, containing technical guidance and biographical information.[76]

While the efforts of Napoleão and White with their Sociedade de Concertos Clássicos and Mesquita with his Concertos Populares were starting to reap their "educational" results in the mid- to late 1880s, Carioca critics like Guanabarino cooperated with their efforts by praising the works of the "classics" in their writings. Nonetheless, even in their most authoritative critiques, the music they preached was an imagined one, a music that they knew very little about, at least in its original format and performance context. This distance from the "original" music and the lack of familiarity with its performance practices were not a disadvantage, but ultimately a given. For it permitted associations with the imported music that were tinted by the imagination, and that as such permitted the tallying of several extra layers of symbolism to música clássica: it added a layer of meaning associated with the music Europeaness that only existed in the new context of imperial Rio de Janeiro; and yet another layer of mysticism that served those enforcing practices and ideas, helping them to keep música clássica near and desirable, but at the same time out of reach of the general public.

NOTES

1. Although Beethoven's First Symphony was performed in 1836 and his Pastoral Symphony in 1856, programs including the music of Mozart and Beethoven at this time were very rare; see Cristina Magaldi, "Concert Life in Rio de Janeiro, 1837–1900" (Ph.D. diss., University of California at Los Angeles, 1994), 45 and 115.

2. *Jornal do commercio*, October 7 and 11, 1854.

3. The idea that classical music is surrounded by an aura of respectability and by a "special mystique" is articulated in Michael Broyles, *Music of the Highest Class* (New Haven, Conn.: Yale University Press, 1992), 1.

4. Jeffrey Needell, "The Domestic Civilizing Mission: The Cultural Role of the State in Brazil, 1808–1930," *Luso-Brazilian Review* 36/1 (1999): 4–6.

5. *Jornal do commercio*, July 21, 1870.

6. Berlioz's article came out in the *Journal du dèbats* on November 19, 1836.

7. *Jornal do commercio*, July 25, 1870.

8. *Jornal do commercio*, July 8, 1870.

9. For an extended study on musical societies in Rio de Janeiro, see Cristina Magaldi, "Music for the Elite: Musical Societies in Imperial Rio de Janeiro," *Latin American Music Review* 16/1 (1995): 1–41.

10. *1868 Estatutos do Club Mozart no Rio de Janeiro* (Rio de Janeiro: Typographia Perseverança, 1868), 3.

11. *1868 Estatutos do Club Mozart*, 6.

12. The following individuals occupied leading positions in the Club Mozart in 1868: President: Ernesto A. de Almeida Campos; secretario José Ferreira Albuquerque; Thesoureiro: Manoel Pereira Barbosa; Archivista: João Augusto da Costa; see *1868 Estatutos do Club Mozart*, 3. In 1872: President, Joaquim da Rocha Fragoso; Vice-President, F. A. Proença; 1° secretario, Manoel José da Fonseca; 2° secretario, José Maria da Cunha Vasco; Thesoureiro, Modesto Augusto da Silva Ribeiro; Archivista, Manoel Joaquim Valentim; see *1872 Estatutos do Club Mozart no Rio de Janeiro* (Rio de Janeiro: Typographia de F. A. de Souza, 1872), 5.

13. *1872 Estatutos do Club Mozart*, 5.

14. *1872 Estatutos do Club Mozart,* 11.

15. Both 1868 and 1872 statutes included regulations for a school of vocal and instrumental music.

16. *Almanak (Laemmert) administrativo, mercantil e industrial da corte e provincia do Rio de Janeiro* (Rio de Janeiro: E. and H. Laemmert & C., 1849–1882); see also Maria Luiza de Queiroz Amancio dos Santos, *Origem e evolução da música em Portugal e sua influência no Brasil* (Rio de Janeiro: Comissão brasileira dos centenarios em Portugal, Imprensa Nacional, 1942), 318.

17. A few programs of the Club Mozart are extant at the Biblioteca Nacional in Rio de Janeiro. For information on the Club Mozart's balls see *Revista musical e de bellas artes,* I/23 (June 6, 1879): 5.

18. *Jornal do commercio*, September 30, 1885.

19. *Jornal do commercio*, July 16, 1881.

20. Concert program extant at the Biblioteca Nacional do Rio de Janeiro, Divisão de Música e Arquivo Sonoro.

21. For a list of musical societies in Rio de Janeiro see Magaldi, "Music for the Elite," 3.

22. The twenty-eight founders of the Club Beethoven were: R. J. Kinsman Benjamin, Dr. Leopoldo Duque-Estrada, Cesar Duque-Estrada, M. J. Amoroso Lima Junior, Louis Droüet, Albert Tootal, Edward Tootal, Otto Warnstorff, Max Krutisch, Harold E. Hime, George Eutis, José Tavares Guerra, P. J. Santos, Manoel Alves Souto, Leandro Sanchez, M. Calogeras, Alfredo Romaguera, Eugenio Tourinho, Edgar James, Dr. Frederico Liberalli, Luiz Barbosa de Coppet, Emilio de Barros, J. S. P. de Meirelles, Dr. Carlos Ferreira França, George Cox, Dr. Arthur Alvim; *Club Beethoven, primeiro relatorio para o ano social de 1882–1883* (Rio de Janeiro: Typ. de G. Leuzinger & Filhos, 1883), 8.

23. *Club Beethoven, Segundo relatorio para o ano social de 1882–1883* (Rio de Janeiro: Typ. de G. Leuzinger & Fillios, 1883), 7.

24. *Almanak (Laemmert) administrativo, mercantil e industrial da corte e provincia do Rio de Janeiro* (Rio de Janeiro: E. and H. Laemmert & C., 1883–1888).

25. My italics. *Club Beethoven, Primeiro relatorio*, 7.

26. *Revista illustrada*, February 4, 1882.

27. From 1886 on, Machado de Assis was the librarian of the Club Beethoven.

28. *Club Beethoven, Segundo relatorio*, 7.

29. In the second year, the German violinist Otto Beck was hired to substitute for Cernicchiaro who left Brazil for a short period. Beck was recommended by Carl Reinecke (1824–1910) of the Leipzig Conservatory, a contact made through Arthur Napoleão. Beck arrived in Rio de Janeiro August 1, 1883, remaining there until his death. In turn, in 1884, Reinecke was granted the title of Honorary Member of the Club Beethoven, together with Arthur Napoleão.

30. *Estatutos da Academia de Musica do Club Beethoven* (Rio de Janeiro: n.p., [1884]), chapter 8, art. 18.

31. A few Club Beethoven concert programs are housed at the Biblioteca Nacional, Rio de Janeiro, Divisão de Música e Arquivo Sonoro.

32. *Revista illustrada*, August 31, 1884.

33. *Club Beethoven, Primeiro relatorio*, 16.

34. *Revista illustrada*, September 15, 1883.

35. See Sanches Frias, *Arthur Napoleão* resenha commemorativa da sua vida pessoale e artistica (Lisbon: n.p., 1913); and Luiz Heitor Corrêa de Azevedo, "Arthur Napoleón 1843–1925: un pianiste portuguais au Brésil," *Arguiros do centro cultural Português*, vol. 3 (Paris: Fundaçaó Caleuste Gulbenkiam, 1971), 572–602.

36. In New York, White performed Mendelssohn's Violin Concerto, Bach's *Chaconne*, and Vieuxtemps's *Ballade*. Critiques of these concerts came out in *Dwight's Journal of Music* of January 8, 1876, 159; February 19, 1876, 184; and April 29, 1876, 224. White also appeared in a "classical concert" at Chickering Hall on December 17, 1875, performing Mendelssohn's B minor piano quartet and Beethoven's sonata for violin and piano in C minor with Mme. Carreno Sauret (pianist). This concert was also documented in *Dwight's Journal of Music*, January 8, 1876, 159. According to the *Dwight's Journal of Music*, April 29, 1876, White was praised for the "perfect purity of his intonation."

37. *Jornal do commercio* of September 30, 1879. For information on José White's activities in Rio de Janeiro see Cristina Magaldi, "José White in Rio de Janeiro, 1879–1889," *Inter-American Music Review* 14/2 (1995): 1–19. White's activities in Chile were extensively documented by Luis Merino in "José White in Chile: National and International Repercussions," *Inter-American Music Review* XI/1 (Fall–Winter 1990): 87–112.

38. See Lourenço Luiz Lacombe, *Isabel, a princesa redentora* (Petrópolis: Instituto Histórico de Petrópolis, 1989), 165 and 196; see also Roderick J. Barman, *Princess Isabel of Brazil: Gender and Power in the Nineteenth Century* (Wilmington, Del.: Scholarly Resources, 2002), 166.

39. *Revista musical e de bellas artes II*, 1 (January 3, 1880): 6.

40. *Revista illustrada*, August 18, 1883.

41. There was no specific season for opera and concerts in the nineteenth-century Brazilian capital. In general, however, theaters, ballrooms, and concert societies were more active after the summer—in Brazil, the period from mid-December to mid-March. When trips to Europe were not possible, the wealthy of Rio de Janeiro headed to the mountains the first week of January to escape the summer heat. After Holy Week, the salons of private societies were reopened for balls and concerts and by the beginning of winter everyone was back to the pleasures of balls and concerts.

42. *Jornal do commercio*, October 13, 1886.

43. *Jornal do commercio*, October 13, 1886.

44. *Jornal do commercio*, September 7, 1885.

45. *Jornal do commercio*, August 29, 1886.

46. The advertisement for the fifth concert included the heading: "Sociedade de Concertos Populares . . . under the protection of Her Majesty, the Princess regent," *Jornal do commercio*, July 24, 1887.

47. Program announced in the *Jornal do commercio*, June 6, 1887.

48. *Jornal do commercio*, June 6, 1887.

49. A copy of this poem is housed at the Music Division, Biblioteca Nacional, Rio de Janeiro.

50. *Gazeta musical*, Anno I, nº 7 (October 1891): 11.

51. *Jornal do commercio*, October 4, 1886.

52. For the influence of European models on Brazilian literature see Maria Elizabeth Chaves de Mello, *Liçoés de crítica: conceitos europeus, crítica literária e literatura crítica no Brasil do século XIX* (Niterói, R.J.: Editora da Universidade Fluminense, 1997).

53. Napoleão's music establishment issued several catalogues listing the music and books for sale. Excerpts from these catalogues were printed on the back covers of sheet music; two full catalogues (1871, 1900) are housed at the Music Division, Biblioteca Nacional, Rio de Janeiro.

54. Henri Blaze was the son of the influential French critic François-Henri-Joseph Blaze (known as Castil-Blaze) who wrote reviews for the *Journal des débats* in 1822, and left an important account of opera in early nineteenth-century France, *De l'opéra en France* (Paris, 1820; 1826).

55. Among his publications are: *Musikalisches Skizzenbuch* (1866), *Musiker-Briefe* (1867), *Beethoven's Leben* (3 vols., 1867–1877), *Neues Skizzenbuch* (1869), *Gluck and Wagner* (1870), *Die Beethoven-Feier und die Kunst der Gegenwart* (1871), *Beethoven, Liszt, Wagner* (1874), *Beethoven nach dem Schilderungen*

seiner Zeitgenossen (1877; English trans. as *Beethoven as Depicted by His Contemporaries*, 1880), *Mozart nach den Schilderungen seiner Zeitgenossen* (1880), *Richard Wagner Bedeutung für die nationale Kunst* (1883), *Das moderne Musikdrama* (1884), *Die geschichtliche Entwicklung der Kammermusick* (1885).

56. His works include *Méthode complète du plain-chant* (1854, 1872), *Histoire génerale de la musique religieuse* (1860), *Méthode d'orgue, d'harmonie et d'accompagnement* (1874; 1894), *Histoire de la musique depuis les temps anciens jusqu'à nos jours* (1885). The following works were also for sale in Rio de Janeiro: *Poésie chrétienne*, *Carmina e poetis christianis*, *Le Paroissien romain*, and *Manuel des tableaux du plain-chant*.

57. The dictionary had four supplements to 1881; a new augmented edition by A. Pougin, *Dictionnaire des opéras* came out in 1897 and 1904.

58. This was a revised edition of *Dictionnaire de musique d'après les théoriciens, historiciens et critiques les plus célèbres*, first published in two volumes in 1844.

59. His writings include: *Curiosités musicales* (1873), *La notation de la musique classique comparée à la notation de la musique moderne, et de l'exécution des petites notes en général*; *L'Art du chef d'orchestre* (1878), *La Société des Concerts de 1860 à 1885* (1887), *De l'exécution d'ensemble* (1888), *Le Passé à propos du présent* (1892), *Mes mémoires* (1890).

60. "Relação mensal dos livros adquiridos pela Livraria Garnier," *Revista popular* (November and December 1859).

61. A second edition of the translation came out in 1859, by Cruz Coutinho (Oporto: Typographia de Sebastião José Pereira); see Ernesto Vieira, *Diccionario biographico de musicos Portuguezes*, vol. 1, 22.

62. Ênio de Freitas e Castro, "Dicionários de música brasileiros," *Revista brasileira de cultura* 2/5 (1970): 12. Castro includes in his article a facsimile of the cover of Machado's dictionary (1842 edition).

63. Liszt, "Uma noite na casa de Chopin," *Revista musical e de bellas artes* I/47 (November 22, 1879): 4; Berlioz, "Os máos e os bons cantores, o publico e a claque," and "Da imitação musical," *Revista musical e de bellas artes* I/48 (November 29, 1879): 6–7.

64. Although the article is not dated, it was probably written in the late 1870s. *Revista musical e de bellas artes* carried the translation in numbers I/17–30 (April–July, 1879).

65. *Revista musical e de bellas artes* I/19 (May 10, 1879): 5.

66. *Revista musical e de bellas artes* I/12 (March 22, 1879): 2–3.

67. *Revista musical e de bellas artes* I/12 (March 22, 1879): 2–3.

68. *Revista musical e de bellas artes* I/12 (March 22, 1879): 2.

69. These reprints of Marmontel's essays were published in 1878 as a book entitled *Symphonistes et virtuoses* (Paris: Imprimerie Centrale des Chemins de Fer).

70. *Revista musical e de bellas artes* II/13 (June 19, 1880): 102.

71. *Revista musical e de bellas artes* II/14 (July 6, 1880): 53.

72. Guanabarino compiled these articles into a 108-page book, published in 1881 by Narciso, Arthur Napoleão & Miguez; see Luiz Heitor Corrêa de Azevedo, *Bibliografia musical brasileira 1820–1950* (Rio de Janeiro: Instituto Nacional do Livro, 1952), 186.

73. *Revista musical e de bellas artes* II/22 (August 21, 1880): 176.

74. *Revista musical e de bellas artes* II/37 (December 11, 1880): 296.

75. Le Couppey's *Les classiques du piano* was offered for sale in Rio de Janeiro in 1865 by Successores de P. Laforge; *Jornal do commercio*, October 15, 1865. Haydn's and Mozart's symphonies arranged by Hummel for piano, flute, and cello, were advertised the following year; *Jornal do commercio*, August 6, 1866.

76. Guanabarino also refers to a "collection of classics" by Moscheles; Georges Bizet's *Le Pianiste chanteur*; and Czerny's edition of Bach's preludes and fugues, *Le clavecin bien-tempéré*.

Chapter 4

Music, Satire, and Politics

AN INTERNATIONAL MUSICAL PHENOMENON

While Bellini, Donizetti, and Verdi reigned in the opera house, another European theatrical musical fashion took Cariocas by storm during the heyday of Pedro II's regime: Offenbach's operettas. Starting with the smashing premiere of *Orphée aux enfers* (1858) on February 3, 1865, and followed by the performance of *La belle Hélène* (1864) on June 26, 1866, Offenbach's music was presented regularly at the Theatro Alcazar Lyrique until the close of the century. Eager for the new Parisian fad, Cariocas flooded the Alcazar for the same reason that they attended the Theatro Provisorio, and with the same aspirations that later drove the elite to the halls of the Club Beethoven: they wanted to use music to imagine they were somewhere else.

More than any other imported fad, Offenbach's operettas fulfilled Cariocas's appetite for "things French." Emanating from the trendy Parisian world, the music was a Parisian craze that could be enjoyed conveniently in a most informal ambiance, far from the social conventions of the opera house and the formalities of upscale musical societies. Francophile Cariocas enjoyed performances at the Alcazar without questioning their authenticity, ignoring the few "minor" changes necessary to adapt Offenbach's scores to the theater's small stage and the restricted local performing forces. Cariocas apparently trusted the Alcazar's French manager, Monsieur Arnaud, not to tamper with the music's "Frenchness." Anyway, no one would dare to doubt Arnaud, whose dowry to the residents of imperial Rio de

Janeiro included the best female French singers with impeccable legs, singing Offenbach's tunes in French for the best ticket prices in town. From the start, the popularity of Offenbach's works helped set the Alcazar apart from other theaters in Rio de Janeiro, for by offering French music at affordable prices the manager of the small theater promoted the taste for the French operetta among audiences at many levels of the socioeconomic scale. It was with great enthusiasm that a fan wrote at the premiere of *Orphée aux enfers* that,

> [For] the larger part of [the Rio de Janeiro] population which does not consist of blue-blood noblemen and has no access to an easy and light genre for entertainment similar to [those] in the European capitals, [and for those for whom the] lyric theater, with its high cost and agonizing dramaticity, is not an option, the Alcazar is the only venue for entertainment. . . . [In the Alcazar] the lively and cheerful operetta *Orphée aux enfers* is being received with great enthusiasm.[1]

Rio de Janeiro audiences were not alone in welcoming with enthusiasm the new Parisian fad. Having reached more people and places than the most popular Italian operatic tunes, Offenbach's music could unquestionably be proclaimed "an international musical phenomenon"[2] during this early stage of globalization. The remarkable spread of Offenbach's operettas in large cities around the world was apparently the result of the composer's personal experience—as a German immigrant who adopted Paris as his home—which was reflected in his music. More than any other composer of his time, Offenbach summoned in his operettas the attractive Parisian cosmopolitanism, providing a music that was at once cosmopolitan, and therefore free from regionalisms, and replete with memorable melodies and captivating rhythms.[3] The large numbers of European immigrants to Latin American cities provided ample audiences for his operettas, and it was not long before Offenbach's music overtook Rossini's and became another musical *lingua franca* on the other side of the Atlantic.

Such an attractive combination of elements—a light, French entertainment offered at a lower price than at the opera house—made Offenbach's music an immediate success in the imperial capital. Cariocas's enthrallment with the Parisian import was also a direct result of their identification with, and consequent reinterpretation of, Offenbach's satirical plots. While the works presented at the opera house were deemed part of a local tradition supported by the status quo, and música clássica represented the new, "cultured" society equated with progress and "modernization," the cunning satires of Offenbach's operettas made them valuable forums for the expression of local politics.

That Offenbach's music and his politically and socially oriented satires found so many devotees in imperial Rio de Janeiro underscores an inherent irony in the construction of this New World empire. Pedro II's most conceited accomplishment, the building of a Brazilian society on par with the European, turned out to determine his fate and heralded the end of the monarchical regime. The governmental policies of midcentury, which sustained an export economy and favored large coffee plantation owners from the Rio de Janeiro province, led to an unprecedented growth of local wealth and bred an expressive middle class in the capital. This new group, who could afford to enjoy at home a wide range of European cultural imports, was also exposed to European politics and ideologies with which they ultimately identified. Now a political force, this middle class composed of intellectuals, professionals, and students followed in the footsteps of European urban middle classes, condemning centralized governments and favoring Republican ideas; they expressed themselves through powerful associations that supported the abolition of slavery and questioned the basic principles of the imperial regime.[4] The tensions, which culminated in 1889 with the proclamation of the Republic, started to escalate exactly in the late 1860s and early 1870s, as the social, economic, and political tribulations caused by the war against Paraguay magnified the contradictions of their forged European society.[5] It was exactly this political climate that helped draw the attention of European-minded Cariocas toward the French operetta.

Of all Offenbach's satirical works, *Orphée aux enfers* was the most popular in the imperial capital and had a particular role in serving as a vehicle for the expression of the new middle class. Not an ephemeral fad, fourteen months after the operetta's premiere Cariocas were proud that *Orphée aux enfers*, "performed 400 times at the Théâtre des Bouffes Parisiens, was presented 255 times at the Alcazar."[6] Such an enduring success, which transformed the Alcazar into "the God of the century,"[7] was not merely the result of a blind commitment to a Parisian fashion. Cariocas, who revealed a peculiar familiarity with Greek gods and goddesses, understood particularly well *Orphée*'s mythological scenes and allegories, and the symbolism of the operetta's songs and dances. If they were not yet able to display their political criticism openly, they could surely revel in the daring social and political commentaries that saturated the French work.

THE INFERNAL DANCE

Orphée's popular finale, the catchy cancan, enticed the emerging Carioca middle class the most. The images and symbols implicit in the witty dance allowed them to voice a veiled, but effective, criticism through political and social satire. As with the reception of other imported fashions discussed in earlier chapters, timing was of the essence for promoting the links between Offenbach's astute satires, the cancan, and the political agenda of Cariocas. Before the presentation of *Orphée*, sporadic performances of the dance in imperial Rio de Janeiro did not strike as politically or socially charged statements. On the contrary, when Gravenstein concluded his bailes à Musard at the Pavilhão Fluminense with the "infernal" gallop and the cancan, his primary goal was to provide the local genteel families with a gay entertainment. Of course, he did not shun exploiting Cariocas's desire to emulate the Parisian bourgeoisie, but he still managed to keep propriety and order as essential ingredients in his bailes. Gravenstein was apparently quite successful in disconnecting his performances of the cancan and the "infernal" gallop in the imperial capital from Philippe Musard's performances of the dance in his masked balls held at the Théâtre des Variétés during the 1830s. For at that time in Paris, the cancan had evolved into a craze as a political dance, used by Parisian youth, romantic bohemians, and other revolutionary bourgeois to express their dissatisfaction with Louis-Philippe's government, and to ridicule its conceited social conventions. According to Kracauer, conservative Parisians perceived the cancan as an "infernal" dance,[8] a social malaise, and complained that,

> [Masked couples] dance it indecently close together . . . they actually throw themselves backwards and forwards . . . to the accompaniment of continual acclamation, laughter and ribald jokes; one can only be filled . . . with horror and revulsion at this mass depravity. . . . [When] the beat of the music is hastened, the dancers' movements become more rapid, more aggressive; and finally the contredanse evolves into a great gallop where dancers form double pairs, four in a row, and gallop

madly round the floor . . . the whole effect of this gallop as it grows wilder and wilder is one of shocking bacchanalian license . . . with their whole moral and physical being poisoned in the heyday of their youth.[9]

If the cancan did not initially arouse similar controversy during Gravenstein's well-mannered re-creations of Musard's notorious Parisian balls, that was not the case after the advent of *Orphée aux enfers*. Cariocas's use of the dance to express derisive political and social criticism in the late 1860s and 1870s indeed reflected Offenbach's and Halévy's use of the dance in the 1850s, as they revived the dance and ingeniously incorporated the cancan into their operettas to rebut the political corruption and social conventions of France's Second Empire. Across the Atlantic, Offenbach's libelous cancan also served the needs of the new Rio de Janeiro society, which was avid for a dance that masked political protest with satire, music, sex, and incessant pleasure. Cariocas clearly understood, and identified with, Offenbach's use of music to convey political satires, and his use of rhythm and dance to describe the inconsistencies and futilities of France's Second Empire. The identification was not forged, for members of the emerging Carioca middle class, who wholeheartedly welcomed Offenbach's operettas, bore a number of resemblances to the new class of Parisian bohemians: both consisted mainly of artists and liberal intellectuals, of well-to-do individuals who strayed from their society but, paradoxically, were dependent on the patronage and political support of the elite.

In 1866, only one year after the premiere of *Orphée*, Cariocas were already using the cancan to display their discontentment with Pedro II's government, and particularly to express their displeasure with the controversial war in the South. In a masked ball held at the Theatro São Pedro de Alcantara, for example, they danced the quadrille "A derrota dos Paraguayos" (The defeat of the Paraguayans) that turned into a brazen "infernal" gallop.[10] The finale to *Orphée aux enfers* also served well as a substitute for a wide array of comic theatrical endings, especially those satirizing local political figures. The Theatro Gymnasio Dramatico, for instance, offered the comedy *Um casamento pelo Jornal do commercio* (A Wedding through the *Jornal do Commercio*), which satirized local events and well-known political figures, concluding with the "great cancan over motives from the popular opera Orphée."[11] The rebellious character of the cancan in the imperial capital did not escape the scrutiny of the press, especially the weekly magazine *A vida fluminense* (1868–1875). In 1871, for instance, when a well-known local judge threatened to keep a group of insubordinate and outspoken students locked up, the case became quite popular and the incident was widely discussed in the press. *A vida fluminense* published a satire of the case in caricatures, which advocated the cancan as the solution to the impasse; "dancing with art and skill," the students engaged in the "infernal" dance to turn the judge's ruling upside down and to transform the courtroom into a lawless but cheerful locale.[12] Alarmed by the popularity of the cancan in Rio de Janeiro and the harmful influence that the Parisian dance exerted over local youth, eighteen months after the opening of *Orpheus* a concerned Carioca had noted that,

> The adoption of this Parisian fashion [cancan] does not fit well with our tropical temperatures. . . . Although I do not understand its choreography, I can affirm, gentlemen, that a people creates the dance it deserves; in other words, in the dance of a people one sees the faithful reflection of its nature, temperament, and intellectual and moral values. Therefore, we should not accept the cancan because it misrepresents our manners and morals; it exposes the ridiculous eagerness with which we imitate foreign fashions; and it betrays the urge with which we inject into our still young society all the viruses that plague and corrupt the old European institutions.[13]

But despite numerous published complaints about the dance's intrusion into the tranquillity of the capital's European life, during Carnival season the French fad could not be stopped, as members of local Sociedades Carnavalescas (Carnival Societies) incessantly danced the cancan through the city's streets accompanied by military bands. Wearing expensive costumes and exhibiting elaborate allegorical floats, for them Carnival was a season to rejoice and celebrate, as well as a re-creation of the exquisite traditions of the Old World in the capital of the New World Empire. But in Pedro II's Rio de Janeiro the celebrations soon took a shape of their own, turning into a forum for self-indulgence as well as group upheaval, for an "inversion of reality"[14] where everything was permitted, for an escape from the discontentment of daily life and the relentless hardships encountered throughout the year, all of which could be masked or compensated for by frantic dancing. The witty imported dance fulfilled this function gracefully, as a reminder that members of the Sociedades Carnavalescas were au courant with Parisian trends. After *Orphée*, however, the cancan helped to magnify the frenzy, causing Rio de Janeiro's Carnival to be characterized as "the domain of madness."[15] If the cancan offered an escape, it also transformed Carnival commemorations into sweeping orgies, as "indecent" women paraded on top of allegorical floats, shamefully waving their bare legs.

Nonetheless, members of the Carnival Societies did not shun engaging in the disreputable cancan, for, more than anything else at their disposal, the riotous dance was suitable for voicing the most daring political statements and satires. Blind to the contradictions inherent in their own behavior, they veiled themselves in luxurious costumes and danced the imported cancan to comment on the hypocrisy of the local society, and used the dance to

Figure 4.1. "The 1870 Carnival season: Ready for the gallop; How does one dance at the ball?; The cancan *'desenfreado'* (frantic)." *A vida fluminense* (February 26, 1870). Young Research Library, UCLA.

"openly" criticize the institution of slavery and to support Republican agendas. The parallel between the members the Sociedades Carnavalescas and the bohemians of France's Second Empire was evidenced not only by their gentry backgrounds or their prudent support of the status quo throughout the year, but also in their fantasized sympathy with the urban masses. During Carnival season they madly danced the cancan in the streets of the imperial capital surrounded by "the people" in an attempt to re-create in Rio de Janeiro a pretend local "*Liberté, egalité, fraternité.*"[16]

Following the logic of *Orphée*, the "infernal" dance was most powerful when it was presented at the end of the Societies Carnavalescas's dramatizations. This role of the dance to muster the Carnival frenzy and the intended satire was particularly clear in the literary *puffs* published in local newspapers during Carnival season, which summarized the political agendas of each Carnival Society.[17]According to the puff published in the *Jornal do commercio* by the Bohemios society during their 1871 Carnival celebrations, the goal of their parade was to emphasize their "freedom" from the local aristocracy, a freedom that was expressed exactly by "raising their legs higher than the tower of the Candelaria [cathedral] in a frenzied cancan."[18] In the same year, the Novas Sumidades Carnavalescas criticized the institution of slavery and the status quo by concluding their parade with the satirical cancan. Their "puff" was published in a local newspaper as follows:

> Carnival is the inferno that devours the fools and pedants. . . . [Carnival is a time when] the ridiculed mock the ridiculous, the crazed torment the ignorant, the deranged preach morals!!! . . . Rejoice oh outlawed [black] race [because your] heroes have no wealth; [rejoice] because although you cannot cover yourself with golden brocades . . . your soul stands far above that of the civilized bacchanalians; [rejoice] because in the end, the cancan *de rigueur* will be danced.[19]

Such irreverent behavior and the rebellious performances of the dance, added to the open mockery of public figures, fuelled widespread societal criticism and inevitably resulted in intervention by the imperial police. With "official" warnings published daily in newspapers during the 1875 Carnival season, for instance, the police strove to instill fear by making it illegal to ridicule public figures during outdoor celebrations.[20] However, despite attempts to censor the dance, the cancan remained as the preferred imported fad among Carioca youth far beyond the expectations of the local police. The balls at the Pavilhão Fluminense continued to regularly feature a cancan *"bem remexido"* (very stirred up) and, by the end of the imperial regime in 1889, Cariocas still frenzied while dancing the cancan during Carnival season celebrations in ballrooms and outdoor parades.

THE FINAL NUMBER

By the early 1870s, the cancan had also marked its presence in a less explicit way, inspiring a wide array of local dances, which in turn substituted for the French dance to fulfill the contemporary needs of Rio de Janeiro's new urban society. Interestingly enough, these cancan surrogates were not of European provenance, but mostly derived from the Afro-Brazilian heritage. Through parallel satirical images learned from the imported model and mediated by managers, actors, and musicians, African derived dances gradually replaced the cancan as the joyous and irreverent finale in local theatrical productions. Most important, the use of Afro-Brazilian dances as substitutes for the imported model reveals a most vivid picture of the political, social, and ethnic negotiations taking place at the end of Pedro II's regime.

The first work to successfully explore a dance of Afro-Brazilian derivation as a theatrical finale in the Offenbach way premiered at the Theatro Phenix Dramatica on October 31, 1868, at the height of *Orphée aux enfers*'s success at the Alcazar. The timing was also a given here, for the managers of the Phenix Dramatica, who had already established a reputation for staging parodies, did not miss the chance to capitalize on the success of the French operetta as a recipe for a box office hit in their theater. To compete with the French Arnaud and his singers in the Alcazar, the Phenix Dramatica bestowed on the Carioca public a parody of the popular French work with a Portuguese title: *Orpheo na roça* (Orpheus in the countryside). Sure enough, with a Portuguese libretto by popular comedian Francisco Correa Vasques (1839–1892),[21] the work brought unmatched popularity to the Phenix Dramatica, surpassing the Alcazar in both box office revenues and popularity, and reached a record 100 performances in its first year alone. The parody's success and its implicit humor were utterly dependent on the satirical images created by

Offenbach and Halévy, as *Orpheo*'s libretto overtly follows each section of the operetta without a glitch. Rio de Janeiro audiences could easily associate the character of Zeferino with Orpheus in the operetta, and could readily identify his wife Brigida as a local version of Euridice. Vasques himself parodied Jupiter as Juiz de Paz Mamede de Souza, a local judge and a staggering ladykiller, comparable to the character in the operetta. The connection between the French work and *Orpheo na roça* was further emphasized by having Zeferino and Brigida sing Offenbach's music. As with the plot, the use, and abuse, of Offenbach's most popular and blissful tunes was deliberate, for the imported music was a strong and necessary element strengthening Cariocas sense of familiarity with the European work. At the same time, the use of recognizable songs in different contexts was necessary for the humor of *Orpheo* to work, as Vasques imbued the already familiar music with new meanings.

The work's amazing and enduring appeal was also a result of Vasques's mastery in adapting Halévy's libretto, bringing Cariocas from dark scenes with mythical Greek Gods dressed in French attire to the daylight reality of a farm near Rio de Janeiro. Thus, in the parody Euridice's death is substituted by the abduction of Brigida from her husband Zeferino, who is actually delighted by the unexpected freedom. While enjoying her liberation, Brigida is set to interact with judge Paz Mamede de Souza, who takes advantage of the situation by disregarding the law and keeping Zeferino's wife for himself. To complete the dose of local reality, the libretto is particularly thrilling in the finale, when all the characters are on stage to perform the final number. By replacing the anticipated cancan with an Afro-Brazilian *fado*, or *fadinho* (short fado), Vasques brought the audiences of the Theatro Phenix Dramatica to a frenzy.

Nonetheless, the overwhelming success of the parody's finale did not quite disguise Vasques's reliance on imported models, for his immediate impetus for the inclusion of a fado as *Orpheo*'s final number might also have come from abroad. African-derived dances were delighting Parisians in the theater at least a decade before the premiere of *Orpheo*, and they first arrived in the Brazilian capital with French titles, such as the *Tango chanson avanaise* by the French M. Lucien Boucquet, performed in Rio de Janeiro in the play *L'île de calypso* and available in sheet music as early as 1863.[22] Vasques's use of a fado in his parody also recalled Spanish zarzuelas, which in the late 1860s and 1870s had also made an impression on Cariocas and regularly included dances such as "tango dos pretos" (black tango) and "tango havaneiros" (tango from Havana).[23] By bringing to the stage popular Afro-Brazilian dances in a parody of an imported work, Vasques accomplished the twofold task of exploring the local and of capitalizing on Cariocas's identification with imported models. The score for the final number, provided by novelist and dilettante composer Manoel Joaquim Maria, was crafted to achieve just that: to dress the Afro-Brazilian dance with a cosmopolitan cover.

The goal was achieved through a clever manipulation of plot and music. Although there are several reports of fado dancing among blacks, mulattos, and whites in imperial Rio de Janeiro's poor neighborhoods, there is scarce documentation describing the actual performances.[24] Nonetheless, in rural areas, the fado is known to have engaged the black population since the late eighteenth century, alongside other African-derived dances such as the *lundu,* the

Figure 4.2.   "Batuque," J. B. Spix, *Atlas zur reise in brasilien* (1817–1820). Biblioteca Nacional, Rio de Janeiro.

batuque,[25] and the hybrid *cateretê*.[26] A dance-song with improvised lyrics and a slow tempo, the rural fado's choreography recalled the Afro-Brazilian batuque and the Spanish *fandango*, in which a group of dancers form a ring around one or several couples and surround the dancers with clapping and foot tapping. The choreographic movements of the fado, according to José Ramos Tinhorão, also shared similarities with those of the batuque in the twisting of the hips and the rotating navel movement, *umbigada*. According to a contemporary description, "[The fado] starts slowly and accelerates gradually as the dancers move forwards and backwards, the women moving their bodies and shaking their arms, the men clapping the beat with their hands. As the music quickens, singing and foot tapping become faster and [more] frenzied."[27]

Apparently, Vasques's and Manoel Joaquim Maria's libretto rested on the rural fado, as it indicates that the dance was to be performed with the "characteristic" instrumentation of fado performances in rural areas, including guitar, viola, *adofos* [sic] (a membranophone, similar to a square tambourine), and pandeiros. Nonetheless, the introduction, the four-line stanzas, the short refrain in two, clear-cut four-measure phrases sung in thirds, the plain harmonies and syllabic settings were all tailored to fit the contemporary theatrical cliché and, conveniently, did not stray completely from Offenbach's and Halévy's popular tunes. The Brazilian authors chose to assert the Afro-Brazilian musical language by also stressing note repetition, the dotted eighth/sixteenth note figure, and syncopation in the accompainiment, a practice that was later used repeatedly in other musical portrayals of African-derived dances on stage. These musical elements, which ensured that the final number would be a box office hit for the Theatro Phenix Dramatica, also resulted in good revenues for the publisher Arthur Napoleão, who astutely predicted the success of the theatrical fado and provided Cariocas with numerous prints and reprints of the work for several decades.

But while Cariocas became "prisoners" of the fado, the captivating effects of the dance were not solely the response to a fashion, imported or local. Vasques's fado erupted on the local stage at the same time when the Carioca white bourgeoisie turned its attention to its Afro-Brazilian heritage. On the one hand, it was clear to some that the end of the monarchical regime and the consequent end of

Musical Example 4.1. Fado from *Orpheu na roça*. Biblioteca Nacional, Rio de Janeiro, Divisão de Música e Arquivo Sonoro

Quebra, quebra, bem quebrado	come dance, waddle with swing
O fadinho brasileiro	the Brazilian little fado
Numa roda deste fado	In a ring of fado
Tudo fica prisioneiro	Everyone becomes a prisoner
(Refrain from Orpheu's fado)	

slavery would inevitably lead to a new social and ethnic order. New political circumstances would require them to strengthen their alliance with the large black population and consequently also to accept Afro-Brazilian culture as part of the local fabric. On the other hand, the Brazilian middle class still shunned black religious beliefs and social practices as deviant. European-minded, white, genteel, and "reputable" urban Brazilians did not openly dance any African-derived dance, believed to be rather indecent, even though paradoxically they cherished their stage performances. Rather oblivious and unsympathetic toward the black culture they were claiming to accept and praise, Carioca bourgeoisie could only embrace the Afro-Brazilian heritage inasmuch as they looked at it as outsiders. This ambiguous relationship was clearly delineated in Vasques's libretto, as the plot of *Orpheo na roça* was set in the countryside and the fado choreography followed that performed in rural areas. Consequently, while clearly emulating Offenbach and Halévy, Vasques's implicit satires and intrigues were set to contrast with the "civilized" (and European) imperial Rio de Janeiro.

Explored in *Orpheo na roça* as caricature, as part of a licentious behavior that overtly explored sexuality, Vasques's final fado substituted well for Offenbach's rebellious cancan. The connection becomes clear when Brigida enters the stage dressed in a *Bahiana* (a black woman from the state of Bahia) outfit, and starts a game of seduction by dancing and singing the fado alongside her husband, her abductor, and the judge. In addition, in her performance she overemphasizes the "*quebra*," or hip movement, in erotic gestures that stress sexual pursuit. This overtly exoticized image presented in *Orpheu*'s fado was undoubtedly drawn from Cariocas's perception of the cancan as a dance that tainted social conventions by highlighting sexual freedom. The connection between the choreographies of the two dances became quite useful during Carnival, as members of the Sociedades Carnavalescas started to substitute the fado for the cancan to fulfill the locals' desire for a "modern bacchanalia."[28]

Hence, the replacement of the satirical role of the cancan by the explicit ethnic symbols in the fado as caricature was neither artificial nor coincidental. The parallel between the French cancan and the Afro-Brazilian dance was fabricated and mediated by white, middle-class intellectuals, artists, and playwrights, who used both

Figure 4.3. Carnival of 1868: "Oh Congo! And they say that a Frenchman in-vented the cancan?" *A vida fluminense* (February 1868). Young Research Library, UCLA.

dances to expose and comment on (and satirize) the imminent changes in the local social, ethnic, and political order.

As was to be expected, those in charge of maintaining the status quo rapidly grasped the association between the two dances and strongly reprimanded both:

> In the countryside, where neither the light of gas nor of civilization has penetrated, the fado shines with distinction; [but] in the city [the fado is] despised and looked upon with contempt, perhaps because of its

Figure 4.4. "The cancan during the 1870 Carnival season." *A vida fluminense* (February 1870). Young Research Library, UCLA.

African kinship. [Today] one needs to find [a dance] to replace them [the cancan and the fado], one that is less in dissonance with our century, one that is more patriotic and decent.[29]

The advice was not followed. While the cancan eventually lost its appeal as the preferred dance of the local bourgeoisie, in the theater it continued in the form of the fado and other dances of Afro-Brazilian derivation to symbolize chaotic situations and licentious (sexual) behavior.

Undoubtedly a significant, albeit overlooked, historical work, the fado from *Orpheo na roça* is apparently not only the earliest printed example of a theatrical dance composed specifically for a local production, but also one of earliest songs/dances to become a popular hit in nineteenth-century Rio de Janeiro. Most important, *Orpheo's* final fado marks the beginning of a trend, for it created a specific way in which the new Carioca middle class used music and dance to depict local social and ethnic groups on stage.

Figure 4.5. "The general and his battalion celebrate peace with a 'fadinho requebrado.'" *A vida fluminense* (February 1871). Young Research Library, UCLA.

THE OPERETTA MODEL

The success of Vasques's parody of Offenbach's *Orphée aux enfers* soon prompted a gamut of similar musical productions: Offenbach's *Barbe-bleu* was then transformed into *O Barba de milho* (1869) and later into *Traga-moças* (1869); *La grand duchesse de Gérolstein* became *A baronesa de Caiapó* (1868); and *La belle Hélène* was parodied as *Abel, Helena* (1878). Along with imported realist plays, the imported operetta inspired local playwrights to immerse their own librettos in social and political satire according to the preferences of Rio de Janeiro's new urban society. The acclaimed Brazilian playwright Arthur de Azevedo's (1855–1908) first success, for instance, was an adaptation of Lecocq's *La fille de Madame Angot* (1872) to the Brazilian scene. With the Portuguese title *A filha de Maria Angú* (1876), Azevedo's version retained only the backbone of the French plot. More direct and unswerving than Vasques's parody, Azevedo transplanted the story to a Rio de Janeiro neighborhood, and his characters were individuals of the local society who could be easily recognized by the public despite their theatrical disguise. Lecocq's music with the added Portuguese translation, rearranged for the local performing forces, was retained in its entirety. As with Vasques's *Orpheo*, in *A filha de Maria Angú*, the use of a recognizable imported musical model was a necessary element for Cariocas's identification with the parody. The adaptations and changes in the plot, the satire and criticisms in the lyrics were redeemed by the use of the familiar European music.

It did not take long, however, for local composers to attempt to "nationalize" the genre by also providing original music for local productions. One early example was the "national operetta" in two acts *Trunfo as avessas,* premiered on August 8, 1871, at the Theatro Phenix Dramatica. The work's libretto was by the Brazilian playwright França Júnior (1838–1890), a master of the comic theater and a specialist in political satires,[30] and the music by the Brazilian composer Henrique Alves de Mesquita.[31] Unlike the author of the music of *Orpheu's* fado, Mesquita had studied in the Paris conservatory from 1857 to 1866 and therefore had the compositional skills to fully re-create the musical language of the French operetta in the Brazilian capital. He also had first-hand knowledge of the comedies presented in Parisian theaters such as the Théâtre du Vaudeville, and in less formal and more socially mixed venues such as the Parisian *Café-concerts*. Mesquita's 1861 *Soirée brésilienne,* written while he was in Paris, was contemporary to Sebastián Yradier's *"Aÿ Chiquita"* (1861) and habanera *"El arreglito,"* (1864),[32] which Bizet later included in his opera *Carmen* (1875). Mesquita's awareness of Parisians's interest in exotic, African-derived dances, such as tangos and habaneras, inspired him to pursue the same road at home and to use in his theatrical productions the Afro-Brazilian sources available to him in the imperial capital.

Although not a parody, *Trunfo as avessas* followed Vasques's model, as the action takes place on a farm near the capital, not in the city. Unfortunately, the full libretto for the operetta is not extant and the scant information about this early national operetta is derived from newspaper reports. Nonetheless, there are several printed musical excerpts from *Trunfo as avessas*, which offer a fair idea of Mesquita's musical choices for nationalizing the genre. First it was his mastery of a foreign musical language that most elicited praise by local critics, who observed that Mesquita's operetta "is a proof of the exuberant talent of this Brazilian composer and conductor."[33] But local recognition of his skills as a composer of operettas also rested on his ability to integrate African-derived dances into the backbone of a foreign genre. Thus, in the same vein as Vasques's *Orpheo*, Mesquita concluded *Trunfo as avessas* with a fado, but then he went further by adding a "Coro de negros" (Black chorus) and a "Grande *jongo* accompanied by a batuque."[34] Mesquita's next operetta *Ali-babá* (1872) also included dances of African derivation, among them a tango that became a major sensation.[35] These hits made Mesquita, a composer trained in Paris, one of the most popular composers of Afro-Brazilian music for the local theater in the two decades preceding the proclamation of the republic. His music was profusely published, and with its dotted and syncopated rhythms, note repetitions, juxtapositions of different rhythmic patters, and melodies with leaps and syncopations, it not only came to represent black music on the stage but also set in motion the popularization of Afro-Brazilian music in the imperial capital. Nine years after *Trunfo as avessas*, another local operetta production got the attention of Cariocas: *A princeza dos Cajueiros,* with text by Arthur de Azevedo and music by the Portuguese immigrant Francisco de Sá Noronha (1820–1881). Premiered on March 6, 1880, and advertised as *operetta de costumes* (operetta in the local manner), *A princeza dos Cajueiros* ran for 150 performances in its first year alone, and continued to be staged ten years after its premiere.

Azevedo's libretto for *A princeza dos Cajueiros* unequivocally followed the satires in Offenbach's works as it punctured the social and political life of contemporary Rio de Janeiro. A local reviewer noted that the work followed "the [same] style of the librettos of Halévy and Meilhac . . . with comic scenes and strong satires . . . accentuated by a rich mise en scène and excellent work of the actors."[36] But caution was still necessary in the satire of one's own environment, thus *A princeza dos Cajueiros* was set in the "imaginary" land of Cajueiros, in an unspecified time. The plot, dealing with the princess's love for a fisherman, makes up for its initial social flexibility at the end, when the poor lover reveals himself as a prince, and the princess turns out to be the daughter of a local doctor—who had exchanged them at birth. But although the plot develops in the "imaginary" land of Cajueiros, the characters were easily identified with popular figures of Rio de Janeiro's daily life. The main character, El Rey Caju, for instance, was an unmistakable caricature of Emperor Pedro II, since Caju was supposedly his nickname among the people.[37] Throughout the story, one could pick out other characters such as politicians, artists, and popular figures of Rio de Janeiro's streets. The plot also referred directly to several contemporary issues addressed in the daily newspapers: it commented on the practice of pimping wet-nurses; scorned the exchange of personal favors for royal titles; and ridiculed the emperor, whose laws were implemented according to his personal needs. Azevedo's astute and direct social and political satires in the operetta were further enhanced by the addition of an ingenious musical score. Noronha's understanding of the response to certain imported and local popular musical styles certainly added to the work's favorable reception.

Arriving in Rio de Janeiro in September 1838, Noronha first appeared before Brazilian audiences as a virtuoso violinist. But his performing career was soon eclipsed by the success of his musical compositions, the great majority of which stemmed from collaborations with successful theater men. Working with the highly regarded Brazilian actor/impresario João Caetano in music-theater productions for the luxurious Theatro São Pedro de Alcantara won him credit with the local elite.[38] However, looking for better and faster financial returns, he also provided music to popular comic genres—vaudevilles and comic *intermezzi*[39]—for which he wrote instrumental variations on Portuguese and Spanish themes, lyric and comic songs with Portuguese texts, modinhas, and lundus. When Noronha

returned to Brazil in 1876, after almost twenty years as music director in several theaters in Portugal, the Brazilian capital had turned
into a cosmopolitan center where republican and antislavery agendas of the emerging middle class were constantly in conflict with the
status quo. In the theater, social commentary through satire highlighted the inconsistencies and contradictions of a slave society
adopting European bourgeois standards. Not intimidated by the
new environment, Noronha quickly learned how to use music to
address the demands of the new Carioca society.

When Azevedo approached Noronha with the libretto for *A
princeza dos Cajueiro*s, he asked for newly composed music, not the
usual pastiche of popular operatic numbers to which composers
customarily turned for works of this kind. After all, the work was
subtitled "operetta in the local manner," with a text as a parody of
Rio de Janeiro's reality, and the music should accordingly be built
upon the same stereotypes. But Noronha knew too well the local
public, which was always eager for music *à la* Offenbach. Thus, instead of investing in the composition of totally fresh material, to better convey the ideas of the "local" he turned to the French composer
for inspiration. A local critic, not aware of Noronha's deliberate use
of the foreign model, accused his score of being "a little too redun-
dant in bringing to light several sections already familiar among
us."[40] But the comment was not to be taken as a criticism. As with
the characters in the plot, Offenbach's music appeared in disguise,
but was expected to be easily recognized by the audience. With that
accomplished, Noronha went further by also following Vasques's
Orpheu and closing his *A princeza dos Cajueiros* with an African-
derived dance/song, the tango "Amor tem fogo" (Love Has Fire).

Similar to *tangos americanos* (American tangos), habaneras, and the
like, which were popularized in Rio de Janeiro in the 1870s, the music in the tango-song "Amor tem Fogo" displays a characteristic bass
rhythmic formula of dotted eighth/sixteenth notes throughout the
piece. The melodic line dispensed with the usual Spanish first-beat
triplets in favor of a more polkalike, catchy tune—much easier to
play and sing. The text is brief, topical, and satirical in essence, like a
musical joke. In short, "Amor tem fogo" had all the ingredients necessary for a quick and lasting success. In fact, a contemporary critic
recalling the opening night of *A princeza dos Cajueiros* pointed out that
"the final number had to be repeated several times [and] no doubt
will remain in the memory of all those attending the performance."[41]

Musical Example 4.2. "Amor tem fogo" from *A princeza dos Cajueiros*. Biblioteca Nacional, Rio de Janeiro, Divisão de Música e Arquivo Sonoro.

If, from today's vantage point, songs like Noronha's "Amor tem Fogo" represent a small part of the complex social fabric that makes the local culture, in the nineteenth century the song was saturated with contemporary relevance, for its success reflected the experience of everyday life and its social and ethnic symbols. Although not a Brazilian dance, the tango, with its class and racial connotations, was portrayed on Rio de Janeiro stages as a dance of the blacks and low-class immigrants, usually in satirical situations, similar to the cancan and *Orpheo*'s fado. Thus, it was definitely not accepted in the "respectable" musical gatherings of the local bourgeoisie. Noronha was aware of that, but in *A princeza dos Cajueiros* he nonetheless chose a tango as the final love song/dance of the royal couple. Those dissatisfied with the monarchical regime must have enjoyed seeing a prince singing and dancing a tango, not for the sarcasm alone, but because it masked the social barrier, permitting everyone to freely identify with the lively dance.

More than the operetta from which it was part, Noronha's finale, the closing tango-song "Amor tem Fogo," then became a major hit in imperial Rio de Janeiro: it was heard in the opening and in be-tween acts of plays until the end of the century, it was reprinted sev-eral times, by different publishers, for different instruments, and the tune appeared as the theme for numerous instrumental variations and salon dances. "Amor tem fogo" engendered musical responses such as the polka "Amor tem Gelo" (Love Has Ice); and, according to contemporary commentators, the tune was regularly hummed in the streets and even heard in the church, much to the distress of the local conservative church-goers. In these ways, "Amor tem fogo" was kept in the collective memory long after the plot of A *princeza dos Cajueiros* was forgotten.[42]

Noronha's next collaboration with Azevedo, the operetta *Os noivos* (1880), was also advertised as *"opera-comica de costumes"* (comic opera in the local manner), but the endeavor was not as suc-cessful. Unlike *A princeza dos Cajueiros* (and like *Orpheo na roça*), in *Os noivos* the plot takes place on a farm, not in the city (nor in the "imaginary land of Cajueiros") and, according to the newspaper ad-vertisement, it was "concerned with delineating characters from the countryside and the popular habits on the farm."[43] Noronha in-cluded a *jongo,* another Afro-Brazilian dance, and a catereté, which according to the reviewer of the *Jornal do commercio,* "will have guar-anteed success in the Theatro Phenix Dramatica."[44] Nonetheless, the

Afro-Brazilian dances in *Os noivos* were danced not by royals, but by the local slaves as entertainment for aristocratic families, and as such did not stir up the audiences as did the tango in the finale of *A princeza dos Cajueiros*.

By the 1885 premiere of the *"operetta de costumes brasileiros"* (operetta in the Brazilian manner) *A corte na roça* (The Court in the Countryside), with libretto by Palhares Ribeiro and music by the Brazilian composer Chiquinha Gonzaga (1847–1935), the idea of exploring the local culture by satirizing characters from the countryside, rather than the reality of the capital, was no longer the standard for local music theater productions. Although the manager of the Theatro Principe Imperial announced the operetta as an "Extraordinary novelty!" the reviewer of the *Jornal do commercio* noted that the plot of *A corte na roça* was "very limited" serving only the purpose of an original musical score. Gonzaga's music, which included waltzes alongside a lundu and a cateretê, served to portray the Brazilian hillbilly character, not the urban Carioca. Even so, a few critics saw merit in the score, which, they claimed, had an uncanny "touch of Brazilian style . . . evident in the undulations and rhythmic movements of local [Afro-Brazilian] songs and dances."[45] Thus, in the 1880s local critics were equating a Brazilian (national) musical style with theatrical constructions of Afro-Brazilian songs and dances, constructions that were heavily mediated to become sure recipes for box-office hits, but which also revealed an ambiguous and unwarranted view of Afro-Brazilian culture by the Carioca elite, as well as by the emerging middle class, intellectuals, artists, and policymakers in general.

MUSICAL REVIEWS

In the early 1880s, Afro-Brazilian dances began to play increasingly important roles in the success of theatrical shows, and they soon became a rage by themselves. Playwrights and composers started to fully grasp the effect that Afro-Brazilian dances as final numbers had on a public that was becoming more and more aware of the black culture around them. Thus in the 1880s when the national operetta started to lose its appeal, Afro-Brazilian dances started to appear consistently in a new theatrical genre, the *revista de anno*, or musical review. The revistas were collections of

theatrical episodes satirically portraying, and directly commenting on, the daily life in the imperial capital. They explored a wide
array of subjects that had made the news in the previous year,
from events in the imperial opera house to the constant conflict
between black capoeiras and the police in the city's streets.[46] Unlike earlier occurrences in parodies and national operettas, in revistas Afro-Brazilian culture had a pivotal role in the plot, although following the interpretation and interests of playwrights
and composers.

Revistas, usually in three acts, consisted of several standard numbers: first, there was the *fio conductor* (main thread or main theme),
linking the work's several episodes, and a *prólogo*, or opening number, introducing the characters. Revistas also usually included
quadro fantasticos (fantastic numbers) with allegories, rich scenery
and wardrobe, and music; and each of the three acts ended with an
apoteose, or finale, and the work closed with a grandiose *apoteose final* (grand finale), where the whole cast appeared on stage to dance
and/or sing.[47] Because revistas were based on a variety of facts, their
success rested on the audiences' acquaintance with the city's surroundings and with recent political events. And because of the
genre's reliance on music, the satire was also largely dependent on
the public's familiarity with the sounds used to portray the local milieu. Accordingly, the music for the revistas consisted of a pastiche
of already-popular songs and dances, the majority by European
composers. The role of the music director was to choose and arrange
the European numbers according to the local performing forces and
to provide theatrical versions of African-derived dances in the style
of Vasques's fado and Noronha's tango. Flashily announced in local
newspapers as "grotesque dances" to contrast bluntly with the European repertory, Afro-Brazilian songs and dances were one of the
main attractions of the revistas, appearing as standard numbers either at the end of acts, or as the "final apotheoses" to close the spectacle. Even more than in the national operettas, in revistas Afro-
Brazilian songs and dances bestowed on Cariocas a frenzied comic
finale filled with ethnic caricature.

The first big hit in the revista genre was *O mandarim*, which premiered in January 1884, with text by the famous duo Azevedo and
Moreira Sampaio.[48] Announced as "revista-opereta" (operetta review), *O mandarim*'s several numbers commented on events of the
previous year: the highlights of 1883 being the effects of the rain

and flooding, the local theatrical presentations, political events, and the actions of well-known politicians and other influential figures. *O mandarim* included music "of various authors," a patchwork of European and local numbers: the former consisting of cancans, gallops, waltzes, and operatic arias, and the latter of "grotesque dances" of Afro-Brazilian derivation.[49] The Brazilian musical director Simões Junior was in charge of choosing the musical numbers, of adapting them to the new dramatic situations in the plot, as well as of providing original numbers, such as the tango that concluded the revista. As was customary, Simões Junior chose European songs and dances already popular among Cariocas, including works by Strauss, Offenbach, Lecoq, Suppé, Hervé, Barbieri, and Verdi. He also included an aria from Wagner's *Lohengrin*, which had premiered in Rio de Janeiro in 1883 and that represented the year's most important operatic event. The other European music excerpts, rearranged, translated, and sung by a cast of local artists, were used to portray and lampoon local situations and local characters. To achieve the expected effect, the imported music needed to be familiar to the audience, for it served to portray the "civilized," European Rio de Janeiro, and at the same time to inspire satire as it was presented in new contexts. Most importantly, European works were to contrast with the African-derived "grotesque dances" such as Simões Junior's final tango.

Azevedo and Sampaio continued to release revistas until the turn of the century, always reaching large audiences.[50] The success of their works lay in the appealing story lines that served as background to the dry review of events that characterized the standard revistas.[51] But Azevedo and Sampaio were not alone in creating hits in the genre. On January 13, 1886, the impresario and manager Mr. Heller premiered at the Theatro Sant'Anna the revista *A mulher-homem*, with text by Valentim de Magalhães e Filinto d'Almeida. The revista made history in the annals of Rio de Janeiro newspapers using as a *fio conductor* a local 1885 scandal of a man who disguised himself as a woman to find a job as a maid. *A mulher-homem* also commented on the recent political events in the imperial capital, the central topic being the Saraiva-Cotegipe Law of 1885, or the law of the *sexagenário* (seniors older than sixty)—a law emancipating slaves sixty years of age or older.

To portray the story and to amuse the audience, *A mulher-homem* included thirty-two musical numbers by several authors, a cocktail of original music by local composers and familiar European works: the talents of the Brazilian composers Gonzaga, Mesquita, Henrique de Magalhães, and Cav. Carlos Cavallier were presented side by side with European works by Ponchielli, Meyerbeer, and Lecocq. While Ponchielli's overture for *La Gioconda* served well as an opening piece for the revista, a gallop by Lecocq and Meyerbeer's march from *Le profete* were used as closing numbers for the Prologue and first act, respectively.[52] But attentions were all focused on the final apotheoses: recalling both *Orphée* and *Orpheu*, in the finale of the revista the allegoric character "public opinion" is abducted, and the much-awaited black dance closes the spectacle. Here, instead of a fado, Henrique de Magalhães provided the audiences with a piece titled *"jongo dos pretos sexagenarios"* (jongo of blacks older than sixty) to portray the irony in the new law, which actually aimed at postponing the emancipation of all slaves.

Like early descriptions of fados, several reports refer to the jongo in rural areas of nineteenth-century Brazil as an Afro-Brazilian dance similar to the batuque; like the fado and the batuque, the choreography involves the participants forming a ring (or two lines) with a soloist or a couple dancing in the middle, with movements of the *umbigada* simulating sexual pursuit. It was usually accompanied by drums and had added lyrics, in the format of verse and refrain. In the theatrical rendition of *A mulher-homem's* final jongo, unlike the words in *Orpheu*'s fado, the lyrics openly criticize the imperial government for postponing the emancipation of all slaves. This display of support for the slave population in the theater was nonetheless disguised in the ambiguous way in which the slave character was presented and in the satire associated with the final dance: in *A mulher-homem* the final jongo portrays slaves as helpless and dependent on the local white bourgeoisie, for it appears in caricature to add humor to the final number. In addition, broken Portuguese is used in the lyrics specifically to emphasize the illiteracy of the slaves.

To attract the interest of those who had already seen *A mulher-homem* several times, on February 13, 1886, Mr. Heller announced a new final act added to the revista titled "Um maxixe na Cidade-Nova" (A *maxixe* in the new city), with music by Gonzaga and Magalhães. The word *maxixe* in the title of the new act was used to describe a musical gathering in poor Rio de Janeiro neighborhoods that included "fados, jongos, and cateretês."[53] According to a newspaper

Musical Example 4.3. "Jongo dos sexagenarios" from *A mulher-homem*. Biblioteca Nacional, Rio de Janeiro, Divisão de Música e Arquivo Sonoro.

Lyrics in printed score	Portuguese	English
Nosso de xô nosso té-ra	Nós deixamos a nossa terra	We left our land
Nosso ve-io nim Brazi	Nós viemos para o Brasil	We came to Brazil
Pla us sucà zi tlabaio	Para fazer o seu trabalho	To work for you
		To drink your Brandy
		Olê

Lyrics in printed score	Portuguese	English
Pla bêbê zi palaty	Para beber o seu Paraty	We are not Africans
Olê	Olê	We are now Brazilians
Nosso non é mai fricano		Our grandfather is
Nosso já é brasirêro		[the focus of
Nosso avóla vai ni plaça	Nós não somos Africanos	attentions] in the
Pla blanco faze	Nós já somos brasileiros	public square
Rinheiro	Nosso avô vai na praça	Just so white people
Ai! Uê mam	Para branco fazer dinheiro	can make money
Hum hum hum	Ai! Uê mam	Ai! Uê mam
	Hum hum hum	Hum hum hum

review, "The new act is just an excuse [to bring to the stage] jongos and fados." Magalhães was particularly praised for his "Jongo dos Pretos (black jongo)," which, a commentator noted, "particularly amused the audience."[54] On February 27, six weeks after its premiere, a local newspaper claimed that 45,000 people had seen *A mulher-homem* and that the small theater was not enough to accommodate all those willing to see the revista. Such a smashing success, they repeatedly noted, was unquestionably the result of the final number, a cateretê, which often "had to be repeated four or five times."[55]

THE POLITICS OF REPRESENTATION

According to Ruy Vas, a character in the novel *A conquista* (1899) by Coelho Neto (1864–1934), in the early 1880s the manager of the Theatro Sant'Anna, Mr. Heller, imposed specific conditions on playwrights with respect to the staging of comedies. Ruy Vas, a personification in the novel of writer Aluísio de Azevedo (Arthur's brother), describes Heller's requirements to him as follows: "Mr. Heller thinks that I should arrange a few lyrics and a jongo for a . . . *comédia de costumes* (comedy in the local manner) . . . he wants, at any rate, that blacks enter the stage with *maracás* (rattles) and drums to dance and sing. . . . He says that the audience does not accept a play without *chirinola* (bamboozle) and *saracoteios* (waddling)."[56]

Overstatement or not, Mr. Heller made clear a particular point: the impact of theatrical versions of Afro-Brazilian dances on Cariocas during the 1880s was not to be taken for granted. The success of theatrical productions including such dances, like *operettas de costumes* and revistas, brought large revenues to managers and theater personnel, and opened up a range of new possibilities for local writers, musicians, and actors. Mr. Heller perhaps also foresaw these theatrical productions becoming crucial vehicles for "local self-awareness,"[57] for the more mingling of Afro-Brazilian music into basically foreign musical models, the higher was Cariocas's interest in the revistas. And Mr. Heller was correct. Revistas turned out to be one of the few places in imperial Rio de Janeiro where the complex interplay between the European-minded Cariocas and the Afro-Brazilian culture that surrounded them was truly revealed.

Again, timing was a crucial factor. The success of Afro-Brazilian music in national operettas and revistas could only happen in the two decades before the abolition of slavery and the proclamation of the republic. *Orpheo*'s final fado took Cariocas by storm in 1868; the final tango from *A princeza dos Cajueiros* created a smashing hit in 1880; the closing jongo in *A mulher-homem* brought unprecedented numbers of Cariocas to the Theatro Sant'Anna in 1886. The success of these shows would surely not have been the same four decades earlier.

To be sure, the use of black dances in Rio de Janeiro theaters was not altogether a novelty. Black characters playing roles of musicians, dancers, and singers in comedies were not uncommon in local theaters and reflected a practice that went back to the Iberian Peninsula.[58] In eighteenth- and nineteenth-century Spain, blacks regularly took part in theatrical presentations as musicians, dancers, and singers, introducing dances such as the *cumbé* and *guineo* in the theater.[59] In Portugal, black vendors in the streets provided the earliest examples of street life transferred to the theater. In 1774, for example, the *Entremez da floreira* (1774) presented in the Teatro do Salitre described a scene of a black women selling mussels in the street and singing a song from "her land."[60] In Argentina, the music of blacks started to appear regularly in the theater in the days of the Rosas. With increasing numbers in the 1860s, farces including white musicians with black faces, in the manner of the American minstrelsy, were apparently very popular.[61] Similarly, in the second part of the nineteenth century, black characters, such as the *negrito* and the *mulata*, performed by white actors in black faces, appeared regularly in the Cuban *Teatro Vernáculo*.[62]

In Rio de Janeiro similar examples go back at least to the 1830s. On June 27, 1838, for instance, in the intermezzo of the play *Hum dos muitos*, the Portuguese Victor Porfirio de Borja performed with the Portuguese actress Graciosa Maria Candida de Souza a "Brazilian duet" composed by Gabriel Fernandes, which included a "comic" lundu.[63] Also in 1838, the Brazilian playwright Martins Pena closed his play, *O Juiz de Paz na roça*, with a "toccata and [cateretê] dance characteristic from the outskirts of Rio de Janeiro."[64] These comic *intermezzi* and final numbers occasionally including black dances were introduced in the imperial capital mostly by Portuguese *buffo* actors, who were also singers and dancers.[65] Keeping the traditional Portuguese *entremez*, their numbers invariably included a variety of songs and dances, from Portuguese *saloias*, to Spanish fandangos, *polos, seguidillas*, boleros, and tangos, to habaneras, a great majority of which had already been presented in Parisian theaters. Because Portuguese immigrants dominated the middle sectors of the local economy, they eventually became mediators between the aspirations of the upper high-class, European-minded Cariocas and the pleas of the black population and recently arrived immigrants. Their understanding and attentive participation in the interaction between foreign music and local context in the theater no doubt contributed to the success of their endeavors in the imperial capital.

Not different from the music presented in the opera house or in the bailes à Musard, these early inclusions of black dances in theatrical intermezzi and finales were a reflection of foreign trends imported to Rio de Janeiro from the Iberian Peninsula, mostly via Paris. Before the 1870s the presence of Afro-Brazilian music in the theater reflected more a fashion that tied Cariocas to Paris and to the Parisian curiosity about exotic cultures, rather than a need to represent the local Afro-Brazilian culture. Before *Orpheu*, the bits of black culture spread throughout short farces and musical acts were one of several comic additions to plays, presented as far out of context as possible, and were rarely a part of the plot. Actually, the black character is practically nonexistent before the 1860s. When present at all, the black characters received minor parts, appearing either as stereotypes of faithful and pitiful slaves, or as immoral and disruptive individuals, but rarely as representatives of their own culture.[66]

A good example is the 1857 play *O demonio familiar* (The Demon in the Family) by the Brazilian playwright José de Alencar, in which the main character is a black youngster, Pedro, a slave working as a ser-

vant in a middle-class Rio de Janeiro family. The function of his character was to create conflicts between couples, just to act as a match-
maker later to gain favors for himself. The similarity between the role
of Pedro and that of *Figaro* in Beaumarchais's plot is unmistakable:
both are indiscreet individuals, expert in "matching" games. The parallel is further confirmed in the end when Pedro enters the stage and
sings the aria "La calunia" from Rossini's *Il barbieri di Siviglia*. Because the character of Pedro serves as a focal point in a plot describing the goings-on of a white, middle-class family, his musical culture
is erased in favor of the familiar European operatic idiom.

It was not until the last two decades before the end of the monarchical regime, when abolitionists' voices started to enjoy resonance on
the political scene, that the Afro-Brazilian music presented on the theater started to have a role in the spectacle. Vasques's fado became so
influential exactly because it appeared on the scene at a time when
economic and social changes, both as a world phenomenon and as a
specifically Brazilian manifestation, started to strongly disrupt and
change the local status quo. Republican abolitionists, committed to
forming alliances with the black population, also felt compelled to
represent them, in the belief that by speaking in the name of Afro-
Brazilians they could delineate the roles of each party, emphasizing
authority and dependency. Thus, the constructed black music used in
finales in the comic theater, operettas, and revistas portrayed the Afro-
Brazilian character as joyful, resigned, and, at the same time, disordered and wicked. These final musical numbers were theatrical constructions as well as musical stereotypes of the Afro-Brazilian culture
in Rio de Janeiro presented as Other and perpetuated by the local
bourgeoisie as a caricature.[67] Furthermore, the recurring reference to
"rhythmic, bodily movements" in these songs and dances, and particularly on *"requebros,"* the female hip movement while dancing,
highlighted erotic bodies and sexual pursuits. While to some the music provided in these comic finales revealed a "touch of Brazilianess"
and an "enchantment that comes naturally from our people,"[68] they
actually revealed "an ideological construction of difference associated
with body type and color."[69] In the end, these theatrical constructions
allowed the status quo to place Afro-Brazilian musical practices and
culture in a "displacing logic," "emptied of meaning," to render their
real culture invisible, and to justify their social and economic positions within the new social order.[70] This image of Afro-Brazilian culture has been passed through generations and is still present to this

day. It is commonplace in contemporary Brazil to symbolically evoke the Afro-Brazilian dance, samba, as "festive, joyful, wicked, and resigned," and as the solution for times of social and economic difficulty. The popular saying that "in Brazil everything ends in samba" indeed has precedents that go back to the 1870s and 1880s, a time when everything first ended in a cancan, and then in fados, tangos, and jongos.

There is but scarce data on the ethnicity of those performing these theatrical dances and songs. In the advertisement for a parody of Verdi's *Aida*, presented on January 1883, there is a reference to the participation of "negras bahianas, moleques, negrinhas" (black bahianas and black children).[71] While it is very possible that Afro-Brazilians were actually on stage in these productions, they were certainly not as "active subjects or agents of their culture."[72] The local political and cultural elite used these mediated theatrical numbers to act as spokespersons for them. One of the ways that Carioca intellectuals and politicians brought legitimacy to their role as spokespersons for the Afro-Brazilian population was by acknowledging that the Brazilian (national) culture could somehow be equated with the Afro-Brazilian element—acknowledgment that frequently appeared in the words of newspaper critics when praising the music in theatrical final numbers. Of course, there was a catch. To foster the desired "new urban musical aesthetic"[73] that satisfied the needs of the new status quo, the black number had to coexist on stage with the European musical model, a coexistence that in a twisted way ended up revealing synchronies as well as oppositions.[74] In the case of Vasques's fado, the association with the French "infernal dance," the indecent and rebellious cancan came in handy. Afterwards, the misrepresentation of Afro-Brazilian culture in finales as constantly joyful, disordered, and wicked, and the association with sexual "rhythmic movements" and "primitivism," became particularly emphasized when it appeared side by side with operatic numbers by European composers, those who in the minds of Cariocas were the holders of "civilization" and power.

The pseudo-transparent politics of ethnic representation in the theater in the two decades preceding the abolition of slavery becomes particularly emphasized and contradictory when one looks at how black culture was actually neither accepted nor understood during that same period. If some saw the popularity of theatrical black dances and songs as a way to embrace Afro-Brazilian culture, it was exactly because it was heavily mediated and decontextualized. Outside the theater, capoeiras were still considered outlawed, and *batuques*, associated with black pagan religious practices, were persecuted almost daily.[75] References to them were also abundant in Rio de Janeiro nineteenth-century newspapers: not in the entertainment section, but in police reports.

NOTES

1. *Jornal do commercio,* April 6, 1865. The ideas in the following three sections of this chapter are also articulated in Cristina Magaldi's "Music, Politics, and Satire" in the forthcoming Malena Kuss, ed., *The Universe of Music: A History.*

2. Siegfried Kracauer, *Orpheus in Paris* (New York: Alfred A. Knopf, 1938), 148.

3. Kracauer, *Orpheus in Paris,* 148–50.

4. For information on the social, economic, and political changes in the 1870s and 1880s see Emília Viotti da Costa, "Brazil: 1870–1889," in *Brazil: Empire and Republic, 1822–1930,* ed. Leslie Bethell (Cambridge: Cambridge University Press, 1989), 161–213.

5. The social and political tensions brought about by the Paraguayan war are discussed in Richard Graham, "Brazil: 1850–1870," in *Brazil: Empire and Republic, 1822–1930,* 153.

6. *Jornal do commercio,* June 9, 1866.

7. Procópio Ferreira, *O ator Vasques* (Rio de Janeiro: FUNARTE, Serviço Nacional do Teatro, 1979 [1938]), 97.

8. Kracauer, *Orpheus in Paris,* 29–32.

9. Kracauer, *Orpheus in Paris,* 29–32.

10. *Jornal do commercio,* March 3, 1866.

11. *Jornal do commercio,* February 8, 1880.

12. *A vida fluminense,* December 9, 1871.

13. Leonardo Alfonso de Miranda, *Jornal do commercio,* June 30, 1866.

14. Pereira, *O carnaval das letras* (Rio de Janeiro: Coleçao Biblioteca Carloca, 1994), 123–24.

15. Pereira, *O carnaval das letras,* 121.

16. Pereira, *O carnaval das letras,* 149.

17. According to Jota Efegê, the English word *puff* was used by the Sociedades Carnavalescas meaning "to blow with great arrogance"; see *Maxixe, a dança excomungada* (Rio de Janeiro: Conquista, 1974), 21.

18. *Jornal do commercio,* February 19, 1871.

19. *Jornal do commercio,* February 19, 1871.

20. *Jornal do commercio,* January 25, 1875.

21. Vasques's biography and the full text of *Orpheo na roça* is published in Ferreira, *O ator Vasques.*

22. Baptista Siqueira, *Três vultos históricos da música brasileira: Mesquita, Callado, Anacleto* (Rio de Janeiro: D. Araujo, 1970), 79. The advertisement for the printed version of Boucquet's *tango avanais* appeared in the *Jornal do commercio* of May 31, 1863. For more information on tangos in Brazil see Paulo Roberto Peloso Augusto, "Os tangos urbanos no Rio de Janeiro: 1870–1920, uma análise histórica e musical," *Revista música* 8/1–2 (São Paulo, May–November, 1997): 105–28.

23. An example is Francisco Asenjo Barbieri's zarzuela *El relampago* (1857), which became popular at the Theatro Phenix Dramatica in the early 1870s and included a "tango dos pretos" and concluded with a "tango havaneiro," *Jornal do commercio,* July 10, 1870.

24. According to José Ramos Tinhorão, the fado dance emerged in Rio de Janeiro at the end of the eighteenth century. Apparently a reference to the dance appeared in the 1825 book *Voyage autour du monde . . .* by the French Louis Claude Desaulces de Freycinet, who visited Rio de Janeiro in 1818. In his romance *Memórias de um Sargento de milícias* (1854–1855), Manuel Antônio de Almeida offers a most detailed description of the dance; see Tinhorão *Fado: dança do Brasil, cantar de Lisboa; o fim de um mito* (Lisbon: Editorial Caminho, 1994), 49–54.

25. References to these dances in titles of sheet music publications are intertwined, and later further tangled with imported dance titles such as tango and habanera. The word *lundu* appears in late eighteenth- and early nineteenth-century sources as "dança de negros" (dance of the blacks) and is often interchanged with batuque. Apparently both have Bantu (from Angola) origins. While "batuques" were often heard in the slave quarters and in plantations, the lundu was later stylized and performed with a songlike character in the parlor and in intermezzi and finales in the theater. In the nineteenth century, *batuques* also became a generic word to describe black dances associated with religious practices.

26. The word *cateretê* was used interchangeably with fado in sheet music publications, possibly because of the kinship in terms of instrumentation (viola accompaniment) and choreography, which involved foot tapping and hand clapping. The word cateretê was also used in nineteenth-century periodical literature to generically refer to dance gatherings in the countryside. Although the *Enciclopédia de música brasileira* defines the cateretê as a dance with Amerindian roots, several nineteenth-century Brazilian operettas and *revistas* (reviews) included a cateretê in the context of an African-derived musical gathering in the countryside. The use of musical instruments derived from the Iberian peninsula (such as the viola and the guitar) suggests their appropriation by Afro-Brazilians.

27. Quoted in José Ramos Tinhorão, *Os sons dos negros no Brasil* (São Paulo: Art Editora, 1988), 63.

28. Pereira, *O carnaval das letras*, 121.

29. *Jornal do commercio,* February 8, 1880.

30. For information on França Junior see Edwaldo Cafezeiro, Carmem Gadelha, and Maria de Fátima Saadi, eds., *Teatro de França Júnior* (Rio de Janeiro: FUNARTE, Serviço Nacional de Teatro, 1980).

31. Mesquita returned to Brazil from Paris in 1866 and worked as trumpeter at the Alcazar Lyrico Fluminense. After 1869, Mesquita frequently conducted the orchestra of the Theatro Phenix Dramática, where he was appointed chief conductor in 1872. In 1872, apart from his duties in the theater, Mesquita was appointed teacher at the Imperial Conservatory, and organist and composer for S. Pedro church. Mesquita was one of the Brazilians composers best represented in local publishers' catalogues; he was a versatile composer, leaving many sacred pieces as well as operettas. For a biography of Mesquita see Siqueira, *Três vultos históricos da música brasileira,* 35–90.

32. *El Arreglito* is part of Yradier's collection *Fleurs d'Espagne, Chanson Espagnoles* (no. 3).

33. *Diario de noticias*, August 10, 1871.

34. Early printed music for these numbers are extant in Music Division, Biblioteca Nacional in Rio de Janeiro.

35. See Augusto, "Os tangos urbanos no Rio de Janeiro," 109.

36. *Jornal do commercio*, March 8, 1881.

37. Because the nickname for the emperor was well known, it had to be changed to El-Rei Tatu during the operetta's premiere.

38. Noronha provided incidental music for the 1843 Rio de Janeiro premiere of Almeida Garret's *Um auto de Gil Vicente* (1838); for the commemoration of Pedro II's coronation (1843), Noronha's music substituted for the original French score of *O triumpho de Trajano,* an old French *tragédie lyrique* by Esmenard (first performed in Paris in 1807 with luxurious scenery and music by Persuis and Lessueur); see Décio de Almeida Prado, *João Caetano: o ator, o empresário, o repertório* (São Paulo: Editora Perspectiva, Editora da Universidade de São Paulo, 1972), 58–59.

39. The following are dramas and short comic acts with music by Noronha: *Arthur*, vaudeville in two acts (1843); *A graça de Deos; O artista e o soldado; A filha do cego; Cosimo—la na minha aldea . . . já de pansa cheia.*

40. *Jornal do commercio*, March 8, 1881.

41. *Jornal do commercio*, March 8, 1881.

42. While the text for *A princeza dos Cajueiros* has been reprinted several times—mostly due to the scholarly interest in Arthur de Azevedo's literary works—only one printed piano arrangement for "Amor tem Fogo" is extant in Brazil. The autographed score for the operetta is housed in the Lisbon Conservatório Nacional; see Ernesto Vieira, *Diccionario biographico de musicos*

portuguezes (Lisbon: Typographia M. Moreira & Pinheiro, 1900), II, 134. The manuscript parts for the entire operetta, formerly in a private collection, were donated to the Biblioteca Nacional at Rio de Janeiro in 1996.

43. *Jornal do commercio*, October 7, 1880.

44. *Jornal do commercio*, October 7, 1880.

45. *Jornal do commercio,* January 18 and 23, 1885.

46. For the history of the *revistas* in Brazilian theaters see Flora Süssekind, *As revistas de ano e a invenção do Rio de Janeiro* (Rio de Janeiro: Editora Nova Fronteira, 1986); Neyde Veneziano, *O teatro de revista no Brasil: dramaturgia e convenções* (Campinas, Spain: Editora da Universidade Estadual de Campinas, 1991); and Roberto Ruiz, *Teatro de revista no Brasil: do início à I guerra mundial* (Rio de Janeiro: INACEN, 1988).

47. Veneziano, *O teatro de revista no Brasil*, 87–92.

48. According to Ruiz, *O mandarim* "started the process of imposition of the revista [in Rio de Janeiro;]" see *Teatro de revista no Brasil,* 20.

49. *Jornal do commercio*, January 9 and February 1, 1884.

50. Among Azevedo and Sampaio revistas that became large successes before the proclamation of the republic include *Cocota* (1885), *O Bilontra* (1886), and *O Carioca* (1886).

51. Faria, *Idéias Teatrais*, 167.

52. *Jornal do commercio*, January 13, 1886.

53. Although it is clear that the word *maxixe* is used here as a general term for a gathering that included tangos, fados, and jongos, the word was already being used to designate a choreography and a dance that had similar characteristics to the fado, tango, and so on. For a documentary study on the emergence of the *maxixe* in Rio de Janeiro, see Efegê, *Maxixe,* 5.

54. *Jornal do commercio* February 13 and 16, 1886.

55. *Jornal do commercio,* February 25, 1886.

56. Faria, *Idéias teatrais: o século XIX no Brasil*, 167.

57. Augusto, "Os tangos urbanos no Rio de Janeiro," 107.

58. Earlier accounts abound of music composed in Latin America with generic titles of *negro, negritos,* and *guineos*; see Robert Stevenson, "The Afro-American Musical Legacy to 1800," *Musical Quarterly*, LIV/4 (October 1968): 475–502; and "Black Dance Types in Spanish Dominions, 1540–1820," *Inter-American Music Review* IX/2 (Spring–Summer 1988): 105–13.

59. See Fernando Ortiz, *Los negro curros* (La Habana: Editorial de Ciencias Sociales, 1986); quoted in Tinhorão, *Fado*, 18–19.

60. Intermezzo attributed to Leonardo José Pimenta e Antas; see Tinhorão, *Os sons dos negros do Brasil*, 43–36 and 39. The text of the intermezzo is reproduced in Tinhorão, *Fado*, 34–35.

61. Vicente Gesualdo, *Historia de la música en Argentina* (Buenos Aires: Editorial Beta, 1961), vol. 2, 870–73.

62. Robin D. Moore, *Nationalizing Blackness: Afrocubanismo and Artistic Revolution in Havana, 1920–1940* (Pittsburgh: University of Pittsburgh Press, 1997), 45–56.

63. *Jornal do commercio*, June 27, 1838.

64. *Jornal do commercio*, October 3, 1838. When staged again in 1877, the presentation emphasized the end of the second number as a cateretê and *fado de roda* "with guitar, and pandeiros, according to the customs of the countryside." *Jornal do commercio*, March 4, 1877.

65. For information on Portuguese *buffo* actors in nineteenth-century Rio de Janeiro, see Prado, *João Caetano*, 11.

66. Miriam Garcia Mendes, *A personagem negra no teatro brasileiro (1838–1888)* (São Paulo: Editora Ática, 1982), 174–201. For an analysis of blacks as themes in nineteenth-century Brazilian literature and poetry, see Raymond S. Sayers, *The Negro in Brazilian Literature* (New York: Hispanic Institute in the United States, 1956), 65–222.

67. Moore makes similar observations regarding the presence of black characters in the Cuban *Teatro Vernáculo*; see *Nationalizing Blackness*, 45.

68. *Jornal do commercio*, February 15, 1886.

69. Ronald Radano and Philip V. Bohlman, "Introduction: Music and Race, Their Past, Their Presence," in *Music and the Racial Imagination*, ed. Ronaldo Radano and Philip V. Bohlman (Chicago: University of Chicago Press, 2000), 5.

70. Aparicio, "Ethnifying Rhythm, Feminizing Cultures," in *Music and the Racial Imagination*, ed. Ronaldo Radano and Philip V. Bohlman (Chicago: University of Chicago Press, 2000), 107 and 99.

71. *Jornal do commercio*, January 2, 1883.

72. Aparicio, "Ethnifying Rhythm, Feminizing Cultures," 96.

73. Augusto, "Os tangos urbanos no Rio de Janeiro," 105.

74. Augusto, "Os tangos urbanos no Rio de Janeiro," 107.

75. The following reports were found daily in the local newspapers: "Yesterday, those who followed the music band making capoeiragem exercises were taken into police custody," *Jornal do commercio*, January 24, 1875. "The residents continue to complain about the noise of a nearby batuque in the region near the beach. The foot tapping and hand clapping and enthusiastic singing are so loud that no one can sleep," *Jornal do commercio*, February 4, 1880. For police persecution of Afro-Brazilian culture during the Second Empire, see Carlos Eugênio Líbano Soares, *A negrada instituição: os capoeiras na corte imperial, 1850–1890* (Rio de Janeiro: Access Editora, 1999).

Chapter 5

The National, the European, the Local, and the Foreign

FOREIGN MUSIC AS A NATIONAL SYMBOL

In March 1870, Cariocas received two pieces of good news: first, they heard about the defeat of the Paraguayan troops in the South and the death of Paraguayan leader Solano López. As with the rest of the Brazilian population, Cariocas had a lot to celebrate, for the victory not only asserted the country's hegemony in the southern cone, but also ended a lengthy conflict that had exacerbated internal political strife and left a mark on the local economy. Only nineteen days later, another piece of good news reached the imperial capital: the successful premiere in the Teatro La Scala in Milan of the opera *Il Guarany* (1870) by the Brazilian composer Antônio Carlos Gomes. Gomes's international triumph added immensely to the already fervent feeling of national pride. After all, he was the first Brazilian to win acclaim as an international composer and thus to elevate Brazil to the status of "civilized" nation. Gomes was then welcomed back to Rio de Janeiro as a national hero and his *Il Guarany* was received as an object for patriotic display.

While the timing of the opera's Italian premiere launched *Il Guarany* on the path of becoming a national icon, the opera's libretto is also said to have contributed to the process. Based on the Brazilian nineteenth-century Indianist novel *O Guarani* (1857) by José de Alencar, the opera's plot tells the story of the love of a Guarany Indian, Peri, for the daughter of a Portuguese nobleman, Ceci, and thus glorifies the formation of the Brazilian race through the unification of the Amerindian and the European. Paradoxically, given the work's seemingly nationalistic plot, *Il Guarany*'s musical language was conspicuously modeled on the contemporary Italian operatic idiom. And since there was nothing particularly Brazilian about the music, twentieth-century Brazilian nationalists were quick to target Gomes as a mere composer of foreign music.[1]

These contradictory roles that Gomes's *Il Guarany* has historically fulfilled reflect the distinct agendas that have guided the local "cultural managers"—politicians and intellectuals—over the years. The controversy is in itself telling, for it shows the different meanings ascribed to the notion of "nationalness" at a time when the idea of national identity in Brazil was just starting to be negotiated. The history of *Il Guarany*'s reception in the imperial capital and in Europe shows the conflicting roles that Gomes's music had to fulfill to satisfy the needs of audiences "here" and "there." Most importantly, the opera serves as a unique example of the ways in which nineteenth-century Cariocas perceived the European musical language as part of their own cultural fabric.

Although not a native of Rio de Janeiro, Gomes left his provincial home city of Campinas (state of São Paulo) in June 1859, and went to the capital to study music in the imperial conservatory. He arrived with a considerable musical background acquired through his father, who was the director of the Campinas band. But it was in Rio de Janeiro that Gomes was first exposed to staged versions of Italian and French operas in vogue, from Rossini, Bellini, Donizetti, and Verdi, to Auber and Meyerbeer. Opera soon became central in Gomes's musical studies and in his career as a composer. He deeply absorbed the idea of music and opera as a single entity and rapidly grasped the prestige attached to the imported genre.

Significantly, the period of Gomes's stay in Rio de Janeiro coincided with the most productive years of the Academia Imperial de Música e Opera Nacional (Imperial Academy of Music and National Opera) (1857–1863), later Opera Lyrica Nacional (National Opera). An institution organized by the Spanish immigrant José Amat (1810?–1870?) and the Brazilian composer Francisco Manuel da Silva, the academia had the patronage of the imperial government and prominent members of the local society.[2] The goal of the Opera Lyrica Nacional was to promote the performance of operas in Portuguese—translations of Italian and French operas and operettas, and Spanish zarzuelas—and to commission operas with librettos on Brazilian subjects. While the use of the Portuguese language reinforced the connection between the imported music and a larger spectrum of the audience, librettos based on Brazilian history were greatly valued by Carioca critics who argued for their native character.[3] The Opera Lyrica Nacional also provided the means for local composers to master the imported musical idiom and offered lessons for local singers, helping them perform side by side with foreign divas. In short, the Opera Lyrica Nacional equipped Rio de Janeiro with the means to produce homemade European opera. In 1863, the imperial sponsors merged the Opera Lyrica Nacional with the Italian Lyric company, forming the Opera Nacional e Italiana (National and Italian Opera). As one entity, the institution received from the government, in 1863 alone, the proceeds from no fewer than thirteen lotteries. In spite of the political dispute involved in the Opera Lyrica Nacional,[4] in six years, Amat managed to present a long list of operas and zarzuelas translated into Portuguese. The Opera Lyrica Nacional also produced two original operas by foreign composers living in Brazil and five by Brazilians, including two works by the young Carlos Gomes: *A noite do castelo* (1861, libretto by José Fernandes Reis), dedicated to Pedro II, and *Joana de Flandres* (1863, libretto by Salvador de Mendonça), which earned him a scholarship to study in Europe.

Gomes left Rio de Janeiro for Milan in 1863, after signing a fellowship contract with the Brazilian government that required him to send to Rio de Janeiro at least one large work to be performed by the Opera Lyrica Nacional. During Gomes's early years in Italy he produced a few short *intermezzi* for comic plays that were quite successful, but only with *Il Guarany*, a full-length opera in the dominant musical language, was he able to fulfill the terms of his fellowship contract. While in Italy, however, Gomes gave away his previous plan for a Rio de Janeiro premiere for *Il Guarany* in favor of a more daring performance at the famous Teatro La Scala—daring because, in Italy, Gomes faced expectations of a different nature than in Rio de Janeiro. In Milan, he found an Italian translation of Alencar's novel and started to work with an Italian librettist to set music to *Guarani, storia dei selvaggi del brasile.*[5]

Drawing inspiration from the Italian success of Meyerbeer's *L'Africaine* (1865), which premiered in Milan on March 1, 1866, Gomes consciously explored the exotic aspect of *Il Guarany*'s subject matter in order to appeal to Italian audiences. Granted a generous subsidy by Pedro II to cover the high costs of the Italian production,

Gomes enhanced the exotic scenery by including specially crafted indigenous instruments made to order for the opera's *bailado* (ballet).[6] The work, premiered on March 19, 1870, attracted the attention of international critics exactly because of the Brazilian plot and the exotic aspects of the performance mise en scène. Gomes's Brazilian nationality was itself a reason for general curiosity in the Italian press, which reviewed the opera favorably, highlighting that Gomes was a *selvaggi del brasile,*[7] "a savage who can write opera!"

Il Guarany premiered in the imperial capital on December 2, 1870, a presentation honored by the presence of Emperor Pedro II. Gomes, who assisted in the rehearsals, manifested his own bias against his "uncivilized" fellow citizens, with fierce complaints that the local singers and dancers acted "[like] frogs, jumping instead of dancing," and that the cast "consisted of soldiers from Rio de Janeiro's headquarters." Skeptical about the performance, he mentioned to his friend Carlo D'Ormeville that "the premiere will undoubtedly be an event for laughter."[8] But that was not the case, at least not according to the local chronicles. A contemporary commentator reported that on the opening night, "Commotion and delirium invaded the audience; the composer was called back in the stage eight or ten times; . . . D. Pedro II was moved, he called [Gomes] into his box and enthusiastically praised Gomes and his *Il Guarany.*"[9]

The local press continually praised the composer and the opera. Yet, such a warm welcome was hardly an expression of impartial acceptance. *Il Guarany's* success in Rio de Janeiro lay above all in its previous validation by the Italian audience at the La Scala premiere. Gomes's initial success in Rio de Janeiro was primarily a result of his international image. Henrique Alves de Mesquita, also a recipient of a grant by the imperial government in 1857, had sent some works from Paris, including an opera, *O vagabundo,* staged in the Theatro Lyrico Fluminense in 1863. Mesquita's opera had limited resonance in the imperial capital, apparently because the work was not based on a Brazilian subject, but most probably because it did not reach the Parisian stage and therefore had no international status.[10]

The immense success of *Il Guarany's* premiere in imperial Rio de Janeiro did not happen without a few glitches, however. Some dared to complain that the work was "boring," others even speculated about the similarity between the beginning of the *bailado* and Offenbach's *La belle Hélène,* and between Cecilia's *ballada* (ballad) and a lo-

cal *modinha* (lyrical song with Portuguese text).[11] Belligerent about
the libretto, the author of the novel, José de Alencar, commented to
a friend that, "Gomes made a big mess out of my *Guarani*, [it is now]
full of nonsense . . . [Gomes made] Ceci sing duets with the Aimoré
cacique, who offers her the throne of his tribe, and convinced Peri to
be the lion [king] of our forests."[12]

It was precisely the subject matter of *Il Guarany*'s libretto that most
disturbed the local audience. If Cariocas shared the Italians's appreciation for the exotic in *Il Guarany*'s libretto and the work's mise en
scène, the portrayal of the native Brazilian as the exotic Other in the
opera was viewed with reservation. Not that they felt uncomfortable
exoticizing the native in the opera house. Rio de Janeiro elite were re-
luctant to accept the image of the savage as praiseworthy, for the real
thing was very near them and threatened their view of themselves as
Europeans. The feeling was not a new one. In 1861, commenting on
the work of a local composer who attempted to write an opera based
on the history of the Indians in Brazil, Machado de Assis declared that
"I'm not one of those who make faces when an indigenous enters the

Figure 5.1.   "Oh God, what is this! A savage in my box? This is not a savage, Sr.
Selmi, but the tenor who, after having enchanted our ears, now come to disen-
chant our pockets." *A vida fluminense* (December 1870). Young Research Library,
UCLA.

scene. . . . I do not want to know to which nation or civilization the characters belong to."[13] That was not the case in 1870. While the elite were reserved about *Il Guarany*'s libretto the press was quick to mockingly equate the "Aimorés [Indians] that sing on the stage" to the "[Indians] that applaud in the audience."[14] The idea of a tenor dressed as an Indian, "in costume," singing in Italian did strike Cariocas as an unpleasant contradiction, as they realized the threatening situation of a "savage" invading the sanctuary of their opera house.

Nonetheless, if the Indian character Peri made Cariocas uncomfortable, the opera's very "familiar" bel canto melodies, sung in Italian, made up for the few initial flaws and boosted *Il Guarany*'s general approval. It was exactly the work's foreign musical language, and not its exotic libretto, that Carioca elite appreciated the most. For writing an opera was an exercise in aligning Brazil with Europe. Gomes's task was not to display Brazilian uniqueness in terms of musical language, but to attempt some kind of equivalence with European composers—to produce music as good as, understood in this sense to be as similar as possible to, imported operas brought to Rio de Janeiro by European lyric companies. There was no contradiction in asserting Brazilianess exactly by stressing a European connection. Carioca critics never recalled the foreignness of Gomes's work as cause for distaste. On the contrary, a comparison with Verdi always was to Gomes's advantage.

Yet, the writing of a good Italian opera did not automatically bring national fame to Gomes. To become an icon in Brazil, he and his opera *Il Guarany* had to be in the right place at right time. That the premiere of the work in Milan coincided with the defeat of Paraguayan troops in the south was just one of the ingredients that boosted the work as a national icon. *Il Guarany* premiered in Rio de Janeiro as a gala event, part of the celebrations of the Emperor's birthday. At the same time, Cariocas heard the opera one day before the publication of the manifesto of the Republican Party, which was signed by no fewer than three enthusiastic devotees and organizers of the Opera Lyrica Nacional: Quintino Bocayuva, Saldanha Marinho, and Salvador de Mendonça.[15] Thus, as Marcus Góes perceptively points out, while *Il Guarany* marked the zenith of the Brazilian Empire, it also announced the ascendance of the Republican Party.[16] In the midst of such passionate moments, Peri's "savage" character was overlooked and the focus was switched to his heroic acts, narrated in the elegant Italian operatic language. To Cariocas, *Il Guarany* recalled Verdi's popular midcentury operas, which were loaded with ideas of unification and moments of patriotic display.

A few months after the opera's premiere, Gomes replaced the original overture with a new sinfonia, or *Protofonia*, as it is known today. Looking for an introduction that would have a better effect as an opening to the opera, Gomes carefully chose popular excerpts of the work and pasted them together, following a common practice in nineteenth-century Italian operas. At the time the new sinfonia was added, the opera already carried with it a whole set of symbols associated with glory, heroism, and national pride, and the new sinfonia was born already embodying those meanings. To enhance that effect, in the work's very opening Gomes used a fanfarelike short section that displayed all the musical effects one has historically associated with civic events. Since then, the *Protofonia* from *Il Guarany* has been regularly performed in Brazil in moments of national unity, sometimes even substituting for the national anthem.[17]

The path followed by *Il Guarany* in becoming a symbol of national identity in Brazil was a process not altogether clear for those twentieth-century intellectuals who were sure to find a symbol of Brazilianess in the popular music of the streets, never in an imported elite music such as opera. Viewed by historians solely as a work destined to fulfill the aspirations of the local elite, Viotti da Costa noted that *Il Guarany* represented "not only the divorce between upper and lower classes but the alienation of the intelligentsia from a country in which 79 percent of the adult free population did not know how to read or write."[18]

This interpretation, while socially and statistically correct, overlooks one important aspect of the opera's reception. The history of *Il Guarany*'s staged performances, with their unilateral evocation of national pride, does not offer a complete picture of the work's popularity. Outside the opera house, excerpts from *Il Guarany* soon emerged as fantasies for the piano and later served as popular dance tunes that circulated widely in sheet music publications. Just one year after the opera's premiere in Rio de Janeiro, the catalogue of a major publishing house listed twelve instrumental fantasies inspired by its tunes.[19] Facilitated versions multiplied quickly, until tunes could be freely hummed in the streets. The popularity of *Il Guarany* continued to grow at the turn of the twentieth century, and by the 1930s, tunes from the opera were popular enough to be included in several Carnival marches and shared by several layers of the population.[20] It is fair to say that the spread of tunes from *Il Guarany* contributed immensely to boosting the operatic subculture that developed independently from the staged operas, librettos, and printed music, and that influenced, by oral transmission, popular musicians in the streets of the capital.

Gomes died unaware of his opera's power as a tool for national symbolism. After all, the work's musical language was unquestionably Italian, and the native elements of *Il Guarany* were the result of his attempts to impress Italian audiences rather than a preoccupation with characterizing Brazil musically. Having received financial support from Emperor Pedro II throughout his life, Gomes saw himself in great financial difficulty when the imperial patronage came to an end in 1889. Even so, he remained loyal to the imperial regime and refused an invitation to write the anthem for the new Republic. Nevertheless, outside his control *Il Guarany* became a national anthem anyway, a work that embodies the history of Brazil's attempts to define itself as an independent nation, exactly by aligning its culture with that of Europe. If, from an international vantage point, Gomes played a shadowy role in the general European music canon,[21] in the imperial capital it was exactly his international reputation and his skills as a composer of European/universal music that gained him recognition as a national icon.

IMPORTED MUSICAL NATIONALISM

The emphasis on opera did not detract Cariocas's attention from local melodies and rhythms. Local composers quickly adopted the ideas brought to Rio de Janeiro by European visitors and immigrants, who followed the trends in European romanticism. As foreigners, Europeans saw the local musical material from their own perspective: as exotic elements that contrasted with the European musical language and set it apart from the "civilized" music. Cariocas learned to use and appreciate their own local music accordingly. Thus, a decade before songs and dances of African derivation started to make a furor in the comic theater, they served as raw material for the earliest manifestations of a local romantic musical nationalism. However, compared with the comic theater, the local element inserted in piano pieces destined for the parlor had less explicit sociopolitical and ethnic connotations. As contradictory as it

may seem, the local musical material reinforced the connection between a European musical trend and the penchant for European musical fashions.

The Austrian composer Sigismund Neukomm, who visited Rio de
Janeiro between 1816 and 1821, was the first of a long list of European visitors inspired by the exotic in the local music: his fantasy for
flute and piano *L'Amoureux*, based on a lyrical modinha,[22] and his
caprice *L'amour brésilien*, which uses a local lundu, are in the Viennese classical style: after a short introduction the theme is followed
by sectional variations with only a few added ornaments and a constant *Alberti* bass accompaniment. Neukomm's early (Brazilian) "nationalistic" pieces, published by Breitkopf & Härtel in Leipzig upon
his return to Europe,[23] were apparently not immediately echoed in
Brazil, for neither the fantasy nor the caprice went on sale at any
contemporary Rio de Janeiro music outlet.

The idea nonetheless caught on. Early in the 1830s, the piano music of the French Henri Herz started to cross the Atlantic, achieving
great success in the New World.[24] Herz personally visited North and
South America giving concerts and selling his pianos. An accomplished composer of variations and fantasies on operatic themes, he
also mastered the virtuoso diplomacy of reaching out to foreign audiences by performing fantasies based on their local themes. His vis-
its to the United States, Mexico, Peru, Chile, and Brazil resulted in a
large number of such compositions.[25]

Herz's contact in Rio de Janeiro was Arthur Napoleão, whom he
had met in Paris and from whom Herz probably learned that the
imperial capital was an excellent market for both his piano compositions and his pianos.[26] Even before his New World tour, Herz had
dedicated his *Grand duo brillant sur um motif del'ópera L'elisire
d'amore*, for four hands, Op. 113, to "Leur Altesses Impériales
Donna Januaria et Donna Francisca, Princesses du Brésil" (Leipzig:
Breitkopf & Härtel, c. 1840).[27] Herz's polka *La brésilienne* Op. 195
(Meyence: Schott, 1860) circulated widely in Rio de Janeiro and
served as inspiration for a long list of piano dances titled "Brazilian
Polka" published in Rio de Janeiro during the second half of the
century.[28]

As with other European visitors, Herz was particularly intrigued
by the presence of African culture in the New World. In his 1866
book *Mes voyages en Amérique* (My Travels in America*)*, Herz
recorded his North American experiences with African American

music, indicating that he was also captivated by the music of blacks from Brazil:

> The banjo is the favorite instrument of the blacks in the United States, just as the marimba[29] is of the blacks of Brazil. . . . Negroes are very appreciative of music, and their souls are far from being closed to the beauties of poetry. . . . In obeying the need to put rhythm in their music the blacks act by some sort of instinct, and it is this very instinct for rhythm that has always intrigued philosophers and scientists.[30]

Apparently, Herz did not leave a musical account of his encounter with black culture, but several contemporary Parisians attempted their own musical interpretations of the African "instinct for rhythm" as described in Herz's memoirs. The Dutch composer and pianist Joseph Ascher is a case in point.[31] Settled in Paris in 1849, where he was active at courtly circles, Ascher was appointed pianist of Empress Eugénie, wife of Napoleon III. He was a prolific composer of piano music, profusely published, and well-accepted in Paris. Of particular interest were his pieces based on Iberian themes and his evocative compositions emulating African music.[32]

Although Ascher seems never to have visited Latin America, his piano compositions started to circulate in Rio de Janeiro as early as the 1850s, most probably because of his acquaintance with Arthur Napoleão, whom he had also met in Paris.[33] Ascher's pieces were advertised daily in Brazilian newspapers and were reprinted several times for more than twenty years. His *Danse nègre, caprice caracteristique*, Op. 109 (ca. 1860), for example, came out in *O Brasil musical* n° 553 (mid- to late 1860s). In this stylized dance Ascher emphasizes several drumlike effects, note repetitions, strong accentuation on first and third beats, extensive use of dotted notes, and syncopated rhythms to simulate in the piano the effects of the African music that he learned second-hand. His caprice lacks an introduction in the virtuoso fashion; instead, the opening twelve measures of his *Danse nègre* use the piano keyboard as a percussive instrument. A pentatonic tune and the repetition of the dotted quarter/eighth note rhythmic pattern also serve well his personal characterization of African music.

Ascher's *Dance nègre* and other similar pieces[34] were already circulating widely when, in 1869, the North American composer Louis Moreau Gottschalk arrived in the imperial capital. Reared in New

Musical Example 5.1. Ascher's *Danse nègre*. Biblioteca Nacional, Rio de Janeiro, Divisão de música e arquivo sonoro.

Orleans, Gottschalk studied in Paris from 1842 to 1850. He toured throughout his life, collecting tunes and using them in his piano fantasies: he was in Spain in 1851–1852; spent 1854 in Cuba; toured Cuba, Jamaica, Haiti, and Puerto Rico in 1857, returned to Havana in 1858; on September 18, 1865, he left for South America, visiting Lima, Santiago, and Buenos Aires, and arriving at Rio de Janeiro on May 3, 1869. Gottschalk's "Louisiana" pieces, using melodies and rhythms of African American flavor—*Le bananier* (1845–1846), *chanson nègre*; *La Savanne, ballade créole* (1845); and *Bamboula, dance nègre* (1844)—won the unconditional approval of Parisians. According to the rigorous critic Hector Berlioz, the pieces' "curious chants from the Creoles and Negroes" fulfilled Parisians's "restless and insatiable passion for novelty."[35] Accordingly, Gottschalk's pieces with African-American flavor, already circulating in the imperial capital before his arrival,[36] also satisfied Cariocas's urge for novelty, but, above all, they fulfilled Cariocas's Parisian aspirations.

With such impeccable Parisian credentials, and as another personal friend of Arthur Napoleão,[37] Gottschalk's success in Rio de Janeiro was thus somewhat predictable. He reported his astounding welcome by the imperial capital in a letter to a friend in Boston: "My concerts here are a perfect *furore*. All my houses are sold eight days in advance. . . . The Emperor, imperial family, and court never yet missed one of my entertainments."[38]

Gottshcalk's *Bamboula, danse de nègre, fantaisie pour piano*, Op. 2 (dedicated to Queen Isabele II of Spain) particularly attracted Cariocas. The title refers to the *Bamboula* dance, popular among the blacks of Louisiana and the West Indies, which was accompanied by drums bearing the same name. George W. Cable described the dance in 1886 as the "booming of African drums and blast of huge wooden horns."[39] *Bamboula*'s formal structure recalls the choreography of the dance, alternating between the dancelike refrain and more songlike middle sections, which make use of two Creole melodies that Gottschalk recalled from his childhood in New Orleans.[40] As with Ascher's *Dance nègre*, instead of an elaborate introduction typical of operatic fantasies, in the twelve opening measures of *Bamboula* Gottschalk uses the keyboard to evoke drumlike effects to emulate African music. There is little variation and no transformation of the refrain in its various presentations; only in the finale does the refrain appear amplified *con bravura*, in the style of operatic-fantasy finales.

The charm, therefore, resides in the transparency of the melodies, which are surrounded by refined pianistic elaboration such as the constant hand crossings necessary to maintain the rhythmic pattern of the bass and sustain the melody on top, producing an attractive visual effect. The magic of Gottschalk's *Bamboula*, as with other such pieces evoking African music, also lay in the exploration of dotted rhythms and syncopated formulae, along with extensive passages including note repetition and accentuations simulating drum performance. These rhythmic formulae and keyboard effects evoking drumming, surrounded by elegant virtuoso pianistic figurations, became almost a cliché for exploring African music as "exotic" in piano pieces destined for the Parisian parlor. Across the Atlantic, the Parisian provenance and the enchantment roused in Parisian audiences by the "exotic charm" of the pieces stimulated Cariocas's curiosity and swayed them to start doing the same. In this case, for the parallel to work, Cariocas had to be particularly discerning in their distinction between "here" and "there." For a Rio de Janeiro equivalence of the "exotic charm" of Afro-Brazilian music rendered in stylized piano music for the parlor had to rest on the pretense that the music to be enjoyed by the Carioca bourgeoisie as exotic was not really available in its authentic form right outside their windows. The pretense was necessary, for it not only helped Cariocas to relegate the genuine Afro-Brazilian musical practices to the realm of the invisible, but especially it allowed them not to miss the music's Parisian connection.

EXOTIC NATIONAL MUSIC

The Parisian publications of Ascher and Gottschalk were certainly familiar to the young Carlos Gomes. Before he left his home town for Rio de Janeiro in 1859, Gomes had published a piano piece titled *A cayumba, dansa de negros* (*Cayumba*, dance of blacks, 1856).[41] This piece later came out as part of a suite of dances titled *Quilombo, quadrilha sobre os motivos dos negros* (Quilombo, quadrille over black tunes, 1857–1858?),[42] consisting of four dances and a finale, similar in organization to the contemporary European quadrille. Instead of featuring English counterdances, *Quilombo* portrays the Afro-Brazilian heritage by including dances with the following titles: *Cayumba, Bananeira, Quingombô*, and *Bamboula*. Interestingly enough, two of the dances in *Quilombo* are not original Gomes compositions, but facilitated versions of Gottschalk's *Bamboula* and *Le bananier*. Without making any reference to the North American composer, Gomes rearranged *Bamboula* and *Bananeira* for the novice, transposing both pieces, eliminating repetitions, chords, octave doublings, and expression and pedal markings, but leaving Gottschalk's tunes and rhythmic accompaniments intact.

The first piece of the suite, *A cayumba*, is a facilitated version of Gomes's own dance, which, although original, has much in common with Gottschalk's *Bamboula* and *Le bananier*. The three-measure introduction is followed by the presentation of a pentatonic theme in a *tempo de chula*;[43] Gomes does not flinch from the constant rhythmic patterns and the repeated notes abundantly used in Ascher's and Gottschalk's pieces. The other dance in Gomes's suite, *Quingombô*, also appears to be an original composition, with a melody that resembles a *lundu*-song. The suite *Quilombô* closes with the traditional final section with motives deriving from the earlier pieces.

Pieces like *A cayumba* and *Quingombô*, stylized versions of Afro-Brazilian dances, were heavily mediated and dependent on an imported impetus; they were written for internal consumption, to be performed at local family gatherings and *saraus*, and for filling in theatrical intermissions. These works were perceived and recreated in the Rio de Janeiro parlor as European music with an exotic flavor, not as nationalistic pieces aiming to portray a distinctive musical language. Far from unique, the embodied "local" elements in these pieces were not regarded in imperial Rio de Janeiro as "national," or as significant contributions to the contemporary musical repertory.

SINGING IN PORTUGUESE

While the use of African-derived music as exotic elements within a European musical language had European counterparts, the use of the Portuguese language in songs was the sole domain of Brazilians, and by extension of Cariocas. Thus, there was nothing better to characterize a national song than the Portuguese language, a genuinely unique element added by local composers to the European music in vogue to reach a wider number of bourgeois amateurs.

The Rio de Janeiro market for songs in Portuguese never slackened. The first publishers, Laforge and Klier, foresaw the potential

A CAYUMBA*

dança dos negros para piano

Ao amigo E. Mareille

A. CARLOS GOMES

Musical Example 5.2. Gomes's *A Caymba* [1856] (Rio de Janeiro: Funarte, 1986). Reproduced by permission.

profits in commercializing native songs with Portuguese texts and started their business in the 1830s by investing in this genre. Müller's 1837 catalogue already offered lyrical songs in Portuguese by Gabriel Fernandes da Trindade, Cândido Ignácio da Silva, and Francisco Manuel da Silva.[44] By midcentury, all publishing firms in Rio de Janeiro devoted part of their business to songs with Portuguese texts: the most popular being modinhas, with their languid and lyric melodies in regular four-measure melodic lines, and characteristically ambiguous harmonies;[45] second came the lively lundu-songs, with their syncopated lines and melodic leaps that reshaped the Afro-Brazilian lundu dance for the parlor. In most cases, collections of modinhas and lundus came out with the words "Brazilian" or "national" in their titles to emphasize their native quality. In 1851, Filippone & Cia began publishing a series titled *Novo album de modinhas brasileiras*,[46] and three decades later the catalogue of Napoleão's collection entitled *Canto portuguez, collecção de romances, modinhas, lundus, etc.* (1890s), included no fewer than 200 songs with Portuguese texts by local composers.[47]

In addition to his work in the Opera Lyrica Nacional, the Spanish immigrant Amat was also a prolific composer of songs with Portuguese lyrics. During his stay in Rio de Janeiro he set to music a massive number of poems by Brazilians, including many by the prominent poet Antônio Gonçalves Dias (1823–1864). Ironically, Amat's masterwork in the genre was an album with a French title, *Mélodies brésiliennes* (Brazilian melodies), printed in Paris in 1852, and dedicated to the Empress Dona Thereza Maria Christina. This luxurious 123-page publication, bound with green velvet and gold and carrying the imperial symbols on the front cover, opens with "A canção do exílio," an early setting of Golçalves Dias's poem, which became a landmark in early literary romantic nationalism.[48]

The Portuguese immigrant Raphael Coelho Machado also left a considerable number of songs with Portuguese texts. Machado, who began in Rio de Janeiro as a music dealer and later served as organist in the Candelária Church, also taught piano, organ, voice, and composition privately.[49] But his most valued accomplishment was his early association of the use of the Portuguese language in songs and a unique national musical production. In his *Breve tratado d'harmonia* (1852), Machado includes a chapter "Poetry and music," in which he advocates the use of the Portuguese language in songs and provides instructions for setting music to Portuguese texts.[50] He strongly condemns Brazilian performers who "sing in a foreign language without knowing the meaning of the words," and criticizes composers even more severely:

> What bigger nonsense than composing in a strange idiom. . . . Concerning profane music, it is remarkable that every nation sings in its own language. . . . After Italian, the Portuguese language is the one most adequate for singing. . . . But to compose with Portuguese text one need not repeat the barbarisms which are evident in a great part of the compositions now in circulation.[51]

To solve the problem, Machado proposes basic rules of prosody to avoid cacophony and punctuation mistakes, and to improve thereby the standards of the local song.

Although he was the author of several modinhas, Machado believed that the Brazilian song, a song with Portuguese text, should be more sophisticated than the popular but "trivial modinhas and lundus." Like Amat, Machado preferred texts by renowned Brazilian poets, especially Gonçalves Dias and Joaquim Manuel de Macedo. The songs in his two collections, *Canto nacional* (ca. 1863), *Album de canto nacional* (ca. 1866) all favor styles such as romance, *recitativo*, *ballada*, and *melodia*, rather than modinha. Moreover, Machado's idea of a national (Brazilian) song did not stem from the musical language of the modinha, but from the direct adaptation of the melodic lines of Italian arias to the Portuguese language. He provided several practical examples in collections such as *Saudades da Norma* (Longing for *Norma*, 1850),[52] *O trovador brasileiro* (the Brazilian *Il trovatore*, 1857), and *Delicias da traviata* (Delights of *La traviata*, ca. 1856), where he adapted arias from Bellini and Verdi to Portuguese. Furthermore, in his laudable efforts to construct a genuinely national, Brazilian song Machado was also careful not to lose the link with the European element; in his publications of "national" songs he provided both Portuguese and Italian versions of the lyrics.

Machado's attempt to promote the use of Portuguese was reliant on the "high standards" that informed his parallel between national song and European arias. Because the use of Portuguese in songs was viewed as secondary to the "natural" Italian language, Machado's preaching fitted perfectly the cultural agenda of the status quo. For his idea of a national song not only permitted a far-reaching spread of the European song style, but it also reinforced the power of the

Carioca political and cultural elite in maintaining their agency in the management of the local culture vis à vis the European. In other words, the accessibility provided by the familiar language was welcomed, so long as it did not interfere with the music's Europeaness. Machado's efforts to institutionalize a local song by inserting Portuguese in the husk of a European musical genre were in essence not different from the idea behind one of the most revered music institutions of the Second Empire: the Imperial Academia de Música e Ópera Nacional (and Opera Lyrica Nacional). Despite the claim of some organizers of the Opera Lyrica Nacional that "music is not the same in all nations" and that "Brasil has its own music, cultivated and worth our great civilization,"[53] by encouraging the translations of operas, operettas, and zarzuelas to make European music accessible on a larger scale, the director of the Academia and his patrons also geared a local music production toward the maintenance of the European musical language. Within this context, it was not at all out of place that the first production of the Opera Lyrica Nacional was not an opera based on a Brazilian story, or a work that incorporated popular, native tunes. Instead, they offered Cariocas Joaquín Romualdo Gaztambide's (1822–1870) zarzuela *La estrea de un artista* translated into Portuguese as *A estreia de um artista.* The work, which premiered in the Theatro Gymnasio Dramatico on July 17, 1857, was followed, on August 31, by Francisco Asenjo Barbieri's *Jugar con fuego,* translated into Portuguese as *Brincar com fogo.*[54] A long list of zarzuelas and Italian operas translated into Portuguese followed; they were to be received, if not as national operas—following the name of the institution—surely as familiar, "nationalized" European musical works.

Given this emphasis on singing in Portuguese, it seems paradoxical that Carlos Gomes's choice for a libretto in Italian for his opera rather than one in Portuguese, for *Il Guarany* rather than *O Guarani,* fostered more than hindered the work's acceptance in imperial Rio de Janeiro. If, from today's vantage point, the Italian libretto might be perceived as a major impediment to the opera's Brazilianess, in the 1870s it was quite the opposite. Italian was still the most "natural" language for singing; Portuguese came second. As Góes points out, even if Gomes was interested in a Brazilian story and originally had in mind a Rio de Janeiro premiere, he had envisioned an Italian libretto from the beginning.[55] The Italian translation of Alencar's novel that Gomes found in Milan, *Guarani, storia dei selvaggi del brasile*, and his work with an Italian librettist to set music to the Italian version of Alencar's novel, was thus part of the original inception of the opera. Every nineteenth-century opera composer aspiring to a successful international career, regardless of their nationality, preferred librettos in Italian to facilitate presentations in European capitals. Gomes was no exception. Portuguese translations would eventually follow, but the original work had to be conceived in the "natural" operatic idiom that enjoyed a higher status.[56] In fact, Gomes's deliberate choice for *Il Guarany* was part of the opera's appeal for the Carioca elite, whose unequivocal taste for things European let them immediately identify with an opera in Italian. Only in 1937, more than sixty years after the Rio de Janeiro premiere, was a Portuguese translation of *Il Guarany* published by Carlos Marinho de Paula Brito. The translation, however, did not gain public acceptance and was actually the reason for much local debate and discontentment.[57] The unwillingness to accept a Portuguese version of *Il Guarany* lay in the attempt to provide the opera with a local association that clashed with the work's very foundation. Gomes was educated in Rio de Janeiro toward building compositional skills to produce European music. He was not a composer of Brazilian music, but a Brazilian composer of (Italian) opera, even if the two overlapped at some point. To audiences in imperial Rio de Janeiro the use of the Portuguese language in Gomes's *Il Guarany* would hinder the international, and consequently the national, appeal of the work.

A FLEXIBLE BORDER

The ambiguous nineteenth-century perception of *Il Guarany* as both a national (local) and a foreign (European) work was also manifested in its predominantly Italian musical language. The lack of local musical elements in a work deemed national by both monarchists and republicans always troubled twentieth-century Brazilian nationalists, whose ideological construction of a national Brazilian culture was based on a putative synthesis of European, Native American, and Afro-Brazilian elements. Accordingly, Gomes's Italian musical language and the nineteenth-century penchant for operatic music in Rio de Janeiro only asserted an aspect of the local culture that needed to be remedied. Hence, to guarantee Gomes's music a role in the history of Brazilian music, twentieth-century music historians have attempted, without much success, to demonstrate *Il Guarany*'s "hidden" nationalistic musical elements. Mário de Andrade saw a "native feeling" in Gomes's music, including "a few coincidences with our popular melodies."[58] Ironically, it was exactly the modinha-like character of Ceci's aria that was singled out by those who attended the opera's early presentations in Rio de Janeiro as an example of the work's lack of originality.[59] To them any association with the local was an unwelcome tinting of a truly Italian opera. And since for a composer from the Southern Hemisphere producing an opera was to follow the European path to development and progress, and to consequently eliminate one's peripheral status,[60] the more "European" the musical composition the easier it was for work to gain local (and national) recognition.

Gomes's piano music, particularly his *A cayumba*, *dansa de negro*, offers a different, perhaps opposite, perspective of the ambiguous perceptions of "local" and "foreign," "national" and "European." If *A cayumba* portrayed the local (Afro-Brazilian) music by excessive use of ostinato rhythmic patterns not prevalent in European music, the work did not afford Gomes the status of a national or international composer as did his success in the operatic field. The work was not mentioned by any contemporary critic as a local landmark, nor was it a hit in sales, as were piano fantasies based on themes from *Il Guarany*. In fact, Gomes's piano pieces, demeaned by twentieth-century modernists as "European music, nothing else!"[61] were indeed that, although they were not perceived in the imperial capital as trivial for their Europeaness. Direct replicas of the Parisian sheet music publications, piano pieces based on local material were produced locally and performed in the houses of the local bourgeoisie without aspiring to an international appeal or an eventual sanctioning as national works. One might argue that it was exactly the local aspect in these pieces, perceived as exotic within a predominantly European musical language, that served to emphasize the European more than to describe the local or embody the national. The suggestive Afro-Brazilian music portrayed in stylized piano pieces destined for the parlor were far enough from their own musical framework and original performative milieu that they were comfortably part of a European imaginary exotic that attracted elite Cariocas a great deal. In addition, the exotic pieces helped Cariocas pretend that the Afro-Brazilian music performed nearby could also be as compliant and lenient. The idea that stylized piano pieces evoking Afro-Brazilian and African-derived music were conceived as local counterparts to European works is supported by the per-forming instructions in the sheet music publications. One of the most prolific local composers of such pieces, Henrique Alves de Mesquita not only brought Afro-Brazilian "rhythms and bodily movements"[62] to the Carioca parlor in printed format, but his fados, tangos, batuques, and cateretês were presented with performing in-structions in Italian: amateurs should play his polka from *Trunfo as avessas* in *tempo di fado* and *scherzando*; and his *Batuque, tango charac-teristico* in a tempo *Molto moderato*.[63] The exotic appeal of Afro-Brazilian music with European cover was also central in the works of several other composers, such as Joaquim Antonio da Silva Callado (1848–1880) and later Ernesto Nazareth (1863–1934).[64]

Yet the idea of what constituted a local (and ultimately national) music, as opposed to European, was not totally absent from the is-sues that interested music critics during the last decade of the monarchical regime. On February 28, 1879, an article titled "O Zé Pereira" came out anonymously in the *Revista musical e de bellas artes*. The author describes the popularity in Rio de Janeiro of the *zabumba*, commonly known in Brazil as *Zé Pereira*, a membranphone used then mostly by Afro-Brazilians in street parades. Commenting on the music produced by the zabumba, the author also stresses the im-portance of rhythm in music, without which, he claims, "melody and harmony cannot produce any worthy musical effect." However, the author bluntly adds, "the less civilized the people, the more con-spicuous the rhythmic basis in their chants,"[65] inevitably allotting Afro-Brazilian music lower rank within his hierarchical divisions. The author continues by observing:

> Rhythm belongs to both savages and civilized man; melody is the mu-sical effect most accessible and easily accepted by the human ear, and is therefore preferred by the people of the Southern Hemisphere, who prefer everything demanding little work; harmony is the most per-fected art; its beauty and scientific elements indicate the level of artis-tic development of a race. . . . Rhythm is for all, melody for several, and harmony for some.[66]

This ranking conspicuously follows a contemporary logic, explicitly articulated in the imported music literature circulating in Rio de Janeiro, that operatic music was trivial, but harmony and its "beauty," as rendered in the music of the (German) "classical" com-posers, is related specifically to the "development of a race" from the

Northern Hemisphere and has superior qualities. In the 1880s, this assumption served well the purposes of the prevailing "cultural managers" in imperial Rio de Janeiro, particularly of the selective group of habitués that gathered in private musical societies such as the Club Beethoven, the group of a privileged few who supposedly could appreciate the harmonic complexities of música clássica. But there was more in the hierarchy above that concerned critics than the choice of different European musical styles. For them, the centrality of rhythm in the musical practices of Afro-Brazilians was a signifier of difference that strategically displaced the Afro-Brazilian element as "non-European," and therefore less "civilized," "primitive," and less worthy.

Arthur Napoleão understood these rankings like no other individual in Rio de Janeiro. Any local identification with African-derived melodies and rhythmic patterns as "non-exotic," any deviation from the European musical structures as presented in the works of the "classics" was to be made with caution. The admiration for Gottschalk's pieces in the capital is an example. Despite his personal links with the North American composer, Napoleão warned his contemporaries in Rio de Janeiro that Gottschalk "is a composer to be admired but not imitated."[67] If Napoleão recognized and appreciated the novelties in Gottschalk's compositions, in his biography he stressed that their "lack of classic taste" gave him pause. The need to keep the European musical taste of Cariocas untainted by the local musical element was also the headline in the preaching of the composer and critic Oscar Guanabarino. Concerned with the growing popularity of polka-lundus, tangos, and other "hideous compositions," and the possible identification with their African-derived rhythms as an identifier of the local, he was pungent in his warnings that "music taste [in Rio de Janeiro] does not mean appreciation for high art."[68]

The musical hierarchy presented by the *Revista* article above also fitted the view of those following the growing popularity of Afro-Brazilian dances in the comic theater. For them, "rhythms and *requebros*" were the domain of the people, and were to be placed in contrast with the "civilized" European harmonic complexity appreciated by selective groups. In fact, the *requebros*, the black women's hip movement while dancing, particularly attracted the (male) audiences not only because it was rendered as caricature in satirical theatrical finales, but also because it was presented as a "forbidden sexuality," something viewed by the Carioca (male) elite as the domain of the

Other, but which, perhaps because of the possibilities aroused by its physical nearness, stirred in them an uncunny desire for conquest.

As the seat of a monarchical government in the New World, as the center of the political decisions, and as a growing metropolis at a time when the cultural implications of globalization just started to make a mark, imperial Rio de Janeiro was the main stage for these cultural negotiations.[69] In spite of the geographical, economical, and cultural distance between the city's Europeanized culture and the rest of the country, which was marked by agricultural areas and cultural isolation from the metropolis, it was in the capital that the imported ideas about music and the aspirations of a "Europeanized national culture" were managed and negotiated. Those in charge of fostering this local culture used music with specific associations in mind, associations that were dependent on a mythical view of various European musical styles and genres as "civilized" and modern, and by implication of a deliberate unapprised image of the various cultures around them as exotic and outlandish.

The perception of European music as "national," or "not foreign," and the understanding of "local" music as exotic and disconnected from "national" were the result of cultural constructions heavily mediated by the imperial government and local intellectuals, the "cultural managers" who guaranteed that the capital became and remained "civilized," modern, and European. Music, with its power to subjectively create and (re)create meaning, was central in fostering these notions, but above all in creating a flexible border between them.[70] Because the symbolic meanings in these concepts were ideological constructs that reflected social and political changes, the flexibility in the understanding of what was and what was not European or Brazilian, foreign or local, was itself saturated with profound political and cultural significance. The flexible border between "European," "national," "local," and "foreign" inform us about the impetus behind the appropriation, re-creation, production, and especially the perceived "value" of a wide range of European, and by extension non-European, musical fashions in imperial Rio de Janeiro. Both politically and conceptually, the interpretation of the role of European and non-European music in the making of the imperial capital's cultural milieu was guided by shifting perceptions of difference and sameness.[71]

This continued to be true in the twentieth century. By the 1920s, the understanding of what "national" music should be shifted drastically. To nationalist intellectuals "national" music, produced by composers of "art" music, should be linked to the cultural experiences of "the people." Accordingly, their interest in the past was limited to a "search" for musical works that showed Afro-Brazilian and other local musical manifestations of the urban low classes, the music of the "popular." Because the genuine music growing out of the cultural interaction between blacks, mulattoes, and immigrants in the poor neighborhoods of Rio de Janeiro in the last decades of the monarchical regime was seldom retained in print, nationalists' search for a past "national" music had to rest on the available printed music. They resorted to bestowing "national" auras on a few extant printed works in which reminiscences of Afro-Brazilian and other local musics appeared alongside European musical styles.

A good example is the reception history of *A sertaneja* (ca. 1869), a piano piece by Brasílio Itiberê da Cunha (1846–1913). The work is an elaborate piano fantasy, similar to several others in the same vein circulating in Rio de Janeiro. Exploring the piano in the bravura style, Itiberê makes use of the popular Brazilian song "Balaio, meu bem balaio" and also the habanera rhythm, including a variety of pianistic figurations, much in the style of Gottschalk's lavish pieces. Like Gomes's *A cayumba*, *A sertaneja* seldom appeared in contemporary publishers' catalogues and was rarely performed in concerts. The work was not recalled by the historian Cernicchiaro in his 1926 *Storia della musica nel Brasil*; Itiberê da Cunha's name was not even mentioned in the 1926 edition of Renato de Almeida's *História da música brasileira*. According to Helza Camêu, who studied the piece extensively, "It was the nationalists, and later the national composers, who consciously argued for the consecration of Brasílio Itiberê da Cunha's name, using his *A sertaneja* as model for a national work."[72]

Thus, in 1930, João Itiberê da Cunha (1870–1953), younger brother of Brasílio—under the pseudonym of Iwan d'Hunac—published the article "Um precursor da música brasileira" (A forerunner of Brazilian music), in which he discussed the "national value" of *A Sertaneja*.[73] Two years later, Andrade Muricy commented on the role of Itiberê da Cunha in creating a Brazilian music in his study "Música brasileira moderna."[74] In the 1942 revised edition of *História da música brasileira*, Renato de Almeida includes Itiberê da Cunha as the "forerunner of Brazilian music,"[75] an idea that remains in music history books to this day. The inclusion of Gomes's *A Cayumba* in the nationalistic canon follows a similar path.

By avoiding the study and interpretation of the prevalent European culture from which these "national" pieces emerged, nationalists (re)created past images that became manipulated twice. Firstly, they were forged images that reflected the cultural and political elite's urge to contrast the local Afro-Brazilian element with the European as Other during the last years of the monarchy. Secondly, by stripping the "chosen nationalistic" works from all their satirical connections and exotic meanings, by "cleaning" them from their thorny origins, nationalists imposed on their invented nationalistic canon an artificial aura of authenticity and purity that fitted perfectly their ideals. As "cultural managers" of their time, nationalist intellectuals avoided the European element not only for its foreignness, but also as a convenient political choice.

NOTES

1. See Mario de Andrade, *Pequena história da música,* 9th ed. (Belo Horizonte: Editora Itatiaia Limitada, 1987), 165–66. An expanded version of this section will appear in Cristina Magaldi's "Musical and National Identity in Brazil: Two Perspectives" in *Brazil in the Making*, eds. Carmen Nava and Ludwig Lauerhaas (forthcoming, Rowman & Littlefield).

2. See Ayres de Andrade, *Francisco Manuel da Silva e seu tempo*, vol. 2 (Rio de Janeiro: Edições Tempo Brasileiro, 1967), 104–07.

3. For a discussion of the use of local topics and the Portuguese language in nineteenth-century theatrical works, see Cristina Magaldi, "Alguns Dados sobre o Canto em Português no Século XIX," in Annals of the 1995 annual meeting of the ANPPOM (Associação Nacional the Pesquisa e Pós-Graduação em Música) (Universidade Federal de Minas Gerais [full text online].

4. For the controversies regarding Amat's administration of the Opera Lyrica Nacional, see Luiz Heitor Correa de Azevedo, "As primeiras óperas: *A noite do castelo* (1861), *Joana de Flandres* (1863)," in *Carlos Gomes: uma obra em foco* (Rio de Janeiro: FUNARTE, Instituto Nacional de Música, 1987). See also Ayres de Andrade, *Francisco Manuel da Silva e seu tempo*, vol. 2, 89–109.

5. Marcus Góes, *Carlos Gomes, a força indômita* (Belém: SECULT, 1996), 91.

6. Góes, *Carlos Gomes*, 91.

7. Góes, *Carlos Gomes*, 99. Gomes's Italian friend and librettist Ghislanzoni also referred to Gomes as "a savage, walking along through cold Italian streets"; see Gaspare Nello Vetro's "Correspondências Italianas recolhidas e comentadas," in *Antônio Carlos Gomes* (Rio de Janeiro: Instituto Nacional do Livro, 1982), 317. The Italian newspaper *Gazzeta musicale* also commented on Gomes's temperament, much evident during *Il Guarany's* rehearsals: "He

puts his hands on his vast hair and starts to run on the stage as if he is possessed, and he screams like a savage very similar to the Guarany [Indians];" quoted in Vasco Mariz, *História da música no Brasil,* (Rio de Janeiro: Nova Fronteira, 2000), 80–81. The parallel of Gomes's persona with his "savage" operatic character was also explored in the recent novel by Rubem Fonseca, *O selvagem da ópera* (São Paulo: Companhia das Letras, 1994).

8. Góes, *Carlos Gomes,* 99

9. Report by Luís de Guimarães Jr., in *Diário do Rio de Janeiro,* December 4, 1870; quoted in João Roberto Faria, *José de Alencar e o teatro* (São Paulo: Editora Perpectiva, 1987), 138.

10. While in Paris, Mesquita also wrote the operetta *La nuit au chateau,* with text by Paulo Kock, which was staged in Paris; but as a small-scale work, it did not have the same repercussion as the presentation of a full-length (Italian) opera like *Il Guarany* in the Teatro La Scala.

11. Article signed by A. de C., and published in *A vida fluminense,* December 17, 1870.

12. Faria, *José de Alencar e o teatro,* 138.

13. *Diário do Rio de Janeiro,* November 10, 1861; quoted in Azevedo, "As primeiras operas," 101–2; Ayres de Andrade identifies Machado de Assis as the author; see *Francisco Manuel da Silva e seu tempo,* vol. 2, 102.

14. *O mosquito* (November 4, 1876) included in the section *"Coisas que eu Gosto"* (Things that I like) caricatures by Rafael Bordalo Pinheiro of several scenes from *Il Guarany;* see Herman Lima, *História da caricatura no Brasil,* vol. 2 (Rio de Janeiro: José Olympio, 1963), 564–66.

15. Quintino Bocayuva translated into Portuguese the libretto for Bellini's *Norma,* which was presented by the Opera Lyrica Nacional on August 12, 1858. Salvador de Mendonça provided lyrics for Gomes's *Joana de Flandres.*

16. Góes, *Carlos Gomes,* 136.

17. Since the 1930s, *Il Guarany* has been performed every weekday at seven p.m., in a national broadcast titled *A voz do Brasil* (The voice of Brazil)—a government-sponsored program aimed at publicizing the daily acts of the president and parliament. President Getúlio Vargas initiated this nationwide broadcast in the late 1930s to unite the vast country and its diverse population in a one-hour act of patriotism. Substituting for Brazil's national anthem, Gomes's *Il Guarany* is heard daily, from the bustling cities of the Brazilian coast to the most remote villages in Brazil's Northwestern territory.

18. Viotti da Costa, *The Brazilian Empire: Myths and Histories* (Chicago: Chicago University Press, 1985), 154.

19. *Catalogo das musicas impressas no imperial estabelecimento de pianos e musicas de Narciso & Arthur Napoleão* (Rio de Janeiro: Imprensa Nacional, 1871).

20. Vicente Salles has investigated the influence of Gomes's *Il Guarany* on Brazilian folklore, on the repertory of bands in Brazil's rural areas, as well as on Carnival marches; see "Carlos Gomes: passagem e influência em

várias regiões brasileiras," in *Carlos Gomes: uma obra em foco* (Rio de Janeiro: FUNARTE, 1987), 7–11. In 1934, the famous popular singer Lamartine Babo launched a carnival march titled "A historia do Brasil" (The History of Brazil) (Victor 33 740-b) in which the opera characters are mixed in topics familiar to the daily life of Cariocas. Another carnival march "Defendendo a raça" (Defending our race), written by Manoel Dias e Floriano Correa and sung by Januário de Oliveira in the carnival of 1939, opens with *Il Guarany*'s Protofonia. For a study of *Il Guarany*'s tunes in carnival marches, see Hélio Damante "O Guarani, o folclore e o carnaval," *Revista brasileira de folclore* 11 (May–August, 1971): 171–78.

21. Gomes's name is seldom mentioned in general music history books in languages other than Portuguese.

22. Neukomm's pieces uses the modinha *La mélancolie* by the Brazilian mulatto Joaquim Manuel da Câmara.

23. The Biblioteca Nacional in Rio de Janeiro and the Bayerische Stadtsbibliotek in Munich hold copies of these works.

24. In Brazil, Herz's compositions were performed in a concert in Rio de Janeiro as early as June 6, 1832; and, by 1837 his Opp. 1 through 91 were for sale at several locations in the Brazilian capital. In the United States, a Charleston paper offered evidence of his popularity in 1847: "There is not a house, in which there are refined inmates, who play the piano, in which his music will not be heard"; *Charleston Courier*, January 23, 1847, quoted in R. Allen Lott, "The American Concert Tours of Leopoldo de Meyer, Henri Herz, and Sigismond Thalberg" (Ph.D. diss., City University of New York, 1986), 73.

25. In his 1849 visit to Mexico, Herz paid special homage to Mexicans through a *Marcha Nacional à los Mexicanos*, Op. 166 (1849); and a *Polka del Siglo* (1849) dedicated "a las Señoritas Mexicanas" (to Mexican ladies); see Esperanza Pulido, "Marcha nacional dedicada a los Mexicanos," *Heterofonía* 88/18 (1985): 45–52, and Donald Garvelmann, ed. *Variations on Non più mesta from Rossini's La Cenerentola* (New York: Music Treasure Publications, 1970), 9. In his *Fantaisie méxicaine, Op.* 162 (1849), Herz built variations on the popular Stephen Foster tune *Oh Susanna*; Herz also included *Oh Susanna* alongside J. Bland's *Carry Me Back to Old Virginny* in his *Impomptu burlesque sur des mélodies populaires de Christy's Ménestrels*, a piece also published as Op. 162; see Lott, "The American Concert Tours of Leopoldo de Meyer, Henri Herz, and Sigismond Thalberg," 183. For the United States, Herz wrote *Variations brillantes et grande fantaisie sur des airs nationaux américains*, Op. 158 (1846), which comprise variations on *Jackson's march*, *Hail Columbia*, and *Yankee Doodle*; the polka *La Californienne,* Op. 167, documented his visit to San Francisco at the beginning of 1850, though not through direct musical quotations; Herz's *Mélodies de Christy* is a simpler setting of the minstrel tunes "Oh Susanna," and "Stop dat knocking;" see John G. Doyle, *Louis Moreau Gottschalk,*

1829–1869 (Detroit: Information Coordinators, 1983), 328–29. For South America Herz wrote *La Tapada, polka caractéristique du Perú*, Op. 171 (Brussels: Schott & Cie., 1850–1851), a piece which circulated widely in Brazil, and was included in Napoleão's 1871 catalogue. Recording his stay in Santiago, Chile, from December 1850 to February 1851, Herz left a piano piece titled *Las flores de Santiago*. His first concert in Santiago bore the title "Musical panorama, or a review of the most famous operas and songs from all countries since the 15th century to the present" and included fantasies on themes by Beethoven, Weber, Rossini, Bellini, Donizetti, Auber, Meyerbeer, Verdi, alongside popular songs such as "Canciones chistosas y muy simples de los esclavos negros," "El jarabe" (from Mexico), and a "Canción nacional" (from Chile). In a second Chilean concert, titled "Viaje musical de Herz," when he described through music his soujourn to the Americas, he included the Chilean *La zamacueca*; see Salas, *Historia de la música en Chile,* 113.

26. It was in Herz's concert hall that Napoleão debuted in Paris; Napoleão voiced his admiration for Herz in his autobiography. Although Rio de Janeiro daily newspapers did not report Herz's visit, Marmontel mentions his stay in Rio de Janeiro in his *Les pianistes célèbres, silhouettes et médaillons* (Paris: A. Chaix et Cie., 1878), 38.

27. The UCLA Young Library, Special Collections, houses one copy of this work.

28. *Catálogo das musicas impresas no imperial estabelecimento de pianos e musicas de Narciso & Arthur Napoleão.*

29. The *marimba* is an idiophone of African derivation, with wooden planks being performed with two sticks.

30. *Mes voyages en Amérique* (Paris: Achille Faure, 1866); translated as *My Travels in America,* trans. Henry Bertram Hill (Madison: The State Historical Society of Wisconsin, 1963), 75–76.

31. According to Fétis, Joseph Ascher was born in London, where he began his music studies, completed later in Leipzig. He studied piano in London with Moscheles, whom he accompanied in 1846 to the Leipzig conservatory; see F.-J. Fétis, *Biographie universelle des musiciens*, vol. 1 (Paris: Firmin-Didot, 1877), 153. According to *Bakers's Biographical Dictionary* (1992) Ascher was born in Holland to German parents. The latter information is confirmed in Theo Stengel's *Juden in der Musik* (Berlin: Bernard Hahnefeld Verlag, 1943), 19.

32. Herz left a *Capriche danse Andalouse,* a *Bolero Le Muletier de Tolède,* and a *Capricho La Sevillana. Fétis, Biographie universelle des musicians*, vol. 1, 153.

33. In his autobiography, Napoleão recalls having met Ascher in Paris and even taking some lessons from him; see "memórias de Arthur Napoleão," *Revista brasileira de música*, 42.

34. Ascher's *Dance nègre* did not lack parallels in local publications. *O Brasil musical* n° 247 (ca. 1860) is a *Fantasia brasileira* (Brazilian Fantasy), writ-

ten by the Italian immigrant composer and teacher Ercole Pinzarrone (1826–1924), based on an eight-bar local lundu melody.

35. Hector Berlioz, "Mr. Gottschalk's Concert," *Journal des débats*, April 3, 1851; quoted in Jeanne Behrend, ed., *Notes of a Pianist* (New York: Da Capo Press, 1979), xxii.

36. *Le Bananier, chanson nègre*, first performed at the Theatro São Pedro de Alcantara in a concert August 8, 1850, was circulating as sheet music in the mid-1850s. *La Savanne, ballade créole* was published in the collection *A familia imperial* around 1862.

37. Gottschalk rented a room in Napoleão's music shop where he practiced and composed during his stay in Brazil. Narciso & Arthur Napoleão's 1871 catalogue listed no fewer than 46 compositions by the American composer, from his *Bamboula*, Op. 2, to a piano reduction of the celebrated *Nuit des tropiques* (andante de la *Sinfonie romantique*).

38. Jeanne Behrend, *Notes of a Pianist*, 320.

39. Richard Jackson, ed., *Piano Music of Louis Moreau Gottschalk* (New York: Dover, 1973), ix.

40. The two Creole melodies were *Quand patate la cuite* and *Musieu banjo*; see Richard Jackson, *Piano Music of Louis Moreau Gottschalk*, ix; see also Gilbert Chase, *America's Music from the Pilgrims to the Present*, rev. 3rd ed. (Urbana: University of Illinois Press, 1992), 290. For data on the first publication of *Bamboula* and its immediate success, see Doyle, *Louis Moreau Gottschalk, 1829–1869*, 264–65. For a well-documented history of *Bamboula* and the use of Creole melodies, see S. Frederick Starr's *Bamboula: The Life and Times of Louis Moreau Gottschelk* (New York: Oxford University Press, 1995), 39–45.

41. Advertisement for the piece appears in *Jornal do commercio*, October 8, 1856. Gomes's *A Cayumba* was "discovered" by Carlos Penteado de Rezende in 1967 when he found an advertisement for the dance in the 1857 *Correio Paulistano*: "*A Cayumba*—negro dance, original music and of an entirely new taste for piano."

42. Gomes's collection was published in the *Ramalhete das quadrilhas* (Filippone & Tornaghi, 1857–1858). The word *quilombo* refers to a shelter for fugitive black slaves.

43. *Chula* is a song-dance of Portuguese origin in cut meter introduced in Brazil by the beginning of the nineteenth century. The chula could also be sung by a soloist accompanied by a guitar and had choreography similar to that of the fado and batuque. The use of the word chula here exemplifies the Iberian influences on Afro-Brazilian traditions.

44. The early publications by J. B. Klier and Pierre Laforge are mentioned in Mercedes Reis Pequeno's "Brazilian Music Publishers," *Inter-American Music Review* 9 (1988): 91–104. Two modinhas by Cândido Ignácio da Silva are reprinted by Mário de Andrade in *Modinhas imperiais* (São Paulo: Casa

Chiarato, 1930); one by Cândido Ignácio da Silva ("Minha Marilia") and three by Gabriel Fernandes da Trindade ("Do Regaço da Amizade," "Se o Pranto Apreciares," and "Erva Mimoza do Campo") are reprinted in Gerhard Doderer's *Modinhas Luso-Brasileiras, Portugaliae Musica,* vol. 44 (Lisbon: Fundação Calouste Gulbenkian, 1984).

45. Mário de Andrade, *Modinha imperiais*, 9.

46. Mercedes Reis Pequeno, ed., *Musica no Rio de Janeiro Imperial, 1822–1870* (Rio de Janeiro: Ministério da Educação e Cultura, 1962), 71.

47. The collection is extant in the music section of the Biblioteca Nacional at Rio de Janeiro.

48. Ayres de Andrade mentioned a musical setting by Adolpho Maersch of the same poem, but withheld the exact date; see Ayres de Andrade, *Francisco Manuel da Silva e seu tempo,* vol. 1, 45.

49. Machado was the organist at the Candelária Church in 1845 and again from 1855 to 1866. On September 7, 1854, a conservatory for religious music training was founded under the auspices of the Bishop of Rio de Janeiro; among the teachers were Padre Joaquim do Amor Divino, conductor of the choir of the Candelária church, Adolpho Maersch, and Francisco Xavier Muniz; Raphael Coelho Machado was the provisional director, according to an announcement in the *Jornal do commercio* of September 28, 1854.

50. This chapter is probably a revised version of his *Principios da arte poetica (ou medição dos versos uzados na lingua portugueza),* advertised in the cover of his *Methodo de afinar o piano,* rev. 3rd ed., 1849).

51. *Breve Tratado de Harmonia* (Rio de Janeiro, 1852), 115.

52. *Jornal do commercio,* April 26, 1850.

53. Azevedo, "As primeiras óperas," 93–94.

54. Both works were translated into Portuguese by José Feliciano de Castilho (1822–1870).

55. Góes, *Carlos Gomes,* 91–92.

56. Mesquita's *O vagabundo* was translated to Portuguese by Vicente di Simoni for the Rio de Janeiro presentation, but in 1871 was presented with its original Italian libretto.

57. A Portuguese translation of *Il Guarany* was published in 1937 by Carlos Marinho de Paula Barros (Rio de Janeiro: Imprensa Nacional), much to the discontent of Gomes's daughter who expected the opera to continue to be performed as her father conceived it. See Itala Gomes Vaz de Carvalho, *A vida de Carlos Gomes,* 3rd ed. (Rio de Janeiro: A. Noite, 1946). For the nationalistic impetus behind the translation see Carlos Marinho de Paula Barros, "A tradução do libretto d'*Il Guarany,*" *Revista brasileira de música* 3/2 (1936): 429–31.

58. Mario de Andrade, *Compendio de historia da música* (São Paulo: L. G. Miranda, 1933), 170.

59. *A vida fluminense,* December 17, 1870.

60. Orlove and Bauer discuss this aspect in the reproduction of imported manufactured goods in Latin America; see "Giving Importance to Imports" in *Imported Goods in Postcolonial Latin America* (Ann Arbor: University of Michigan press, 1977), 13.

61. Liner notes for the LP *O piano brasileiro de Carlos Gomes* (Rio de Janeiro: INM, 1979), performed by Fernando Lopes. According to Bruno Kiefer, *A Cayumba* is "too repetitive and the black element is only displayed in the title, as was common in pieces of this period"; see "A obra pianística de Antônio Carlos Gomes," in *Carlos Gomes, uma obra em foco* (Rio de Janeiro: FUNARTE, 1987), 42.

62. *Jornal do commercio*, February 15, 1886.

63. The Biblioteca Nacional in Rio de Janeiro, music division, holds copies of these pieces by Mesquita.

64. Gerard Béhague explores the local, Afro-Brazilian musical elements that composers such as Callado, Gonzaga, and Nazareth introduced in imported polkas and waltzes; see "Popular Musical Currents in the Art Music of the Early Nationalistic Period in Brazil, circa 1870–1920" (Ph.D. diss., Tulane University, 1966), 90–163.

65. *Revista musical e de bellas artes* I/8 (February 28, 1879): 1.

66. *Revista musical e de bellas artes* I/8 (February 28, 1879): 1.

67. Sanchez Frias, *Arthur Napoleão resenha commemorativa da sua vida pessal e artistica* (Lisbon: n.p., 1913), 221.

68. *Revista musical e de bellas artes*, II/22 (August 21, 1880): 176.

69. Ulf Hannerz, *Cultural Complexity studies in the Social Organization of Meaning* (New York: Columbia University Press, 1992), 198.

70. Benjamin Orlove and Arnold Bauer, "Giving Importance to Imports," in *The Allure of the Foreign*, 13.

71. Akhil Gupta and James Ferguson's "Beyond Culture: Space, Identity, and the Politics of Difference," in *Culture, Power, and Place: Explorations in Critical Anthropology*, ed. Akhil Gupta and James Ferguson (Durham, N.C.: Duke University Press, 1997), 49.

72. See Helza Camêu, "A importância histórica de Brazílio Itiberê da Cunha," *Revista brasileira de cultura* 2/4 (1970): 34.

73. Yoão Itiberê da Cunha, *Illustração musical*, 1/i (August, 1930), 5.

74. Andradi Muricy, "Musica brasileira moderna," *Revista da Associação Brasileira de Música*, 1/i (Rio de Janeiro, 1932): 2–14.

75. Renato de Almeida, *História da música brasileira* (Rio de Janeiro: F. Briguiet, 1942), 424.

Bibliography

NINETEENTH-CENTURY PERIODICALS

A vida fluminense
Ba-ta-clan
Dwight's Journal of Music
Gazeta musical
Jornal do commercio
Revista illustrada
Revista musical e de bellas artes
Revista popular
Revue et gazzette musicale
Semana illustrada

NINETEENTH-CENTURY SOURCES

Almanak administrativo, mercantil e industrial da corte e provincia do Rio de Janeiro. Rio de Janeiro: E. and H. Laemmert & C., 1849–1882.

Almanak administrativo, mercantil e industrial da corte e provincia do Rio de Janeiro. Rio de Janeiro: E. and H. Laemmert & C., 1883–1888.

Blake, Sacramento. *Dicionário bibliográfico brazileiro*. Rio de Janeiro: Typografia Nacional, Imprensa Nacional, 1883–1902 [rpt. 1970].

Catalogo da biblioteca musical de J. C. Müller e H. E. Heinen: fornecedores de musica de sua Magestade. Rio de Janeiro: Typographia Imp. e Const. de J. Villeneuve e Cᵃ, 1837.

Catálogo das musicas impresas no imperial estabelecimento de pianos e musicas de Narciso & Arthur Napoleão. Rio de Janeiro: Imprensa Nacional, 1871.

Club Beethoven, primeiro relatorio para o ano social de 1882–1883. Rio de Janeiro: Typ. de G. Leuzinger & Filhos, 1883.

Club Beethoven, segundo relatorio para o ano social de 1883–1884. Rio de Janeiro: Typ. de G. Leuzinger & Filhos, 1884.

Estatutos da academia de musica do Club Beethoven. Rio de Janeiro, 1884(?).

1868 Estatutos do Club Mozart no Rio de Janeiro. Rio de Janeiro: Typographia Perseverança, 1868.

1872 Estatutos do Club Mozart no Rio de Janeiro. Rio de Janeiro: Typographia de F. A. de Souza, 1872.

Fétis, F. J. *Biographie universelle des musicians.* Paris: Firmin–Didot, 1877.

Kidder, Rev. Daniel Parish. *Sketches of Residence and Travels in Brazil.* Philadelphia: Sorin & Ball, 1845.

Machado, Raphael Coelho. *Methodo de afinar piano.* Rev. 3rd ed. Rio de Janeiro: Typ. Francesa, 1849 (1843).

———. *Breve tratado de harmonia.* Rio de Janeiro, 1852.

Marmontel, Antoine-François. *Les pianistes célèbres, silhouettes et médaillons.* Paris: A. Chaix et Cie., 1878.

———. *Symphonistes et virtuoses.* Paris: Imprimerie Centrale des Chemins de Fer., 1878.

Vieira, Ernesto. *Diccionario biographico de músicos portuguezes.* Lisbon: Typographia M. Moreira & Pinhero, 1900.

TWENTIETH-CENTURY SOURCES

Abreu, Martha. *Império do Divino: festas religiosas e cultura popular no Rio de Janeiro, 1830–1900.* Rio de Janeiro: Nova Fronteira and Fapesp, 1999.

Alencar, Francisco. *História da sociedade brasileira.* Rio de Janeiro: Livro Técnico, 1981.

Almeida, Renato de. *História da música brasileira.* Rio de Janeiro: F. Briguiet, 1926. 2nd ed. rev., Rio de Janeiro: F. Briguiet, 1942.

Andrade, Ayres de. "Um rival de Liszt no Rio de Janeiro." *Revista brasileira de música* I/I (1962): 27–50

———. *Francisco Manuel da Silva e seu tempo*, 2 vols. Rio de Janeiro: Edições Tempo Brasileiro, 1967.

Andrade, Mário. *Ensaio sobre a música brasileira.* São Paulo: Livraria Martins Editora, 1963 [1928].

———. *Modinhas imperiais.* São Paulo: Casa Chiriato, 1930.

———. *Compendio de historia da música.* São Paulo: L. G. Miranda, 1933.

Atwood, William G. *The Parisian Worlds of Frédéric Chopin.* New Haven, Conn.: Yale University Press, 1999.

Augusto, Paulo Roberto Peloso. "Os tangos urbanos no Rio de Janeiro: 1870–1920, uma análise histórica e musical." *Revista música* 8/1–2 (May–November, 1997): 105–28.

Auler, Guilherme. *Os bolsistas do imperador*. Petrópolis: Tribuna de Petrópolis, 1956.

Azevedo, Moreira de. *O Rio de Janeiro*. 3rd ed. Vol. 2. Rio de Janeiro: Livraria Brasiliana Editora, 1969.

Azevedo, Luiz Heitor Corrêa de. *Bibliografia musical brasileira 1820–1950*. Rio de Janeiro: Instituto Nacional do Livro, 1952.

———. "Arthur Napoléon: Un pianist portugais au Brésil," Arquivos do Centro Cultural Português. Vol. 3. Paris: Fundação Calouste Gulbenkian, 1971, 572–602.

———. "As primeiras óperas: *A noite do castelo* (1861), *Joana de Flandres* (1863)." In *Carlos Gomes: uma obra em foco*. Rio de Janeiro: FUNARTE, Instituto Nacional de Música, 1987.

Bahia, Juarez. *Jornal, histórica e técnica: história da imprensa brasileira*. 4th ed. São Paulo: Ática, 1990.

Barman, Roderick J. *Citizen Emperor: Pedro II and the Making of Brazil 1825–91*. Stanford, Calif.: Stanford University Press, 1999.

———. *Princess Isabel of Brazil: Gender and Power in the Nineteenth Century*. Wilmington, Del.: Scholarly Resources, 2002.

Barros, Carlos Marinho de Paula. "A tradução do libretto d'*Il Guarany*." *Revista brasileira de música* 3/2 (1936): 429–31.

Béhague, Gerard. "Popular Musical Currents in the Art Music of the Early Nationalistic Period in Brazil, circa 1870–1920." Ph.D. diss., Tulane University, 1966.

Behrend, Jeanne, ed. *Notes of a Pianist*. New York: Da Capo Press, 1979.

Bernard, Elisabeth. "Jules Pasdeloup et les Concerts Populaires." *Revue de musicologie* 57/2 (1971): 150–78.

Bethell, Leslie. "The Independence of Brazil." In *Brazil: Empire and Republic 1822–1930*. Cambridge: Cambridge University Press, 1989.

Bhabha, Homi. "Of Mimicry and Man: The Ambivalence of Colonial Discourse." In *Tensions of Empire: Colonial Cultures in a Bourgeois World*, ed. Frederick Cooper and Ann Laura Stoler. Berkeley: University of California Press, 1997.

Bispo, Antonio Alexandre. "O século XIX na pesquisa histórico-musical brasileira: necessidade de sua reconsideração." *Latin American music review* 2/1 (Spring 1981): 130–42.

Brito, Manuel Carlos de. *Estudos de história da música em Portugal*. Lisbon: Imprensa Universitária, Editorial Estampa, 1989.

Brito, Manuel Carlos de and David Crammer. *Crónicas da vida musical portuguesa na primeira metade do século XIX*. Lisbon: Imprensa Nacional-Casa da Moeda, 1990.

Broyles, Michael. *Music of the Highest Class: Elitism and Populism in Antebellum Boston*. New Haven, Conn.: Yale University Press, 1992.

Burns, E. Bradford. *A History of Brazil*. New York: Columbia University Press, 1993.

Cafezeiro, Edwaldo, Carmem Gadelha, and Maria de Fátima Saadi, eds. *Teatro de França Júnior.* Rio de Janeiro: Serviço Nacional de Teatro, FUNARTE, 1980.

Canclini, Néstor García. *Hybrid Cultures: Strategies for Entering and Leaving Modernity,* trans. Christopher L. Chiappari and Silvia L. López. Minneapolis: University of Minnesota Press, 1995.

Carvallio, Itala Gomes Vazde. *A vida de Carlos Gomes,* 3rd ed. Rio de Janeiro: A Noite, 1946.

Castro, Ênio de Freitas e. "Dicionários de música brasileiros." *Revista brasileira de cultura* 2/5 (1970): 9–20.

Cernicchiaro, Vincenzo. *Storia della musica nel Brasil.* Milan: Stab. Tip. Edit. Fratelli Riccioni, 1926.

Chase, Gilbert. *America's Music From the Pilgrims to the Present.* Rev. 3d. ed. Urbana: University of Illinois Press, 1992.

Coaracy, Vivaldo. *Memórias da cidade do Rio de Janeiro.* Rio de Janeiro: Livraria José Olympio, 1965.

Cooper, Jeffrey. *The Rise of Instrumental Music and Concert Series in Paris 1828–1871.* Ann Arbor, Mich.: UMI Research Press, 1983.

Costa, João da Cruz. *History of Ideas in Brazil: The Development of Philosophy in Brazil and the Evolution of National History,* trans. Suzette Macedo. Berkeley: University of California Press, 1964.

Damante, Hélio. "O Guarani, o folclore e o carnaval." *Revista brasileira de folclore* 11 (May/August, 1971): 171–78.

Diniz, Edinha. *Chiquinha Gonzaga: uma história de vida.* Rio de Janeiro: Editora Codecri, 1984.

Dizikes, John. *Opera in America: A Cultural History.* New Haven, Conn.: Yale University Press, 1993.

Doderer, Gerhard. *Modinhas Luso-Brasileiras, Portugaliae Musica.* Vol. 44. Lisbon: Fundação Calouste Gulbenkian, 1984.

Doyle, John G. *Louis Moreau Gottschalk, 1829–1869.* Detroit: Information Coordinators, 1983.

Dunn, Christopher. "The Relics of Brazil: Modernity and Nationality in the Tropicalia Movement." Ph.D. diss., Brown University, 1996.

Efegê, Jota. *Maxixe, dança excomungada,* Rio de Janeiro: Conquista, 1974.

Escobar, José Ignácio Perdomo. *La ópera en Colombia.* Bogotá: Litografía Arco, 1979.

Farwell, Arthur. "Keeping in Touch with World's Musical Growth through the Piano." *Musical America,* November 5, 1910.

Faria, João Roberto. *José de Alencar e o teatro.* São Paulo: Perspectiva, 1987.

——. *O teatro realista no Brasil: 1855–1865.* São Paulo: Perspectiva, 1993.

——. *Idéias teatrais: o século XIX no Brasil.* São Paulo: Perspectiva, Fapesp, 2001.

Faria, Paulo Rogério de. "O pianismo do concerto no Rio de Janeiro, no século XIX." Master's thesis, Universidade Federal do Rio de Janeiro, Escola de Música, 1996.

Fazenda, José Vieira da. "Antiqualhas e memórias do Rio de Janeiro." *Revista do Instituto Histórico e Geográfico Brasileiro*, t. 93, v. 147 (1923), Rio de Janeiro, 1927.

Ferreira, Procópio. *O ator Vasques*. Rio de Janeiro: FUNARTE, Serviço Nacional do Teatro, 1979 (1938).

Fleiuss, Max. *Paginas de historia*. Rio de Janeiro: Imprensa Nacional, 1924.

Fonseca, Aleilton Santana da. "Enredo romântico, música ao fundo." Master's thesis, Universidade Federal da Paraiba, 1992.

Fonseca, Rubem. *O selvagem da ópera*. São Paulo: Companhia das Letras, 1994.

França, Jean M. Carvalho. *Literatura e sociedade no Rio de Janeiro oitocentista*. Rio de Janeiro: Imprensa Nacional, 1999.

Freire, Gilberto. *Inglêses no Brasil: aspectos da influência britânica sôbre a vida, a paisagem e a cultura brasileira*, Documentos Brasileiros 58. Rio de Janeiro: José Olympio, 1948.

―――. *Vida social no Brasil nos meados do século XIX*. Recife: Instituto Joaquim Nabuco, 1964.

Frias, Sanches. *Arthur Napoleão: resenha comemorativa da sua viada pessoal e artística*. Lisbon: n.p., 1913.

Garvelmann, Donald, ed. *Variations on 'Non più mesta' from Rossini's La Cenerentola*. New York: Music Treasure Publications, 1970.

Geertz, Clifford. *The Interpretation of Cultures*. New York: Basic Books, 1973.

Gesualdo, Vicente. *Historia de la música en Argentina*. 2 vols. Buenos Aires: Editorial Beta, 1961.

Góes, Marcus. *Carlos Gomes, a força indômita*. Belém: SECULT, 1996.

Gordon, Eric A. "A New Opera House: An Investigation of Elite values in Mid-Nineteenth-Century Rio de Janeiro." *Inter-American Institute for Musical Research Yearbook* 5 (1969): 49–66.

―――. "Opera and Society: Rio de Janeiro, 1851–1852." Master's thesis, Tulane University, 1969.

Graham, Richard. *Britain and the Onset of Modernization in Brazil: 1850–1914*. Cambridge: Cambridge University Press, 1968.

―――. "Brazil: 1850–1875." In *Brazil: Empire and Republic, 1922–1930*, ed. Leslie Bethell. Cambridge: Cambridge University Press, 1989.

Gupta, Akhil, and James Ferguson. "Beyond Culture: Space, Identity, and the Politics of Difference." In *Culture, Power, and Place: Explorations in Critical Anthropology*, ed. Akhil Gupta and James Ferguson. Durham, N.C.: Duke University Press, 1997.

Hannerz, Ulf. *Cultural Complexity: Studies in the Social Organization of Meaning*. New York: Columbia University Press, 1992.

Hahner, June E. *Poverty and Politics: The Urban Poor in Brazil, 1870–1920*. Albuquerque: University of New Mexico Press, 1986.

Hallewell, Laurence. *O livro no Brasil*. São Paulo: Editora Universidade de São Paulo, 1982.

Harding, James. "Paris: Opera Reigns Supreme." In *Music and Society: The Late Romantic Era*, ed. Jim Samson. Upper Saddle River, N.J.: Prentice Hall, 1991.

Herz, Henri. *My Travels in America.* Trans. Henry Bertram Hill. Madison: the State Historical Society of Wisconsin, 1963.

Illari, Bernardo. "No hay lugar para ellos: los indígenas en la capilla musical de La Plata." *Anuario* (Sucre, 1997): 73–108.

———. "Les hacen lugar? Y como? La representación del indio en dos villancicos chuquisaqueños de 1718." *Data* 7 (1997): 165–96.

Kallberg, Jeffrey. *Piano Music of the Parisian Virtuosos 1810–1860.* New York: Garland, 1993.

Kiefer, Bruno. "A obra pianística de Antônio Carlos Gomes." In *Carlos Gomes: uma obra em foco.* Rio de Janeiro: FUNARTE, 1987.

Kozeritz, Carl von. *Imagens do Brasil.* Trans. Afonso Arinos de Melo Franco. Belo Horizonte: Ed. Itatiaia; São Paulo: Ed. da Universidade de São Paulo, 1980.

Kracauer, Siegfried. *Orpheus in Paris.* New York: Knopf, 1938.

Krims, Adam. *Rap Music and the Poetics of Identity.* Cambridge: Cambridge University Press, 2000.

Jackson, Richard, ed. *Piano Music of Louis Moreau Gottschalk.* New York: Dover, 1973.

Lacombe, Lourenço Luiz. *Isabel, a princesa redentora.* Petrópolis: Instituto Histórico de Petrópolis, 1989.

Lange, Curt. "Vida y muerte de Louis Moreau Gottschalk en Rio de Janeiro (1869)." *Revista de estudios musicales* 2/4 (1950): 76.

Leite, Míriam Moreira. *A Condição feminina no Rio de Janeiro.* São Paulo: HUCITEC, Instituto Nacional do Livro, 1984.

Lévi-Strauss, Claude. *Tristes tropiques.* Trans. John and Doreen Weightman. New York: Penguin Books, 1992 [1955]).

Levine, Lawrence. *Highbrow/Lowbrow: the Emergence of Cultural Hierarchy in America.* Cambridge, Mass.: Harvard University Press, 1988.

Lima, Herman. *História da caricatura no Brasil.* 2 vols. Rio de Janeiro: José Olympio, 1963.

Lobo, Eulalia M. L. *História do Rio de Janeiro.* Vol 1. Rio de Janeiro: IBMC, 1978.

Loesser, Arthur. *Men, Women and Pianos: A Social History.* New York: Dover, 1990 (1954).

Los Rios Filho, Adolfo Morales de. *O Rio de Janeiro imperial.* Rio de Janeiro: Editora Noite, 1945.

Lott, R. Allen. "The American Concert Tours of Leopoldo de Meyer, Henri Herz, and Sigismond Thalberg." Ph.D. diss., City University of New York, 1986.

Macedo, Joaquim Manuel de. *Memórias da Rua do Ouvidor.* Rio de Janeiro: Garnier, 1925.

Magaldi, Cristina. "A disseminação da música de Mozart no Brasil (séc. XIX)." *Revista Brasileira de Música* 19 (1991): 15–32.

———. "Concert Life in Rio de Janeiro, 1837–1900." Ph.D. diss., University of California at Los Angeles, 1994.

———. "Music for the Elite: Musical Societies in Imperial Rio de Janeiro." *Latin American Music Review* 16/1 (1995): 1–42.

———. "José White in Rio de Janeiro, 1879–1889." *Inter-American Music Review* 14/2 (1995): 1–19.

———. "Alguns Dados sobre o Canto em Português no Século XIX." Annals of the 1995 annual meeting of the Associação Nacional the Pesquisa e Pós-Graduação em Música. Belo Horizonte: Universidade Federal de Minas Gerais, 1996.

Malerba, Jurandir. *A corte no exílio: civilização e poder no Brasil às vésperas da independência (1808 a 1821).* São Paulo: Companhia das Letras, 2000.

Mallon, Florencia. "The Promise and Dilemma of Subaltern Studies." *American Historical Review* 99/5 (1994): 1510–11.

Mariz, Vasco. *História da música no Brasil.* Rio de Janeiro: Nova Fronteira, 2000.

Márquez, Gabriel García. *Love in the Time of Cholera.* Trans. Edith Grossman. New York: Penguin Books, 1989.

McLamore, Laura Alyson. "Symphonic Conventions in London's Concert Rooms, circa 1755–1790." Ph.D. diss., University of California at Los Angeles, 1991.

Mello, Maria Elizabeth Chaves de. *Lições de crítica: conceitos europeus, crítica literária e literatura crítica no Brasil do século XIX.* Niterói, R.J.: Editora da Universidade Federal Fluminense, 1997.

Mendes, Miriam Garcia. *A personagem negra no teatro brasileiro (1838–1888).* São Paulo: Editora Ática, 1982.

Merino, Luis. "José White in Chile: National and International Repercussions." *Inter-American Music Review* XI/1 (Fall–Winter 1990): 87–112.

Merrick, Thomas William, and Douglas Graham. *Population and Economic Development in Brazil, 1808 to the Present.* Baltimore, Md.: Johns Hopkins University Press, 1979.

Moore, Robin. *Nationalizing Blackness: Afrocubanismo and Artistic Revolution in Havana, 1920–1940.* Pittsburgh: University of Pittsburgh Press, 1997.

Napoleão, Arthur. "Memorias de Arthur Napoleão." *Revista brasileira de musica* 3 (1962), 4–6 (1963).

Needell, Jeffrey D. *A Tropical Belle Époque: Elite Culture and Society in Turn-of-the-Century Rio de Janeiro.* Cambridge: Cambridge University Press, 1987.

———. "The Domestic Civilizing Mission: The Cultural Role of the State in Brasil, 1808–1930." *Luso-Brazilian Review* 36/1 (1999): 1–18.

Olavarria y Ferrari. *Reseña histórica del teatro en México.* 3d. ed. Mexico City: Editorial Porrúa, 1961.

Orlove, Benjamin, and Arnold Bauer. "Giving Importance to Imports." In *The Allure of the Foreign: Imported Goods in Postcolonial Latin America*. Ann Arbor: University of Michigan Press, 1997.

Parakilas, James et al. *Piano Roles: Three Hundred Years of Life with Pianos*. New Haven, Conn.: Yale University Press, 1999.

Pequeno, Mercedes Reis. "Impressão musical." In *Enciclopedia de musica brasileira*. Rio de Janeiro: Art Editora, 1977.

———. "Brazilian music publishers." *Inter-American Music Review* 9 (1988): 91–104.

———. *1770–1970: Exposição Beethoven no Rio de Janeiro*. Rio de Janeiro: Divisão de Publicação Biblioteca Nacional, Seção de Música e Arquivo Sonoro, 1970.

Pereira, Leonardo Affonso de Miranda. *O carnaval das letras*. Rio de Janeiro: Coleção Biblioteca Carioca, 1994.

Prado, Décio de Almeida. *João Caetano: o ator, o empresário, o repertório*. São Paulo: Editora Perspectiva, Editora da Universidade de São Paulo, 1972.

Pulido, Esperanza. "Marcha nacional dedicada a los Mexicanos." *Heterofonia* 88/18 (1985): 45–52.

Raeders, Georges. *Dom Pedro II e os sábios franceses*. Rio de Janeiro: Atlantica Editora, 1944.

Rezende, Carlos Penteado de. "Notas para uma história do piano no Brasil, Séc. XIX." *Revista brasileira de cultura* 2/6 (1970): 9–38.

Rosselli, John. "The Business and the Italian Immigrant Community in Latin America 1820–1930: the Example of Buenos Aires." *Past and Present* 127 (May 1990): 155–82.

Rowe, William, and Vivian Schelling. *Memory and Modernity: Popular Culture in Latin America*. London: Verso, 1991.

Rugendas, J. M. *Viagem pitoresca através do Brasil*. Trans. Sérgio Milliet. São Paulo: Editora da Universidade de São Paulo.

Ruiz, Roberto. *Teatro de revista no Brasil: do início à guerra mundial*. Rio de Janeiro: INACEN, 1988.

Sala, Juan Andrés. "Actividad musical en Buenos Aires antes de la inauguración del actual teatro Colón." In *La historia del Teatro Colón 1908–1968*, ed. Roberto Caamaño. Buenos Aires: Editorial Cinetea, 1963.

Salas, Pereira. *Los orígenes del arte musical en Chile*. Santiago: Universidad de Chile, 1941.

———. *Historia de la música en Chile, 1850–1900*. Santiago: Publicaciones de la Universidad de Chile, 1957.

Salles, Vicente. "Carlos Gomes: passagem e influências em várias cidades brasileiras." In *Carlos Gomes: uma obra em foco*. Rio de Janeiro: FUNARTE, 1987.

Santos, Francisco Marques dos. "A sociedade fluminense em 1852." *Estudos Brasileiros* 18 (May/June 1941): 244.

Santos, Luiza de Queiroz Amancio dos. *Origem e evolução da música em Portugal e sua influência no Brasil*. Rio de Janeiro: Comissão brasileira dos centenarios em Portugal, Imprensa Nacional, 1942.

Sayers, Raymond S. *The Negro in Brazilian Literature*. New York: Hispanic Institute in the United States, 1956.

Schultz, Kirsten. *Tropical Versailles: Empire, Monarchy, and the Portuguese Royal Court in Rio de Janeiro, 1808–1821*. New York: Routledge, 2001.

Schwarz, Roberto. *Ao vencedor as batatas*. São Paulo: Duas Cidades, 1977.

Seeger, Charles. "Review of *The Music of Mexico* by Robert Stevenson." *Notes* 10/2 (March 1953).

Shelemay, Kay Kaufman, *Soundscapes*. New York: Norton, 2001.

Silva, Lafayette. *História do teatro brasileiro*. Rio de Janeiro: Serviço Gráfico do MEC, 1938.

Simeone, Nigel. *Paris: a Musical Gazetteer*. New Haven, Conn.: Yale University Press, 2000.

Siqueira, Baptista. *Três vultos históricos da música brasileira: Mesquita, Callado, Anacleto*. Rio de Janeiro: D. Araujo, 1970.

Slobin, Mark. "Micromusics of the West." *Ethnomusicology* 36/1 (1992): 1–87.

Soares, Carlos Eugênio Líbano. *A negrada instituição: os capoeiras na corte imperial, 1850–1890*. Rio de Janeiro: Access Editors, 1999.

Sousa, J. Galante de. *O teatro no Brasil*. Rio de Janeiro: MEC, Instituto Nacional do Livro, 1960.

Starr, S. Frederick. *Bamboula: The Life and Times of Louis Moreau Gotlschalk*. New York: Oxford University Press, 1995.

Stengel, Theo. *Juden in der Musik*. Berlin: Bernard Hahnefeld Verlag, 1943.

Stevenson, Robert. "The Afro-American Musical Legacy to 1800." *The Musical Quarterly*, 54/4 (October 1968): 475–502.

———. "Wagner's Latin American Outreach (to 1900)." *Inter-American Music Review* 9/2 (Spring–Summer 1983): 63–83.

———. "Gottschalk programs Wagner." *Inter-American Music Review* 5/2 (Spring–Summer 1983): 89–94.

———. "Black Dance Types in Spanish Dominions, 1540–1820." *Inter-American Music Review* 9/2 (Spring–Summer 1988): 105–13.

Süssekind, Flora. *As revistas de ano e a invenção do Rio de Janeiro*. Rio de Janeiro: Editora Nova Fronteira, 1986.

Suttoni, Charles Russell. "Piano and Opera: A Study of the Piano Fantasies Written on Opera Themes in the Romantic Era." Ph.D. diss., New York University, 1973.

Táti, Miécio. *O mundo de Machado de Assis*. Rio de Janeiro: Secretaria Municipal de Cultura, Turismo e Esportes, 1991.

Tinhorão, José Ramos. *Os sons dos negros no Brasil*. São Paulo: Art Editora, 1988.

————. *Fado: dança do Brasil, cantar de Lisboa; o fim de um mito.* Lisbon: Editorial Caminho, 1994.

Toussaint-Samson, Adèle. *A Parisian in Brazil; the Travel Account of a Frenchwoman in nineteenth-century Rio de Janeiro.* Trans. Emma Toussaint. Wilmington, Del.: Scholarly Resources, 2001.

Treitler, Leo. "Gender and Other Dualities of Music History." In *Musicology and Difference: Gender and Sexuality in Music Scholarship,* ed. Ruth A. Solie. Berkeley: University of California Press, 1993.

Veiga, Manuel Vicente Ribeiro. "Toward a Brazilian Ethnomusicology: Amerindian Phases." Ph.D. diss., University of California at Los Angeles, 1981.

Veneziano, Neyde. *O teatro de revista no Brasil: dramaturgia e convenções.* Campinas, Spain: Editora da Universidade Estadual de Campinas, 1991.

Vetro, Gaspare Nello. *Antônio Carlos Gomes.* Rio de Janeiro: Instituto Nacional do Livro, 1982.

Viotti da Costa, Emilia. *The Brazilian Empire: Myths and Histories.* Chicago: Chicago University Press, 1985.

————. "Brazil: 1870–1889." In *Brazil: Empire and Republic, 1822–1930,* ed. Leslie Bethell. Cambridge: Cambridge University Press, 1989.

Volpe, Maria Alice. "Compositores românticos brasileiros: estudos na Europa." *Revista brasileira de música* 21 (1994–1995): 51–76.

Weiss, Judith A. *Latin American Popular Theater: The First Five Centuries.* Albuquerque: University of New Mexico Press, 1993.

Williams, Daryle. *Culture Wars in Brazil: The First Vargas Regime, 1930–1954.* Durham, N.C.: Duke University Press, 2002.

Index

About the Author

Cristina Magaldi holds degrees from the University of Brasilia (BS); Reading University, England (MMus); and the University of California, Los Angeles (PhD). She specializes in music of the Americas, Latin American music, and popular music. Dr. Magaldi is a fellow of the Guggenheim Foundation and a research associate of the Latin American Center at the University of California, Los Angeles.

Dr. Magaldi has articles in *The New Grove Music Dictionary of Women Composers* and in the revised edition of *The New Grove Dictionary of Music and Musicians*. She is a contributing editor of the music section of the *Handbook of Latin American Studies* and associate editor for *Women and Music in America Since 1900: An Encyclopedia*. She has presented papers in national and international conferences; in the fall of 2000, she presented a paper at the Annual Meeting of the American Musicological Society (AMS) in Toronto.

Dr. Magaldi's articles have appeared in journals such as *Latin American Music Review*, *Inter-American Music Review*, *Revista de Musicologia*, and *Popular Music*. Her contributed chapters have been published in *The Universe of Music: Latin America and Caribbean* and in *Brazil's National Cultural Identity*.